W9-BKC-369

International Dimensions of

BUSINESS POLICY
AND STRATEGY

THE KENT INTERNATIONAL DIMENSIONS OF BUSINESS SERIES

International Dimensions of
BUSINESS POLICY
AND STRATEGY
Second Edition

John Garland
University of Kansas

Richard N. Farmer
Late of Indiana University

Marilyn Taylor
University of Kansas

THE KENT INTERNATIONAL DIMENSIONS OF BUSINESS SERIES
David A. Ricks
Series Consulting Editor

PWS-KENT Publishing Company
Boston, Massachusetts

PWS–KENT
Publishing Company

Sponsoring Editor: Rolf Janke
Assistant Editor: Kathleen M. Tibbetts
Production Editor: Chris Crochetière
Text Designer: Elise Kaiser
Cover Designer: Julie Gecha
Manufacturing Coordinator: Peter D. Leatherwood
Typesetter: Pine Tree Composition
Printer/Binder: Courier/Stoughton
Cover Printer: New England Book Components

© 1990 by PWS-KENT Publishing Company. © 1986 by Wadsworth, Inc. All rights reserved. No part of this book may be reproduced, stored in a retrieval system, or transcribed, in any form or by any means, electronic, mechanical, photocopying, recording, or otherwise, without the prior written permission of the publisher, PWS-KENT Publishing Company, 20 Park Plaza, Boston, MA 02116.

PWS-KENT Publishing Company is a division of Wadsworth, Inc.

Printed in the United States of America.

1 2 3 4 5 6 7 8 9—94 93 92 91 90

Library of Congress Cataloging-in-Publication Data

Garland, John S.
   International dimensions of business policy and strategy / John
Garland, Richard Farmer, Marilyn Taylor.—2nd ed.
     p.   cm.—(The Kent international dimensions of business
series)
   ISBN 0–534–91942–1
   1. International business enterprises—Management. 2. Strategic
planning. I. Farmer, Richard N. II. Taylor, Marilyn L.
III. Title. IV. Series.
HD62.4.G37 1990   90–34037
658′.049—dc20   CIP

Series Foreword

Prior to World War II, the number of firms involved in foreign direct investment was relatively small. Although several U.S. companies were obtaining raw materials from other countries, most firms were only interested in the U.S. market. This changed, however, during the 1950s—especially after the creation of the European Economic Community. Since that time, there has been a rapid expansion in international business activity.

The majority of the world's large corporations now perform an increasing proportion of their business activities outside of their home countries. For many of these companies, international business returns over one-half of their profits, and it is becoming more and more common for a typical corporation to earn at least one-fourth of its profits through international business involvement. In fact, it is now rather rare for any large firm not to be a participant in the world of international business.

International business is of great importance in most countries and that importance continues to grow. To meet the demand for increased knowledge in this area, business schools are attempting to add international dimensions to their curricula. Faculty members are becoming more interested in teaching a greater variety of international business courses and are striving to add international dimensions to other courses. Students, aware of the increasing probability that they will be employed by firms engaged in international business activities, are seeking knowledge of the problem-solving techniques unique to international business. As the American Assembly of Collegiate Schools of Business has observed, however, there is a shortage of information available. Most business textbooks do not adequately consider the international dimensions of business and much of the supplemental material is disjointed, overly narrow, or otherwise inadequate in the classroom.

This series has been developed to overcome such problems. The books are written by some of the most respected authors in the various areas of international business. Each author is extremely well known in the Academy of International Business and in his or her other professional academies. They possess an outstanding knowledge of their own subject matter and a talent for explaining it.

These books, in which the authors have identified the most important international aspects of their fields, have been written in a format that facilitates their use as supplemental material in business school courses. For the most part, the material is presented by topic in approximately the same order and manner as it is covered in basic business textbooks. Therefore, as each topic is covered in the course, material is easily supplemented with the corresponding chapter in the series book.

The Kent International Dimensions of Business Series offers a unique and much needed opportunity to bring international dimensions of business into the classroom. The series has been developed by leaders in the field after years of discussion and careful consideration, and the timely encouragement and support provided by the PWS-KENT staff on this project. I am proud to be associated with this series and highly recommend it to you.

David A. Ricks

Consulting Editor to the
Kent International Dimensions of Business Series
Professor of International Business,
University of South Carolina

Preface

A central tenet to all business policy and strategic management courses is that corporate strategy cannot be properly designed, implemented, or evaluated without taking into consideration the nature of the firm's external environment. This environment is now, more than ever before, characterized by worldwide economic and competitive pressures. Competition is increasingly global in nature, and even the basic economic conditions under which firms operate domestically are increasingly affected by global interdependencies. The tenfold increase of energy costs in the seventies, the 1979–1982 recession, the more recent financial and monetary turbulence—all were global rather than national in origin.

These developments affected all firms, not merely the large multinational corporations with numerous subsidiaries abroad. It is obvious that industrial leaders such as John Deere, IBM, General Motors, and Caterpillar Tractor Company face international competition. It is less obvious, but just as true, that even the small, privately owned firm that is oriented to the local market is vulnerable to international competitive and economic pressures. The environment of business has become internationalized, and thus the international dimensions of business policy and strategy are as relevant to the small, domestic firm as they are to the multinational. It is therefore crucial for students of business policy, in evaluating corporate strategy, to understand the global competitive and economic factors that shape the environment in which firms operate. Strategies designed without taking such factors into consideration are inevitably less than optimal, and frequently less than tenable.

This text is a revised version of the edition I co-wrote with Richard N. Farmer several years ago. The changes, including a new chapter on the strategic implications of economic integration, reflect perhaps the spirit of my former co-author, but not his active involvement. Dick Farmer, one of the founding fathers of the field of international business studies, died in March 1987.

My new co-author and colleague, Marilyn Taylor, is well known to teachers and students of Business Policy and Strategic Management. She has written numerous cases and several books, the most recent of which is *Divesting Business Units*. She has spent considerable time in Europe during the last several years, exploring how firms are coping with the internationalization of the competitive environment as the European Community moves closer to its target date of 1992 for completing its common market. In so doing, Marilyn is addressing, as all professors of Policy and Strategic Management must, one of the most salient issues of our field. We hope this text facilitates the task for others.

We would like to thank the following for their reviews of the second edition: Maureen Fleming of The University of Montana and Paul Leinenbach of Loyola Marymount University.

John Garland

About the Authors

JOHN GARLAND is an Associate Professor of Business Administration at the University of Kansas, where he teaches International Business. He received his D.B.A. degree from Indiana University and has written three books and numerous articles on international business and economic relations. He is an active member of the Academy of International Business, the Academy of Management, the American Association for the Advancement of Slavic Studies, the Association for Comparative Economic Studies, the Business Association of Latin American Studies, and the GDR Studies Association. His current research focuses on economic reform in Eastern Europe.

RICHARD N. FARMER, fellow and former President of the Academy of International Business, was the author of 30 books and several hundred articles, mostly on international business topics. One of his books was identified by his peers as among the most influential publications in the field. He taught at Indiana University for 22 years before his death in 1987.

MARILYN TAYLOR is an Associate Professor of Strategic Management at the University of Kansas School of Business. Her areas of specialization include management of divestiture, family businesses, and managing significant careers. She received her D.B.A. and M.B.A. (with distinction) from Harvard University Graduate School of Business and her B.A. in Business Administration from the University of South Florida. She was founding Director of the Small Business Development Center at the University of Kansas from 1982–1985 and Director of the Small Business Institute from 1978–1985. She is co-founder and Director of the University of Kansas School of Business Field Studies Program.

Dr. Taylor has written *Business Policy: Strategic, Administrative, and Social Issues* (with Curtis E. Tate, Jr.) and *Divestiture of Business Units—Making the Decision and Making it Work*. She has published articles in several journals including the *Journal of Case Research* in addition to numerous professional presentations and proceedings publications. She is the author of numerous cases including "Marion Laboratories," a classic case widely used in texts of Business Policy. She is active in leadership capacities with several professional associations including Southern Management Association, North American Case Research Association, MidWest Case Research Association, and World Association for Case Research and Application. She is on the editorial board for *Case Research Journal*, the *Journal of Management*, and *Entrepreneurship: Theory and Practice*. She has consulted with numerous organizations on a variety of issues including strategic planning, business plans, competition and industry analysis, and venture capital funding. She participates frequently in management development seminars.

Contents

CHAPTER 1

▼

Introduction and Overview

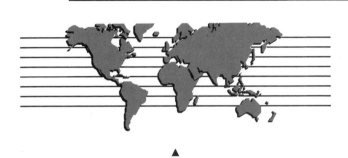

▲

One decade ago, U.S. industry faced exceptionally severe recessionary problems, which were reflected in part by overcapacity in major sectors and relatively high levels of unemployment. During those years, for example, employment in the manufacturing sectors fell by over 10 percent and specific industries faced massive layoffs. Many complex factors were involved in the decline of U.S. industrial performance. Some observers have pointed to deep-rooted structural difficulties, while others have suggested that management has long been concerned only with short-run profits, at the expense of long-term investment in plants and equipment or research and development. Some have pointed the finger at what they consider to be overpaid and undisciplined labor forces, and resultant high-priced, low-quality goods. The U.S. government has been accused of excessive interference through restrictive regulatory practices and faulty tax or economic policies that discourage investment. Conversely, the government has also been accused of neglect, failure to adopt an "industrial policy" for example. International trade policies have also been held accountable for the decline of U.S. industrial performance, although here too, the contentions are not fully consistent. It has been suggested that government negligence has contributed to the rapid diffusion of U.S. technology abroad, which allegedly

1

undermines the international competitive position of U.S. firms, and that the U.S. government has not sufficiently protected industry against what are perceived to be unfair trade practices from abroad. Contrary assertions maintain that excessive trade protection has delayed what should have been a natural adjustment to the mostly beneficial pressures of international competition.[1] More recently, the altogether serious budgetary and trade deficits have focussed attention on the realization that domestic and foreign economic policies, as well as fiscal and monetary policies, are inevitably interrelated. The recession of the early eighties has been overcome, but today's economy faces problems just as severe, if of a different nature.

THE GLOBAL INTERDEPENDENCE

Whatever the merit of these arguments, it is evident that U.S. industry has become directly and indirectly increasingly affected by worldwide economic and competitive pressures. Today, beyond question the United States is more dependent than ever in recent history on foreign sources of raw materials, capital, technology, and markets. The recession of the early eighties was a global phenomenon, not merely an American one, and it reflected the greatly increased interrelationship of all economies, whether rich or poor, developed or less developed, socialist or capitalist.[2]

Most U.S. citizens are fully aware that global developments in the international energy sector have directly affected their business performance. Fewer are aware of the extent to which the international monetary crisis affects them. Similarly, the press has extensively covered foreign competition in the U.S. automobile, steel, textile, and electronics industries. Much less coverage has been focused on the extent to which the general store in a rural area or the small, family-owned business has been touched by global economic and competitive forces.

Between the two extremes of industries dominated by giant firms and industries dominated by very small businesses, lie significant industries essentially comprised of medium-sized firms. One such industry is the machine-tool industry, which has become highly internationalized in recent years. Imported machines accounted for around 40 percent of the U.S. machine-tool market in 1983, up from only 13 percent ten years earlier.[3] In addition, this industry has undergone a rapid surge of investment in production facilities in the United States by foreign firms. U.S.-based companies have watched their share of the Western world's machine tool market fall from 35 percent in the 1960s to only 8 percent by 1988.[4] The industry is exceptionally important, since it supplies equipment to virtually all other manufacturing sectors, directly affecting their productivity and therefore their international competitiveness. U.S. machine-tools producers have lost their once substantial technological lead, and indeed today many are often seeking foreign technology through licensing arrangements or through the direct import of components and machines. Increasingly, businesses, especially small and medium-sized firms, must search the world, not just the United States, for the best available technologies or the least expensive source of other inputs. Those that fail to scan worldwide for sources of technology or critical inputs can quickly fall behind in the competitive race.

The substantial technological gap between the United States and other industrialized nations, which prevailed in the years immediately following the Second World War, no longer exists. European nations and Japan compete directly with U.S. producers in the high-technology sectors. In the more mature industries with relatively standardized products, a number of less developed countries have become extremely competitive, especially in sectors where production is essentially labor-intensive. But apart from specific industries, U.S. economic performance in general is affected by macroeconomic developments abroad. For example, the Latin American debt crisis has had a severe macroeconomic impact on U.S. industrial performance (to say nothing of the performance of U.S. banks). U.S. exports to Latin America, which accounted for 25 percent of total U.S. exports in 1981, fell by 40 percent during the next two years, costing the U.S. economy an estimated 400,000 jobs.[5] By 1990 the debt crisis continued to dampen exports to the region, in spite of many debt relief initiatives undertaken throughout the 1980s.

One can easily see the increased significance of international linkages by considering the present state of the automobile industry. Twenty years ago, the antitrust division of the U.S. Department of Justice was demanding that General Motors be broken up, on the grounds that it was a monopoly or tight oligopoly. The antitrust division focussed on the domestic market and domestic producers. But conditions have changed, and the automobile industry is now a global industry, defined by Porter as one in which the strategic positions of competitors in major geographic or national markets are fundamentally affected by their overall global positions.[6] Today, GM is locked into fierce international competition with American, Japanese, and European companies in the

United States and all over the world, and neither GM nor the government can now ignore foreign competition or competitive developments in foreign markets. Accordingly, as we shall discuss further, GM has significantly shifted its strategy. The Justice Department has relaxed its antitrust rules (especially in regard to joint ventures), and the government provided temporary protection to American automobile companies by negotiating "voluntary" marketing agreements with Japan. While these developments are perhaps most apparent in giant firms, all U.S. industry is affected by international economic and business relations. For example, the considerable strengthening of the U.S. dollar vis-à-vis other currencies in the early eighties did not just adversely affect those American firms that export or are faced with import competition. When Canada won a 40 percent share of the American lumber and plywood market in 1984, the entire Pacific-Northwest of the United States suffered, not just that single industry. When there is a substantial decline of activity in a major regional industry, spillover effects have an adverse impact on general economic activity, for example in the retailing sectors. No matter how domestically insulated a firm might believe itself to be, no firm can fully escape the consequences of the increasing scope and the growing complexity of international economic and business linkages.

A highly beneficial consequence of intensified foreign competition has been that much U.S. industrial innovation in recent years has been undertaken by industries generally considered to be stagnant, "smokestack" industries. Hundreds of thousands of jobs were lost in the automotive and steel industries in the early eighties, but much of that was due to strategic changes aimed at increasing productivity, reducing capacity, introducing much greater flexibility, lowering break-even points, and thus laying the groundwork to fend off foreign competition in the long run. These developments are basically reshaping much of American industry, and they represent a quite rational response to the greater market uncertainties and intensity of competition.

FOREIGN DIRECT INVESTMENT
IN THE UNITED STATES

When the United States began to run continuous and worsening trade deficits in the early 1980s, a significant counterflow of direct investment in the United States by foreign firms also appeared. The total stock of direct foreign investment in the United States rose from $20.6 billion in 1973 to $111.4 billion in 1983, with European firms accounting for two-thirds of the stock purchased. By the end of 1987, foreign investment stock had risen to $262 billion, and the United States had become the single largest recipient of international direct investment (surpassing Canada). Given the size of the U.S. economy, however, this direct foreign investment in the country is a relatively less important factor in economic performance than American direct investment abroad is to the countries of Europe and Canada. Figure 1–1 reflects the relatively greater inflow than outflow of U.S. foreign investment in recent years.

The inflow of foreign investment during the decade of the eighties coincided with sharp increases and decreases in the value of the dollar, which suggests that the direct investment decisions are influenced less by exchange rate variations per se than by the long-term production and marketing strategies of foreign firms. These foreign financial flows

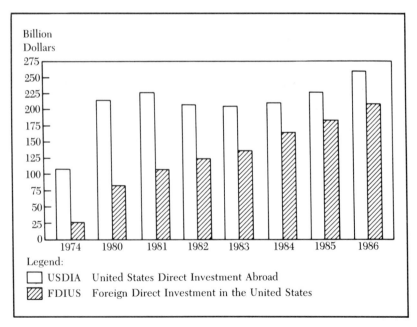

FIGURE 1–1 Stocks of U.S. Outward and Inward Investment (Direct), 1974 and 1980–1986

SOURCE: U.S. Department of Commerce, Bureau of Economic Analysis.

are both a response to and an important contribution to the recovery of the U.S. economy from the recession of the early 1980s.

Much of the foreign inflow has been associated with the formation of joint ventures between American and foreign firms, in contrast to the more passive portfolio investments. One consequence of this is that the distinction between domestic and foreign firms becomes blurred, with one key being the posture that the enterprise takes towards the international product and factor markets and another being the orientation of the management of the joint undertaking to its parent companies.

Most foreign investors come from one of seven countries: Britain, Canada, France, the Netherlands, Japan, Switzerland, and West Germany. Approximately 50 Third-World countries now have their own multinational corporations with investment abroad, but these investments are typically of very small proportions and located in other developing countries, since they are seldom competitive with the more innovative, technology-based multinationals of the industrialized countries.

When economic conditions are favorable there are sound reasons for foreign firms to invest in America. The United States represents the world's largest homogeneous market, and it is presently growing at a faster rate than most other industrialized economies. The United States also offers high quality technological resources at a scale and cost generally competitive with anywhere else. The labor force is highly skilled, and the wage gap with European pay scales has narrowed significantly. Furthermore, the United States offers a degree of political stability unavailable in many other parts of the world, and is relatively free of government regulations in many sectors. Foreign firms have become more confident in their ability to compete in the American market, and corporate restructurings through spin-offs (the sale of a subunit of the larger corporation, usually to outsiders, but occasionally to the managers and/or employees of that same sub-unit) have increased the number of American units available to foreign purchasers.

In the eighties, however, another motive loomed large in the minds of some foreign investors. At least Japanese investments in the United States have been substantially motivated by potential or real protectionist measures by the American government. Mazda has become the fourth Japanese car manufacturer (after Toyota, Nissan, and Honda) to set up car production facilities in the United States, and that was due in part to Japanese concern about the increasingly apparent dissatisfaction among U.S. policy makers regarding the bilateral trade balance between Japan and the United States. Numerous bills had been introduced in the U.S. Congress calling for a variety of protectionist measures such as tighter import quotas, local content requirements, reciprocity regarding open markets, and the like.

THEORETICAL BASIS OF TRADE AND INVESTMENT TRENDS

Early Concepts of Free Trade

Adam Smith, in *The Wealth of Nations* (1776), emphasized the importance of specialization as a source of increased output in a world where productive resources are scarce and human wants cannot be completely satisfied. At the international level, he suggested, each nation should specialize in the production of goods it is particularly well equipped to produce, exporting part of that production and taking in exchange other goods that it could not so readily turn out. This pattern has prevailed for millennia, for no country produces all the goods and services that it desires. Indeed, in today's world most countries depend on a substantial level of imports even to maintain their present living standards; and to receive these imports, they must export.

David Ricardo, in 1817, enunciated his refinement of Smith's concept by postulating the principle of comparative advantage (as opposed to Smith's concept of absolute advantage). The principle suggests that a country has a comparative advantage in the production of those goods that it can produce *relatively* more efficiently than other goods. Thus, although a country might have an absolute advantage in the production of two goods, it should produce for export the good in which it had the greatest comparative advantage and import goods in which it had an absolute disadvantage or even goods in which its comparative advantages were not so great.

The Ricardian concept still serves as the underlying basis of free trade, but it has been refined to argue that countries tend to export those goods whose production requires relatively more of the factor inputs with which a country is relatively well endowed. Ricardo's concept focussed on the flow of goods among nations, assuming that factors like capital and labor were immobile. These assumptions were more realistic for his age than ours. Today the focus is more on why firms

7

rather than nations trade, and more on demand than on supply sides of the equation.

The Product Life Cycle

A theory much more explanatory for modern developments, yet much more complementary than competitive with the Ricardian concept, is Vernon's concept of the *product life cycle.*[7] According to the product life cycle concept, the stimulus to innovation in the development of new products (or processes) is typically provided by some perceived opportunity (or threat) in the major, usually home, market. The home market is not only the source of stimulus for the innovation, but also the preferred location for the product development, for numerous reasons. The expense of research and development precludes "reinventing the wheel" in numerous locations, and such activities are generally highly centralized due to their long-run strategic importance and to the necessity of keeping fully in-house any major breakthroughs, for competitive reasons. There are additional benefits to be gained by centrally locating research and development activities. These benefits include maintaining close communication among the scientists and engineers and tighter coordination between the research and development activities and such functions as financial and production planning. It is necessary also to keep in close contact with prospective customers and to closely monitor competitive developments. The nature of the product development process also strongly influences the decision to begin production first in the home market. As Vernon suggests, the transitions from development to pilot projects to first commercial production are often incremental in nature. Specifications must be continually changed until the proper processes and designs can be established, and the prototype prepared for volume production.

One consequence of conducting the research and development of new products in the home country, as Vernon notes, is that innovations tend to reflect the characteristics of the home market. As a result, U.S. firms have tended to develop and manufacture products that are labor-saving and that respond to relatively high-income wants. Continental European firms, in contrast, have tended to develop and manufacture products that are material-saving and capital-saving. European and Japanese firms have also taken the lead in energy-saving innovations, partly as a consequence of U.S. government policies which delayed immediate response of the private sector to the energy crisis. One upshot of these patterns is that American firms, even though they may have been purely domestically oriented until quite recently, may reap great benefits by licensing from foreign producers the technology that is more compatible with the economic conditions prevalent today. Taking advantage of this technology could mean the difference between success and failure, especially for the small and medium-sized American firms that typically lack economies of scale or scope.

Phase One

During the first stage of the product life cycle, the innovating firm produces and markets solely in the home market. Immediately upon the commercial introduction of the products, costs and prices are high. The innovating firm, however, typically benefits from real or perceived monopolistic advantages (if the product is sufficiently differentiated from other existing products), and the initial buyers are relatively insensitive to price. If the product catches on, there is a rapid expansion of the market, eventually providing increasing economies of scale, lower unit costs, and a further expansion of the market. This very success encourages the entry of competitors, especially as production becomes more standardized. The market eventually becomes saturated and profits decline notably, for competitive reasons.

Phase Two

Vaster markets and greater economies can be gained by exporting, however, and here begins phase two of the product life cycle. The assumption is that there is an imperfect market for knowledge and technology and that the original advantage held by the innovator in his home market may be duplicated abroad. The American producer has typically sought markets in Canada and Europe for two basic reasons; they are large enough to be quite attractive, and the demand patterns among industrialized countries are fairly similar, which precludes having to adapt the product substantially for the foreign market. Success in exporting to foreign markets prolongs the life of the product. Competition eventually emerges from domestic firms in the targeted export market, but at first they are noncompetitive due to the normal start-up problems and to the lack of economies of scale.

Phase Three

Eventually, foreign producers gain a substantial advantage by refining their production techniques and by gaining scales at least sufficient to cause a disadvantage to the original exporter, who has the added costs of distant transportation and communication. The cultural distance also becomes a factor, for the foreign domestic companies are much more familiar with the market. Often, as in the case of the Japanese auto companies now investing in the United States, the foreign government will undertake protectionist actions in order to facilitate development or enhance the competitiveness of local producers. When these factors in aggregate become serious enough to adversely affect exports, stage three of the product life cycle emerges, in which the exporting firm shifts its strategy by locating production facilities abroad in the markets that have been served by exports up to this point. This pattern, until quite recently, has been dominated by American multinational corporations, whose technological lead over the firms of war-devastated Europe and Japan was substantial for the two decades following the Second World War.

Phase Four

For those products that are particularly labor-intensive, and for which mass manufacturing technologies are feasible, a final stage in the product life cycle is for the originally innovating firm to cease all production in the typically high labor cost domestic market (and often also in the foreign markets which it first entered by exports and then production), and to serve the home market through imports from foreign subsidiaries located in low-wage areas abroad. These new production locations will typically be in the most rapidly developing of the Third World countries, such as Brazil, Hong Kong, Singapore, or South Korea, where low labor costs are combined with sufficient infrastructure and generally excellent productivity levels.

The Relevance of the Product Life Cycle Today

As Vernon himself suggests, the predictive powers of the product life cycle model have waned in recent years, essentially for two reasons. First, there has been an increase in the geographical reach of many of the enterprises that are involved in the innovation process, due to their having established subsidiaries abroad already. Second, there has been a change in the national markets of the advanced industrialized countries, which has reduced many of the differences that had previously existed among them.

The very rapid growth of foreign investment during the three decades following the Second World War is a matter of record. For 30 years the process of innovation, export, and foreign investment ran full tilt. One consequence of this pattern is that one rarely finds today major innovative firms that do not already have extensive operations overseas. This in turn has had two significant effects. First, the interval of time between the introduction of any new product in the United States and its first production in a foreign location has substantially decreased. That is, the foreign productive facilities are already largely operative, and the firm has gained substantial experience in the transfer of new technologies abroad. Second, there has grown a considerable reverse flow of technology through innovations by the subsidiaries abroad which are subsequently introduced in the original "home" market.

That has in part been a consequence of the narrowing of differences among the markets of the industrialized countries. Immediately following the Second World War, American firms enjoyed substantial competitive advantages. A technology gap developed, foreign firms were more concerned with reconstruction rather than with innovation, and there was a general scarcity of resources abroad. The technology gap has narrowed significantly over the years, the foreign economies have long since regained their footing, and the per capita income gap among industrialized nations has closed noticeably, thereby decreasing the differences in demand among the various markets. In Europe, the closing of both the technological and income gaps was fostered in part by the creation of the European Community in 1958, which established a "common market" large enough to allow European firms to become competitive with American ones. This competitiveness should be further enhanced by 1992 — the target date for the completion of the common market.

The product life cycle model has less predictive capability than it did for some three decades. It might still be relevant for small firms or others that have not yet established substantial foreign operations. It also holds to some extent for those many domestic firms that could reap substantial benefits from licensing in the technology of foreign firms. And for decades to come, the concept will surely hold for business relations between the developed and less developed countries (the latter in general falling further and further behind in the technology race), or for business relations between the most rapidly developing of the Third World countries and those which show much less promise.

The product life cycle model links the demand side to the theory of comparative advantage, and presents the argument that the pattern of many exports and imports is better explained by competitive factors at the firm level rather than at the national level. That is, international trade follows markets, and international investment responds to potential and real threats to export markets. In other words, the product life cycle concept attempts to describe how the exporting, importing, and manufacturing location of a product changes over time, as firms respond to changing competitive conditions and as domestic and foreign markets for the product grow, mature, and decline over time.

More recent theories of international investment are based on concepts of industrial organization and the existence of market imperfections. They posit that foreign investment is undertaken only by those firms that enjoy some monopolistic or oligopolistic competitive advantage. The reason for this is that under perfect market conditions foreign firms would be noncompetitive due to the cost of operating from a distance (both geographically and culturally). Thus, the firm that invests abroad is presumed to have some unique advantage, whether in product differentiation, marketing or other managerial skills, proprietary technology, favorable access to finance or other critical inputs, and so on. Oligopolistic theory further suggests the phenomenon of defensive investment, which can occur in concentrated industries to prevent competitors from gaining or enlarging special advantages that could then be exploited globally.[8]

SUMMARY AND OVERVIEW

In this book we examine the basic strategic patterns associated with the internationalization of business, for it is clear that this trend has accelerated to the point at which virtually all companies are to some extent, and most to a substantial degree, affected by international linkages and developments. This is a critically significant change in the environment of business, and in the long run the successful firms will be those that have changed their strategies accordingly.

In Chapter 2 we introduce the concept of economic integration that is basic to the internationalization of the business environment. The coverage in this chapter assumes a macroeconomic perspective of economic integration in order to establish the framework for the firm-level discussion that follows throughout the text. Certainly in the Western world the completion of the European Economic Community's "Common Market" in 1992 and the ratification of the U.S.–Canadian free trade agreement in 1989 necessitate basic strategic responses by the business firm. We will give special consideration to the centrally planned economies (with focus on the Soviet bloc) and less developed countries, whose economic integration is strongly influenced by systemic and situational factors, respectively.

In Chapter 3 we address the issue of the global strategic perspective, and how it differs from the perspective of the purely domestically oriented firm and from the perspective of the traditional multinational corporation. Threats and opportunities that affect a business firm are of both foreign and domestic origin, and firms that fail to take this into consideration risk a serious deterioration of their ability to compete. The issue is not simply a question of competition with foreign firms. More basically, it is the fact that neither factor nor product markets are defined by national boundaries. Domestic firms that include such considerations in their strategic planning quickly gain a competitive edge over those which fail to do so.

In Chapter 4 we address the issue of strategy formulation from a global perspective. The policy literature in general distinguishes among strategies at the enterprise, corporate, business, and functional area levels. Enterprise strategy focuses on social-legitimacy concerns, i.e., an examination of the firm's general role in society. Corporate strategy addresses the issue of what businesses the firm is in and how those businesses are integrated into an effective portfolio. Business strategy is concerned with the question of how to compete in a given business, given the resources available and the competitive nature of the industry. Functional area strategy deals with the more specific activities in the areas of production, marketing, finance, and so on. There is a hierarchical relationship among these strategy levels. As one moves from enterprise strategy to corporate strategy to business strategy and to functional area strategy, one moves not only down the organizational hierarchy, but also downward in terms of constraints. That is, the lower level strategies are subordinate to, and supportive of, higher level strategies.

Each of these strategy levels is dealt with extensively in this book. With the exception of the functional strategies, however, we do not categorize them as such, for several reasons. First, the strategies are so closely interwoven that it can be misleading to treat them in isolation. Second, as the reader will discover, quite frequently in international business the tail wags the dog. That is, foreign environmental constraints can force the firm to adopt modes of behavior that let, for example, the means of production determine business and corporate strategies, which reverses the flow of influence generally posited in the literature. Third, there are many strategic issues in international business which assume far greater significance than in a purely domestic context, and it is necessary to address these issues in a slightly different framework in order to put them into proper perspective. Fourth, the focus here is directed often on what is different about strategy in a global context compared to that in the traditional, domestic context. Accordingly, we will intentionally neglect detailed discussion of those areas that the reader is assumed to be fairly familiar with.

The implementation of strategy is discussed in Chapters 5 through 8. Every business is confronted with a series of decisions that are future oriented, and often these lock the firm into patterns that persit for decades. Once such decisions are made, it is very difficult, costly, and time-consuming to change them. These critical decisions are core managerial issues, and they are the concern of Chapters 5 and 6. One such core issue, for example, focuses on entry and ownership patterns for the firms that expand internationally. Should the firm go only into wholly owned subsidiaries abroad, or should it consider joint ventures with local partners? Should it license its technology (either inwards or outwards), do turnkey projects, or be a minority shareholder in foreign companies? It can also be heavily involved in traditional exporting and importing, for none of these forms precludes the other possibilities. Decisions as to what form the company takes in its international activities can be crucial. Another critical core issue addressed here is that of technology transfer, and the many complexities involved when the transfer crosses national boundaries.

In Chapter 6 we address the structural options of the globally oriented firm. As firms assume a global perspective, they may find that their traditional organizational structures are no longer appropriate. Indeed, changes in corporate strategy quite frequently necessitate changes in corporate structure. Particularly for the firm which expands abroad, the choice of a fundamental operating mode becomes critical. Should the firm maintain its local base as the power center, or should it decentralize wherever feasible? To what extent should it attempt to integrate operations, compared to having relatively autonomous foreign affiliates? Disparities in an organization's environment generally encourage selective decentralization, although the nature of the technology involved and the degree of competition are also determinants of the fundamental operating mode. In any event, when a firm adopts a global orientation, its environmental complexity explodes. Instead of looking carefully at one environment, it must look at many, each with its own rich diversity and complexity. Managers must somehow integrate their firms into the world, not just one country. This really is what the internationalization of strategy is all about: responding on the one hand to pressures driving companies towards greater responsiveness to conditions in individual countries, and on the other hand to pressures pulling them towards greater global integration of products and markets. This is the international dimension of the mandate that successful organizational performance derives from the simultaneous achievement of high levels of differentiation and integration, where the degree of local autonomy necessary for successful adaptation to environmental needs is blended with an optimum of corporate control for successful organizational integration.

In Chapters 7 and 8 we examine the implementation of functional strategies. Such functional strategies are more properly studied in detail in the international discussions in courses devoted to them, such as Finance, Marketing, and so on. However, functional strategies cannot be viewed properly in isolation from the general strategic thrust of the firm. Moreover, the functional strategies take on special significance in the global context. It can be argued that functional managers are involved in essentially the same activities worldwide. However, cultural differences are a major source of variation in crossnational managerial behavior, as are the differing degrees of industrial and economic development around the world. More to the point, a global strategic perspective frequently leads to a complete revamping of functional strategies. Hence, an auto manufacturer may decide to produce components wherever they are most efficiently produced. Engines may be made in Mexico, bodies stamped in Canada, electrical items manufactured in Brazil. These components are then transported to various assembly plants in other locations, and the finished products then shipped abroad. Such strategies are now evolving, and they are basically changing the nature of the auto industry.

In Chapter 9 we discuss certain legitimacy issues of the global corporation, which are an extremely complex variant of the corporate social responsibility question. It is at best a challenging task for the firm to respond adequately to domestic legitimacy demands, but when the firm becomes involved with global operations, it encounters decidedly differing views as to what responsible behavior is. For example, governments are rightfully concerned with national issues, so conflicts with a globally optimizing corporation are to some extent inevitable. Thus it might make eminent sense from a corporate perspective to invest in South Africa, but that country's apartheid policies cause great concern in many circles. Under the circumstances of having to answer to competing demands, the corporation must devote increased attention to its conflict resolution strategies.

Thus, our focus in this book is on the rationale, formulation, and implementation of global strategies. The strategies must be global, because they must effectively respond to environmental realities. The strategies must of course also be based on the capabilities of the individual firm, and therefore there are many diverse strategic options for the firms that accept the challenge of competing in an increasingly interdependent world. There are many viable global strategies, and a properly global orientation does not presume any single strategy in particular. That is of course the challenge of any strategic management, but the options on a global scale are immensely rich.

DISCUSSION QUESTIONS

1. Why must even purely domestic companies adopt a global view?
2. How can one explain the recent surge of foreign direct investment in the United States?
3. Many are concerned with what they consider to be a "foreign takeover of America." What are some of the positive consequences of foreign direct investment in the United States?
4. The U.S. government has pressured Japanese automobile manufacturers to restrict their exports of cars to this country. What are the "pros" and "cons" of such an action?
5. What are the stages of the "product life cycle"? What are some of the products which illustrate the final stage? Why does this theory have less relevance today than it did perhaps 25 years ago?

NOTES

1. Robert Z. Lawrence, *Can America Compete?*, (Washington, D.C.: The Brookings Institution, 1984), 1–2.

2. Raymond Vernon, "The Future of Multinational Enterprise in Developing Countries," in *Private Enterprise and The New Global Economic Challenge*, ed., Stephen Guisinger (Indianapolis: Bobbs-Merrill Educational Publishing, 1979), 1–21.

3. Ralph E. Winter, "Making Machine Tools Increasingly Requires Ties to Foreign Firms," *Wall Street Journal* (September 4, 1984), 1.

4. Nick Garnett, "U.S. Machine Tool Makers Face Uphill Grind," *Financial Times* (September 20, 1988), 26.

5. Stewart Fleming, "Debt Crisis in Latin America Costs Jobs," *Financial Times* (November 17, 1983), 6.

6. Michael E. Porter, *Competitive Strategy: Techniques for Analyzing Industries and Competitors* (New York: The Free Press, 1980), 275.

7. See for example: Raymond Vernon, "The Product Cycle Hypothesis in a New International Environment," in *Strategic Management of Multinational Corporations: The Essentials*, eds., Heidi Vernon Wortzel and Lawrence H. Wortzel (New York: John Wiley & Sons, 1985), 16–27.

8. For an analysis of such theories, see; David McClain, "Foreign Direct Investment in the United States: Old Currents, 'New Waves,' and the Theory of Direct Investment," in *The Multinational Corporation in the 1980s*, eds., Charles P. Kindleberger and David B. Audretsch (Cambridge: The MIT Press, 1983), 278–333.

FURTHER READING

1. Bergsten, C. Fred. *America in the World Economy* (Washington, D.C.: Institute for International Economics, 1988).

2. Heenan, David A., and Warren J. Keegan. "The Rise of Third World Multinationals." *Harvard Business Review*, January–February, 1979, 101–109.

3. Kindleberger, Charles P., and David B. Audretsch, eds. *The Multinational Corporation in the 1980s*. Cambridge: The MIT Press, 1983.

4. Lawrence, Robert Z. *Can America Compete?* Washington, D.C.: The Brookings Institution, 1984.

5. Organization for Economic Co-operation and Development. *Recent Trends in International Direct Investment*. Paris: OECD, 1987.

6. Porter, Michael E. *Competitive Strategy: Techniques for Analyzing Industries and Competitors*. New York: The Free Press, 1980.

7. Vernon, Raymond. "The Product Cycle Hypothesis in a New International Environment." In *Strategic Management of Multinational Corporations: The Essentials*. eds., Heidi Vernon Wortzel and Lawrence H. Wortzel. New York: John Wiley & Sons, 1985, 16–27.

CHAPTER 2

▼

The Concept
of Economic Integration

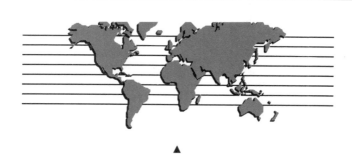

▲

We are mainly concerned in this book with the strategies of firms and corporations that integrate and coordinate their diverse activities across national borders. This cross-national integration of enterprise-level activities, however, would not be possible were it not for the macroeconomic integration within which it occurs. In other words, it presupposes an institutional framework that permits the cross-national flow of people, money, goods, services, and technology. It is therefore important to understand the nature of economic integration in general, and the different forms that it may assume. Only then can enterprise management develop sound strategies for coping with the competitive changes brought about through the increased integration of regional and global markets.

At the macroeconomic level, major integration initiatives are now under way in both North America and Europe. Dozens of other initiatives, though generally smaller in scale and scope, can be found in other parts of the world (notably in East Asia and Latin America), and major efforts are being made to improve the institutional framework of economic integration among the Soviet Union and East European members of the Council for Mutual Economic Assistance (CMEA). In all such cases, the main rationale of integration is to improve economic performance on a regional basis. Similar efforts are being made within the General Agreement on Tariffs and Trade (GATT) to improve economic performance on the global level.

Macroeconomic integration basically alters the competitive position of firms both within and outside the integrated area. It is for this reason especially that firms need to closely monitor the progress of integration initiatives and to develop strategies to cope with the changing competitive environment.

THE MARKET-ORIENTED CONCEPT OF ECONOMIC INTEGRATION

Specialization occurs at the national as well as the enterprise level. Thus, Canada exports wheat and imports coffee and other tropical goods from Latin America. This specialization (division of labor) increases overall output and welfare by permitting each country to focus on the production of goods which it is most suited for. Today, economic integration goes far beyond the internationalization of markets for goods and services; it includes the markets for capital and labor, technology and entrepreneurship, and money and credit.[1] The cross-national flows of labor, managers, finance, and technology have increased substantially in recent years.

The proliferation of regional trading blocs, in which preferential trade treatment is given to member countries, may serve to the detriment of "outsiders." Nevertheless, the further development of trading blocs in general can be viewed as part of a larger process of international economic integration, through which product and factor (input) flows among national economies lead to increased economic interdependence among nations.

Advantages of Economic Integration

Specialization at the country level leads to an improved allocation of production factors; human, financial, and material resources are channeled to their most productive uses. Cross-national economic integration creates larger markets (because firms can now produce for export

19

markets as well as for the domestic market), and thus provides the opportunity for greater scales of economy. Another significant advantage of economic integration is the competitive stimulus which it creates; foreign competition in the home market forces domestic firms to become more efficient and thereby produce higher quality goods at lower cost than would be the case without the competition. Flows of finance and technology from abroad similarly improve economic performance at home.

Trade Creation Versus Trade Diversion

As noted, free trade improves resource allocation and leads to potential gains in economic welfare. However, under certain conditions regional economic integration may have the opposite effect and may lead to a deterioration of economic welfare. Regional economic integration is beneficial when it creates trade and improves welfare by letting consumers shift from the consumption of higher-cost domestic products in favor of lower-cost products from member countries. In such cases the domestic firms either become more efficient and competitive, or they turn to the production of goods in which they are more efficient to begin with.

Regional economic integration may have nondesirable consequences, however, and may reduce economic welfare under certain conditions. This is typically the case when discriminatory treatment against countries that are not members of the trading bloc causes consumers to shift their purchases from low-cost nonmembers of the bloc to higher-cost bloc members. Here one talks of "trade diversion" rather than of "trade creation."

In other terms, if countries A and B form a trading bloc by removing tariffs on imports from each other but retain a tariff on imports from C, a new import from B to A may replace either a product domestically produced in A or an import from C. If it displaces A's domestic product, trade creation results. If it displaces a previous import from C, no new trade is created, but trade is diverted from a cheaper source of supply to a more expensive one (due to the tariff discrimination against C).

Under what circumstances is the beneficial consequence of trade creation likely instead of the adverse consequence of trade diversion?

First, when a high proportion of trade is already conducted with prospective integration partners, since that reduces the probability of trade diversion. Second, when existing foreign trade is at a low level relative to domestic production, because this too suggests that trade creating will be larger than trade diverting effects.

To be sure, the measurement of trade creation and trade diversion is very complex, and industry-specific. In the European Economic Community (EEC), for example, it appears that trade diversion has occurred in such areas as foodstuffs, chemicals, and light manufactures, but was more than offset by the trade creating effects of integration in the areas of heavy machinery and equipment.[2] Clearly the EEC's highly protective Common Agricultural Policy has penalized both foreign suppliers and domestic consumers.

Statistical Indicators of Integration

One may measure, and should distinguish between, either the conditions or effects of economic integration. Conditions of integration are those factors that affect the mobility of goods and factors of production. Effects of integration are the actual movement of goods, services, and factors of production. In this latter category, for example, one might measure changes in the level and composition of trade or in the relative prices of goods and factors of production within a region. These statistical measures give important insights, especially when applied over time instead of at a given moment. On the other hand, one must use a great deal of caution in using any indicator that relies on changes in trade shares among members of a trading group. Surely a decrease in the share in the face of an increase in the absolute volume of intrabloc trade would not indicate a decline in regional integration, just as an increase in the share in the face of a declining volume of intrabloc trade does not signal a higher degree of integration. Thus, trade shares per se tell us very little about the actual degree of integration achieved. If intrabloc trade remains unchanged in the face of decreasing or increasing trade with outsiders, the fall or rise in the ratio of intrabloc trade is not at all indicative of a change in the degree of regional integration. More relevant, but still a far from perfect indicator of the degree of regional integration, is the share of regional trade in the country's domestic production.

The Basic Typology of Economic Integration

The mechanisms, rationale, and objectives of economic integration vary according to the nature of the national economic systems in general. Thus, one must distinguish among market-oriented, centrally planned, and less developed economies in the discussion of economic integration. The typology discussed here is based primarily on integration in the Western, market-oriented context.

1. Free Trade Area. In a free trade area, member states agree to remove all tariffs and quotas on trade passing among them (with the typical exception of agricultural goods), but each party is free to determine unilaterally the level of customs duties on imports coming from outside the area. This latter characteristic raises the possibility of outside imports entering the free trade area through the member country with the lowest external tariff rates; hence, it is important to establish "rules of origin" to ensure that preferential treatment is confined to commodities originating within the free trade area. Without such rules of origin "trade deflection" would result, for nonmember exports would enter high-duty member states through low-duty member states, with the lowest rate for each commodity becoming the effective rate for the entire area.

2. Customs Union. In a customs union, tariffs and quotas on trade between members are removed, but in addition to that, the members agree to apply a common tariff on goods entering the union from outside. Many view the customs union as a compromise between free-traders and protectionists, for on the one hand it recognizes the benefits of free trade, while on the other hand it provides regional protection from outside competition.

3. Common Market. In a common market, the free movement of the factors of production (i.e., labor, capital, technology, and entrepreneurship or enterprise) is added to the free movement of goods within the customs union. Thus, factor as well as product markets are integrated. Ultimately, it is unobstructed factor mobility that creates an integrated economy out of separate national economic entities. This free factor movement has far-reaching consequences for national policies, for when factor movements are unrestricted it is virtually impossible to maintain divergent national economic policies in the basic areas of policy concern.

4. Economic Union. An economic union is a common market in which there is also a relatively high degree of unification of monetary and fiscal policies (typically including the harmonization of taxes and subsidies throughout the bloc). This typically requires the establishment of a supranational authority to control these aspects of the integration. The need for policy harmonization arises naturally from the consequences of liberalizing product markets. For example, after tariff barriers were substantially reduced in the EEC, firms' profit margins and thus competitive positions were more strongly affected by the different systems of taxation among the member nations; it was thus decided to harmonize tax structures within the region.

5. *Monetary Union.* Monetary integration requires fixed exchange rates and free convertibility of currencies among members of the union as well as free movement of capital within the union. Because convertibility of currency is essential for a customs union and capital movement is free in a common market (implying capital market integration), the distinctive element in monetary union is the maintenance of constant exchange rates. This in turn requires that members of the union harmonize their rates of monetary expansion (which consequently removes a basic source of disparate movements in the members' price levels). Thus, entrance into a monetary union requires a nation to relinquish its independent monetary policy. The objective of monetary union is to improve resource allocation by permitting and encouraging the free movement of capital.

6. *Total Economic Integration.* In total economic integration there is complete unification of economic, monetary, and fiscal policies. Conceptually, it would require also the actual utilization of all potential opportunities for efficient division of labor and the complete interdependence of all economic activities. Some theorists would include a final stage of political integration under the taxonomy of integration; here the participating members assume the identity of a single nation, in which the central authority not only controls monetary and fiscal policies but also has a central parliament with the sovereignty of a nation's government.

The typology just described does not preclude alternative approaches. For example, one may distinguish among trade integration, factor (input) integration, policy integration, and total integration. Under virtually all typologies of integration, however, one usually distinguishes between the concepts of negative and positive integration.

Negative Versus Positive Integration

Negative integration, in which the barriers to trade (such as quotas and tariffs) are eliminated, is a basic mechanism among Western industrialized countries; here one relies typically on market mechanisms to stimulate further integration. Positive integration, which entails the explicit governmental creation of coordination mechanisms, is a basic method of integration among centrally planned economies. To be sure, positive integration processes are also very common in the West, but here they typically serve to facilitate the operation of market rather than to replace it. Thus, negative integration policies may be regarded as the essential step in market integration, but the higher levels of integration definitely require the implementation of positive policies even in the West. In the typology previously discussed, it is the free trade area that represents the basic form of negative integration, and to a certain extent, the customs union also. But as early as the common market stage as described above, in which factor as well as product movements are relatively free, we have reached a more developed stage of negative integration and one that requires certain positive measures as well.

Positive integration requires the creation of common institutions and policies that take one of essentially two basic forms. They may take the form of *intergovernmental* initiatives to promote cooperation on specific projects to rationalize production along desired lines (e.g., European collaboration on aerospace projects). While the intergovernmentalist approach is often directed toward economic ends, its reliance on political will rather than economic forces often leads to outcomes not altogether economically rational. Positive integration initiatives may also take the form of *supranational* institutions that create the general economic climate within which private enterprises are encouraged to rationalize production along the desired lines. Examples of this form of positive integration include the removal of impediments to factor mobility, monetary and fiscal harmonization, and so on. Because this form challenges the principle of state sovereignty, it frequently is a central point of conflict among members of the trade bloc.

It is important to note that, although conceptually distinct, the mechanisms for negative and positive integration reinforce each other. That is to say, they are mutually dependent on, rather than substitutions for, each other. Much gain can be made from the early stages of negative integration, but increasingly, further progress depends on positive measures. This is in part a natural consequence of the technological revolution and the increased role of government in modern times. As Pinder notes, "Whereas, in the simpler economy of the earlier industrial revolution, a laissez faire system was possible, the complex modern economy, with its imperfect markets and intricately interlocking parts, requires a more complex form of economic management."[3] As one moves from trade integration (elimination of barriers to trade) through factor integration (liberalization of factor movements) to policy integration (harmonization of national economic policies), the emphasis generally shifts from market forces to governmental action (which, however, is aimed at stimulating market responses). Negative measures clearly constitute an easier route to integration than the positive measures of harmonizing national economic and social policies. This is because the automaticity and anonymity of the market, when available, provide a more effective mechanism for integration than the explicit, inevitably highly politicized coordination of national policies. Furthermore, one can more easily conceptualize integration from the viewpoint of efficiency and general welfare objectives than from the important economic perspectives of integration's impact on employment, the balance of trade, exchange rates, economic growth, and inflation.

Economic Integration: Process or Condition?

Economic integration may be viewed as a process or as a state of affairs. Each of the types we have discussed might well be considered an ultimate objective in its own right, and, to be sure, it appears that the founders of the European Free Trade Association (EFTA) never intended for that arrangement to go beyond the stage of a simple free trade area. If one views integration as a process, however, it is easy to assume that the different types of integration represent stages leading to complete economic (and perhaps also political) integration. As it happens, no integration scheme in reality fully reflects the ideal types discussed above, and one focusses instead on the relative degrees of integration. Thus, the European Economic Community has been described as "a full customs union, a well developed common market, a partly developed economic union, and weakly politically integrated."[4]

The typology is based on increasingly complex integration models, and because each model builds on the previous to expand the scope of integration, it is typically assumed that an organic process is involved. For example, the trade-creating and allocational benefits of tariff elimination in a free trade area or customs union may be substantially reduced if incongruent domestic policies among member countries prevail. In such a case, the benefits of integration can be increased through the harmonization of policies related to such concerns as market and structural balance, income distribution, and monetary and fiscal measures. This is because, for example, trade and payments restrictions are partly interchangeable in terms of their effect on trade flows. A tariff restricts imports by raising their prices, whereas exchange control lowers imports by limiting the amount of foreign currencies available to finance them. Similary, a quota system can discriminate among various commodities and sources of supply by the manner in which import licenses are issued, but the same effect can result by use of exchange controls, multiple exchange rates, and bilateral clearing agreements. Consequently, it is often of little value to remove one type of restriction without removing the other also.

The harmonization of market policies typically addresses the many nontariff barriers to trade, which assume increased relevance once the tariffs are eliminated. Safety and health regulations represent a common nontariff barrier to trade, but more basic, for example, are widely diverse industrial standards (which reduce the potential for economies of scale and thus cost reduction).

Structural policies which frequently need union-wide harmonization in order to increase the benefits of integration include the national treatment of cartels, regional policy, factor mobility, and other rigidities which hamper the functioning of market forces. Regional policy is especially important in this regard, because unless a coordinated approach is taken, the more advanced areas will benefit more from integration than the relatively depressed areas most in need of industrial development.

Income distribution among the member states requires explicit attention because integration aimed solely at allocational and structural efficiency typically favors the most advanced members of the union at the expense of those who are in greater need of industrial development. Economic disparities among the members may well widen unless definitive steps are taken to balance the benefits and costs of integration.

Monetary institutions and financial policies are also critical areas of concern. Without fiscal harmonization, the diverse patterns of subsidies and taxes among member states may counteract the gains expected from tariff elimination. Without monetary and financial harmonization, it is difficult to achieve the allocational objectives of economic integration in general. Perhaps more importantly, monetary harmonization derives from the need to promote economic stabilization objectives. Trade and factor movements induce greater interdependence among national economies, and arguments for coordinating the monetary and fiscal policies at the union level thus become stronger. Financial measures taken by one country to regulate domestic economic activity inevitably spill over and significantly affect the activity in other members' countries.

It is for these reasons that one can easily assume that the establishment of a customs union inevitably sets forces into motion which lead to further integration along the lines of an economic union. It is true that the static economic gains from optimal resource allocation could be increased by integrating factor as well as product markets and by harmonizing domestic policies among the members that affect competition and economic structure. However, such economic gains may be of less priority to the national governments than the pursuit of other quite valid objectives, such as the promotion of domestic regional balance, full employment, a more balanced income distribution, and so on. Governments must pursue multidimensional policy objectives, and thus they might well wish to confine their integration mainly to tariff policy (as happens in a simple customs union or free trade area) while marginally correcting only the most blatantly counterproductive policy incongruencies. There is a trade-off here, although even for customs unions and free trade areas, some degree of harmonization of trade and commercial policies is indispensable if the basic objectives of integration are to be achieved. Strict unilateral quotas on imports from member countries could, for example, completely undermine the advantages to be gained from tariff elimination. If no policy harmonization whatsoever is undertaken, conflicts emerge which either weaken the commitment to integration or call for periodic ad hoc adjustments to the integration mechanisms.

Even the simplest of integration schemes will be hindered in the absence of a monetary system that facilitates foreign payments by securing the convertibility of currencies. But note the dilemma here of complete monetary policy harmonization, which would take away from national governments one of the most effective policy instruments of domestic economic control (e.g., the use of varying interest rates). As a result, the integration arrangements of today have induced governments to use earlier available instruments more aggressively and to develop new policy instruments. Examples of this include the use of (a) taxes and subsidies on investment, employment, and research and development; (b) public capital grants of equity capital and lending priorities; (c) selective import fees and export subsidies; (d) the tying of foreign aid to purchases of goods produced in the granting country; (e) "buy-national" policies; and (f) government use of product and environmental standards and regulations for protectionist means.[5]

Integration and Neo-mercantilist Policies

On the face of it, the measures just mentioned represent steps toward disintegration, for they merely replace tariff protection by nontariff protectionist devices. On the other hand, such measures might be necessary for domestic political reasons in order to prevent more blatant protectionism from arising.[6] Thus, the neo-mercantilist policies frequently seen today represent both a retreat from full commitment to integration and simultaneously a commitment to encourage integration wherever politically feasible. The immediate post-Second World War era witnessed a remarkable commitment to international integration through the releasing of market forces, but these forces in turn became so strong that governments felt compelled subsequently to take steps to ameliorate them. One observer notes that it was as if governments found "that they had, like the Sorcerer's Apprentice, released forces outside their own control."[7]

To be sure, the conflicts noted above are somewhat ameliorated if the integration is limited to the sectoral (single commodity) level. An example of a bilateral arrangement of this nature is the U.S.–Canadian automobile free trade agreement signed in 1965. An example of a multilateral arrangement of this nature is the European Coal and Steel Community, which served as a forerunner to the establishment of the EEC.

One may also distinguish between specialization between sectors (interindustry integration) or within sectors (intraindustry integration). In the EEC especially, one reason why integration has proceeded apace is that the expansion of trade to a large extent has been intrasectoral rather than intersectoral. This in turn means that integration could proceed without much closing down of large parts of industry branches, for domestic reallocations were possible merely by having existing firms alter their product lines. Consequently, serious social problems linked to the reallocations were, to a considerable extent, avoided. Protectionism has been most difficult to remove in the fields where free international competition would have led to intersectoral rather than intrasectoral reallocation of resources, namely in agriculture and labor-intensive products.

At the beginning of this chapter, it was suggested that the emergence of regional integration arrangements represents a suboptimizing, second best alternative to global integration. This does not mean, however, that regional integration necessarily thwarts progress along global lines. Fritz Machlup distinguishes between two modes of utilizing opportunities of efficient division of labor once trading blocs have been established: more intensive exchange within the area in question, versus outward extension of the area to third party countries.[8] In other words, he distinguishes between a partial approach to a wider union versus a more complete approach to a narrower union. Thus, if there already exists a high degree of integration within the bloc, greater overall welfare gains could be achieved by extending trade with the outside world than by intensifying integration within the bloc. On the other hand, if there are still serious obstacles to economic integration within the bloc, then the removal of these obstacles, and, hence, the attainment of greater regional integration, may contribute more to the economic welfare of the area than could be expected from an extension of the division of labor to third party countries. Machlup suggests that the conflict of the alternative policies may be more apparent than real, since the extension of external trade may simultaneously reduce the distintegrating forces within the region. For example, competition from third countries' imports may reduce internal barriers by stimulating greater internal efficiency and competitiveness, so that integration with third parties may at the same time raise the degree of regional integration. To be sure, this effect depends very much on the nature of the domestic barriers to integration, and thus would not hold in all cases. The point is, that regional integration and greater openness to third countries outside the bloc are not necessarily mutually exclusive alternatives.

ECONOMIC INTEGRATION IN CENTRALLY PLANNED ECONOMIES

We have argued that regional economic integration may lead not only to trade creation, but to trade diversion as well. Trade creation results from one partner's importing from another products it previously produced for itself. Trade diversion results from the increase in trade among partners at the expense of third nations which, though more efficient producers, lose their markets as a result of discriminatory measures adopted by the new trading bloc. In the case of the CMEA (Council for Mutual Economic Assistance), a third effect—that of trade destruction—may arise.[9]

Economic integration among the Soviet Union and Eastern European members of CMEA has been retarded essentially due to systemic constraints and deliberate policy choices. Until quite recently all foreign trade was a monopoly of the state; autarkic policies to promote economic self-sufficiency took priority over the efficiency gains to be achieved through the international division of labor. Currency inconvertibility necessitated a bilateral balancing of trade, and irrational prices (i.e., the arbitrary determination of prices that consequently fail to reflect economic costs or to respond to supply and demand forces) made virtually impossible any sound economic comparison of investment or purchasing opportunities. Strong emphasis on plan fulfillment at the enterprise level undermined the ability (and interest) of enterprises to engage in foreign trade. What little integration there was derived from explicit actions of the governments to promote the coordination of plans, technical and scientific cooperation, contractual agreements on cooperation among enterprises, and joint investments in common projects.

Consequently, the model of integration discussed earlier in this chapter bears little relevance to integration in the centrally planned context. To be sure, some progress has been made along the lines of plan coordination and product specialization (through which individual member countries are assigned specific product lines which they then produce for the entire bloc). There has been, however, minimal integration of factor movements (labor, capital, enterprise), and integration within the bloc remains limited largely to the exchange of goods.

Such exchange continues to be thwarted by differences in the development levels of individual members, by the asymmetric pattern of trade flows (the U.S.S.R. clearly dominates the smaller member countries economically), and by the parallel production structures which have arisen from the earlier autarkic policies. More recently, the divergence of reform movements among the member countries has made multilateral planning within the bloc even more problematic, and the increased trade with the West since the early 1970s has to some extent dampened further the willingness to enter bloc-wide agreements. Deteriorating terms of trade for the Eastern European members (who export manufactures to the Soviet Union in return for Soviet supplies of energy and raw materials) have also served to dampen the interest in deepening integration within the bloc, as has the technological stagnation characteristic of centrally planned economies.

As Gottfried Haberler noted long ago,

> There can hardly be a doubt that despite real or alleged monopolies, oligopolies, and other deviations from perfect competition, and despite the disregard of real or imagined externalities, the "invisible hand" of often imperfect competition, impeded though it is by tariffs and other government restrictions of trade, has managed to integrate

the Western economies to a much greater extent than the centrally planned economies of the East have been integrated by their planners.[10]

Some East European leaderships, notably those in Hungary and Poland, have long insisted that the regional integration mechanisms of the CMEA were dysfunctional and ineffective. Early in 1990, in the wake of economic reforms sweeping throughout Eastern Europe and the Soviet Union, virtually all members of the CMEA were urging that new trade agreements should replace those in effect in the region. One target of the new proposals is to make the Eastern European currencies convertible. Until that occurs, a trade surplus with one member country in the bloc cannot be used to wipe out a deficit with another, so that bilateral balancing of trade prevails over the much more efficient multilateral balancing found in the Western economies.

ECONOMIC INTEGRATION IN LESS DEVELOPED COUNTRIES

Regional economic integration among less developed countries (LDCs) differs from that among developed, Western countries in regard to its rationale, mechanisms, and problems. In Western countries, the relative success of regional integration can be largely attributed to the conditions of highly developed productive forces, well developed market relations, a high level of historically evolved division of labor, sophisticated economic and institutional structures, and roughly similar degrees of development among member countries. These conditions have not only fostered economic integration among Western countries, but determined its nature as well. In LDCs, these conditions are generally absent. Here, in contrast, integration is necessitated by economic backwardness and/or the very need for development per se.

The Irrelevance of Orthodox Theory to Integration Among LDCs

Kadar has noted that the idea of integration by means of the market cannot even be proposed rationally if the economic environment is characterized by the general backwardness of market relations.[11] Consequently, economic integration strategies in LDCs must be tailored to the specific characteristics of the economies involved. Market-oriented integration based on orthodox theory may well be (and indeed has been) either dysfunctional or largely ineffective in the LDC context. Even if markets in LDCs were sufficiently developed for Western-style integration, other factors would limit its effectiveness. Orthodox theory holds that greater gains will obtain from regional integration when, (a) existing foreign trade is small relative to domestic production, and (b) a relatively large amount of trade is conducted with prospective integration partners prior to bloc formation. These conditions are precisely the opposite of those typically found in LDCs, whose foreign trade is usually large relative to domestic production and whose intragroup trade is usually a very minor component of total trade. Consequently, economic integration schemes based on the orthodox model may be at best irrelevant and at worst positively harmful for LDCs, except possibly for the more developed of such countries. It may be irrelevant because LDCs rely heavily on the exportation of primary products and thus on world markets, and integration is unlikely except in the very long run to affect significantly the volume of resources allocated to the production of such commodities. It may be harmful because the imports of LDCs consist chiefly of intermediate products and finished manufactures, which many such countries produce either not at all or very inefficiently, so that they cannot compete successfully against the exports of developed countries, even assuming some degree of protection.

It is in this context that one recognizes that the rationale for economic integration among LDCs does not lie in the static gains to be derived from changes in the existing pattern of trade or from the exploitation of comparative advantage based on existing patterns of production. Instead, the rationale for integration among LDCs is based on prospective gains from rationalizing the emergent structure of production, and on the effects of the creation of regional markets on the more fundamental problems of these countries (including the need to increase the opportunities for profitable investment by both domestic and foreign firms, and the need to mobilize unemployed resources). In brief, it is the drive to industrialize that is the primary economic motivation for integration among LDCs, and this shared motivation distinguishes regional integration in the Third World from that among Western countries. Integration is thus viewed as an integral part of development policy rather than as a logical consequence of development once achieved.

Orthodox theory holds trade diversion to be harmful because it implies the misallocation of (assumedly) fully employed resources from more efficient to less efficient pursuits. In LDCs, however, the domestic labor drawn into trade-diverting activities may have been formerly unemployed or grossly underemployed, so that its opportunity cost is at or near zero. Trade diversion resulting from regional integration among LDCs may be viewed favorably also if the only viable alternative is a policy of import substitution pursued individually by the members of the union, each with a small national market; or if it results in substantial savings of scarce foreign exchange (i.e., when foreign exchange has a scarcity value in excess of its market value). In contrast to orthodox integration theory, among LDCs one objective of integration might well be not to terminate protection, but to increase its scale and effectiveness.

This is because integration among LDCs is a potential means of creating a sufficiently large, protected market that will stimulate the regional production of import substitutes, create opportunities for profitable investment, and ultimately increase the export competitiveness of the region. Under these conditions, the short-run economic losses stemming from trade diversion are an acceptable cost of investment aimed at long-run competitiveness on world markets. Yet this rationale is the same as for infant industries, and thus subject to the same qualifications. Often protection of an industry is as likely to inhibit its development through the lack of competitive stimulus as it is to stimulate it, and the selection of sectors to protect is highly arbitrary.

Given the high priority of industrialization and development as objectives of regional integration among LDCs, one must address the issue of great disparities in the development levels of member states. Under such conditions, reliance primarily on market mechanisms would be detrimental to the less developed members, for economic activity and the benefits of integration would tend to concentrate in the relatively developed member countries. Thus, integration efforts among LDCs typically include the planned allocation of scarce resources and investment activities, with unilateral benefits and concessions extended to the less developed members. Typical compensatory policies have involved preferential treatment in regard to tariffs, taxes, income redistribution, and capital flows. None of these measures to date has been successful in substantially stimulating industrialization among the less developed members of LDC regional blocs, yet at least some have taken bold steps to explicitly allocate new industry in favor of the less developed members.

To be sure, the implementation of such compensatory mechanisms is very complex, and it greatly complicates integration policies and institutions. Disparities in the level of development involve many structural variances, including the structure of traditional exports and nature of their markets; the degree of diversification of exports; import-dependence; role of the state in the production and distribution of goods and services; differences in social structure and social policies, especially affecting enterprise management; and differences in rates of inflation. Where substantial differences along these lines prevail, integration designs must seek new instruments appropriate to the heterogeneity involved. Whether through complementarity agreements (trade liberalization for selected existing industries or product groups) or industrial programming (trade liberalization for selected new industries or product groups), integration among LDCs typically involves the deliberate, planned rationalization of production and targeted specialization among group members; and policy instruments rather than the market determine the pattern of production.

Existing patterns of trade have hindered economic integration among LDCs. The success of Western European integration has been based in part on the historically developed higher degree of regional division of labor already existing when integration was launched in Western Europe; at the time, members were already conducting around one-third of their foreign trade with each other. When the integration schemes were launched in Latin America, however, the ratios of trade among members were 9 percent for the Central American Common Market, 8 percent for the Latin American Free Trade Association (LAFTA), and only 3 percent for the Andean Group. Thus, existing trade patterns tended strongly to support regional cooperation in the EEC, but to undermine it in Latin America. Under these conditions, the immediate welfare gains from the allocative effects of integration are small, although integration could possibly create the conditions for subsequent rapid increases in intraregional trade through spill-over effects on infrastructure, such as transportation networks, the present underdevelopment of which has been a significant deterrent to regional integration.

Given the existing trade patterns, the only viable integration arrangement among most LDCs is one which complements, rather than substitutes for, a strategy of more active participation by the LDCs in the world economy.[12] Economic integration in this context is thus conceived as a means of removing external barriers to development through the deepening of import substitution (on a regional scale). Especially in Latin America today, integration models must explicitly be designed to ameliorate the serious balance-of-payments problems. To be sure, the strategy of import substitution generally changes the composition rather than the quantity of hard-currency imports (by replacing imports of goods that can be produced within the region with those of capital and intermediate goods and basic inputs). Moreover, a balance of export promotion with import substitution must be achieved, since Western markets for LDC exports are a crucial component of debt reduction.

Relations between a trading bloc and the external world can be of immense importance in explaining the degree of political commitment to integration. However, the causal relationship is seldom clear-cut. Perceptions of being victimized by the global system tend to foster regional integration among LDCs as a defensive measure, but perceptions of heavy dependence on the larger system may be so pervasive as to be a disincentive to regional integration efforts. When a single extraregional state wields strong influence on the economies of the integrated region, its role in influencing integration is indeterminate. That is, it may tend to undermine regional integration efforts (as has been alleged of the United States in dealing with several Latin American integration efforts) or to support them (as in the case of the U.S.-sponsored Caribbean Basin initiative). The existence of trading blocs themselves may foster the formation of new trading blocs: thus EFTA was created largely as a response to the creation of the EEC, and Latin American integration efforts similarly have been given an impetus by the EEC's protectionist policies and preferential treatment of other LDCs through the Lome Convention (through which the European Community extends privileged access to its market for former colonies in Africa, the Caribbean area, and certain Pacific island nations).

The continuing economic and financial crisis in Latin America during the 1980s surely creates conditions unfavorable to regional integration. Between 1980 and 1984 intraregional trade among LDCs in the Western Hemisphere declined by 27 percent in value, mainly because of import austerity programs and because the heavily indebted countries were compelled to shift their exports away from regional arrangements towards convertible currency markets. On the other hand, the severity of the situation has perhaps convinced many in Latin America that regional economic integration is the only viable solution to the region's problems. Consequently, there has been a renewed push in Latin America for regional economic integration.

IMPLICATIONS OF ECONOMIC INTEGRATION FOR THE FIRM

International economic integration occurs most obviously on two separate levels. One is the macroeconomic level, at which market forces and government action, on either a regional or global basis, induce the transnational flow of factor inputs and final products. This has been the focus of the present chapter. The other is at the microeconomic level, at which multinational enterprises coordinate and integrate diverse activities among their geographically dispersed units. Such firm-level initiatives comprise the basic focus of this book. It is important to keep the macroeconomic forces in mind, however, because they both reflect and make possible the international strategic thrusts of individual firms. The horizontal and/or vertical integration of corporate activities across national borders assumes the configuration enabled by the specific nature and conditions of the larger economic system under which it occurs.

As countries integrate economically to increase efficiency and to improve economic performance, so do enterprises integrate their international activities in order to improve profitability and long-term competitive positions.[13] The two developments are inseparable, and reinforce each other. Successful macrolevel integration is based on the behavior of firms, and successful firm-level integration derives from strategic responses to changes in the macroeconomic environment. When major developments ensue such as that of the U.S.–Canadian Free Trade Agreement or of the completion of the European integration scheme in 1992, it is essential that firms respond proactively to ensure viable competitive positions. Threats as well as opportunities emerge under such changing conditions and the nature of competition changes. Firms adjust their strategies to cope with the new circumstances, and shifts in relative positions are likely.

It is important to note that no single generic strategy will succeed globally, given the widely diverse natures of integration schemes throughout the world. It may result, for example, that a single company opts for fully owned subsidiaries in the European Community, for industrial cooperation agreements in Eastern Europe, and for joint ventures or partnerships in Latin America. One unit of the firm may integrate vertically, and the other horizontally. Marketing channels will differ, and finance policies in different regions will be difficult to reconcile. The environment is complex, as are the functional strategies of individual firms. Regulatory regimes and competitive conditions will vary widely across regions, so that strategic planners must assume a multifocus in trying to coordinate and integrate corporate activities.

All this creates a tremendous challenge for those who are responsible for the strategic direction of firms, and also for those who are responsible for implementing the strategic and policy initiatives given them. In subsequent chapters, we discuss potential specific responses to such challenges.

SUMMARY

Major initiatives are now underway (e.g., in North America and West Europe) at the macroeconomic level that will fundamentally alter the competitive positions of firms engaged internationally. Economic integration at the national level is causing firms to reconsider their own strategic initiatives and to adjust policies in view of the changing realities. Basic environmental changes necessitate strategic reorientation at the enterprise level.

Economic integration at the macroeconomic level is a highly complex phenomenon, however, and its specific configuration varies widely over time and across regions. In general, one must distinguish among market-oriented integration as found in the West, integration among the centrally planned economies of Eastern Europe, and the numerous integration schemes found among less developed regions. In each case, one will find numerous integration options even at the disaggregated level.

The integration and coordination of enterprise-level activities will typically reflect the opportunities and challenges inherent in integration at the macroeconomic level. Firms adjust or lose their competitiveness. The variety of integration schemes across regions, however, means that no single corporate strategy is feasible in responding to the competitive challenges which arise. Strategies must be adapted to the specific conditions in individual markets, and this makes it difficult at the highest levels of the firm to coordinate widely dispersed initiatives. In subsequent chapters we discuss a variety of possible responses to the increasingly complex nature of the corporate environment for international operations.

DISCUSSION QUESTIONS

1. In the Western context, economic integration may be viewed as either a state of affairs (condition) or a process. Discuss.
2. Distinguish between the trade creating and trade diverting consequences of economic integration at the regional level.
3. Distinguish between negative and positive integration, and explain the connection between the two.
4. Compare economic integration in the Soviet bloc to that found in Western Europe.
5. Why have market-oriented integration schemes generally failed when applied to less developed countries?
6. Compare the rationale for integration at the macro- and microeconomic levels.
7. Western Europe has established the year 1992 as the target date for completing its regional economic integration. What implications does this have for American firms just entering the market?

NOTES

1. Paul Marer and John Michael Montias, eds., *East European Integration and East–West Trade* (Bloomington: Indiana University Press, 1980), "Theory and Measurement of East European Integration," pp. 3–38.
2. Bela Balassa, "Types of Economic Integration," in *Economic Integration: Worldwide, Regional, Sectoral*, ed., Machlup (London: Macmillan, 1976), pp. 17–31.
3. John Pinder, "Integration in Western and Eastern Europe: Relations Between the EC and CMEA," *Journal of Common Market Studies* (December, 1979), pp. 114–134.
4. Peter W. Wood and Robert F. Elliott, "Trading Blocs and Common Markets," in *Handbook of International Business*, ed., Ingo Walter (New York: John Wiley and Sons, 1982), pp. 4:3–4:44.
5. Assar Lindbeck, "International Economic Integration," in *The International Allocation of Economic Activity*, eds., Ohlin, Hesselborn, and Wijkman (London: Macmillan, 1977), pp. 216–226.
6. An analogy is found in the plight of the U.S. Administration, which has frequently been placed in the position of having to compromise with the most highly protectionist Congress, granting limited protection in the hopes of avoiding more damaging and permanent restrictions on trade.

7. Lindbeck, *op. cit.*, p. 225.

8. Fritz Machlup, "Conceptual and Causal Relationships in the Theory of Economic Integration in the Twentieth Century," in Ohlin et al., *op. cit.*, pp. 196–215.

9. Franklyn D. Holzman, "Comecon: A 'Trade-Destroying' Customs Union?," *Journal of Comparative Economics* (December, 1985), pp. 410–423.

10. Gottfried Haberler, "Theoretical Reflections on the Trade of Socialist Economies," in *International Trade and Central Planning*, eds., Alan A. Brown and Egon Neuberger (Los Angeles: University of California, 1968), pp. 23–48.

11. Bela Kadar, *Problems of Economic Growth in Latin America* (London: Hurst and Co., 1980), p. 127.

12. Luciano Tomassini, "The Disintegration of the Integration Process: Towards New Forms of Regional Cooperation," in *Regional Integration: The Latin American Experience*, ed., Altaf Gauhar (Boulder: Westview Press, 1985), pp. 210–233.

13. A superb analysis comparing integration at the macro and micro levels is found in John H. Dunning and Peter Robson, "Multinational Corporate Integration and Regional Economic Integration," *Journal of Common Market Studies* (December, 1987), pp. 103–125.

FURTHER READING

1. *The Journal of Common Market Studies* provides excellent analyses of integration schemes of all types.

2. Machlup, Fritz, ed. *Economic Integration: Worldwide, Regional, Sectoral.* (London: Macmillan, 1976).

3. Marer, Paul, and John Michael Montias, eds. *East European Integration and East-West Trade* (Bloomington: Indiana University Press, 1980).

4. Robson, Peter. *The Economics of International Integration* (London: George Allen and Unwin, 1980).

5. Wood, Peter W., and Robert F. Elliott. "Trading Blocs and Common Markets." In *Handbook of International Business*, ed., Ingo Walter (New York: John Wiley and Sons, 1982), pp. 4:3–4:44.

CHAPTER 3

▼

The Global Strategic Perspective

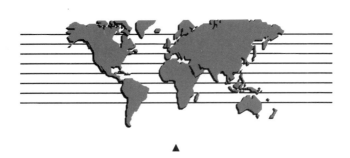

▲

Organizations are formed to accomplish a purpose, and it is only in relation to goal achievement that corporate strategies may be adequately assessed. Privately owned firms may have many goals and objectives, but typically long-term profit maximization, growth, and survival have high priority. For private firms, profitability is of course one of the most basic business indicators and an overriding consideration in virtually all strategic decisions. It is a key criterion in investment decisions, the selection of marketing strategies, and the evaluation of managerial performance.

THE GLOBAL ENVIRONMENT

For two decades following the Second World War, companies could succeed, quite well, simply by managing efficiently the businesses they ran. In the 1950s there was a seller's market for most commodities, due to the pent-up demand resulting from war-time scarcities and relatively high levels of personal savings. Moreover, there was virtually no competition in the United States by foreign firms, which were fully preoccupied with the reconstruction of war-torn countries. The seller's market disappeared in America by the 1960s, but firm growth rates were in many cases maintained through a series of mergers among the major firms. The most forward-looking firms went abroad, but it was really not until the 1970s, "the decade of the multinationals," that American involvement in international trade doubled from 12 percent to 24 percent as a share of the gross national product (GNP).

In today's economic environment, managing efficiently may not suffice. Indeed, given the intense international competition, environmental turbulence, and the total restructuring of many basic industries, the key to success today quite often appears to be the management of change instead of the management of growth. The focus is more on quality than on quantity, more on entrepreneurship than on administration. No longer is the entrepreneur incompatible with long-standing, relatively large organizations (if indeed he or she ever was); instead, large organizations have rapidly learned how to manage innovation within their well-established hierarchies. The emergence of this qualitative change within U.S. industry has been prompted to a great extent by economic forces and competition that are international in nature.[1]

The reorientation of European companies toward the global strategic perspective has been prompted in large part by the European Community's decision to complete the integration of its internal market by 1992. Although the European Economic Community was established in 1958, nationalistic industrial policies have hindered the development of strong, world-class companies in Europe (with notable exceptions, such as in chemicals, pharmaceuticals, and the aerospace industry). The current emphasis on positive integration measures (e.g., harmonization of economic policies and the creation of continent-wide industrial standards), as defined in the previous chapter, has fundamentally altered the competitive environment of Europe and, consequently, the strategic orientation of European companies. Part of the reorientation is defensive in nature, as the expansion of the internal market leaves previously protected companies exposed to foreign competition. Essentially, however, the reorientation focuses on the opportunities which emerge through the broadening of markets and general deregulation.

Japanese companies have also very recently become much more multinational in their approach to production, marketing, and investment decisions. Their heavy foreign investment in East Asia, for example, is moving into a new phase, as Japanese companies shift assembly work from higher labor-cost countries (Taiwan, South Korea, Singapore, Hong Kong) to lower (e.g., Malasia, China). This restructuring includes a greater horizontal division of labor, as the focus is now on the foreign manufacture of components rather than on merely assembly work. Economic integration in Europe and North America has also induced considerable investment by Japanese companies in those areas. The reorientation does not derive solely from integration efforts, but from currency movements, relative changes in competitive positions, and industrial restructuring as well.

Consequently, because of these changes in the environment, corporate policies that proved quite successful a few decades ago are not necessarily appropriate for conditions in the 1980s. All firms, small, medium, and large, must assume a global orientation if they are to seek optimal performance. There will of course be wide variation in the extent to which firms are actively involved internationally, because environmental threats and opportunities (of both foreign and domestic origin) affect different firms in different ways. But the failure to recognize that input and output markets are not confined to national boundaries, or that the economic climate is largely dependent on international economic forces, can lead to the adoption of strategies that are inevitably less than optimal.

This is not to say that all industries are global in nature, for they are not. Furthermore, it is not necessary that a firm have foreign operations in order for it to become globally oriented. Even a purely domestic firm might, and we contend should, adopt a global perspective. And we stress here also the importance of the fact that assuming a global perspective does not in itself presume the adoption of any specific strategy. There are many viable strategic patterns, as students of business policy are well aware.

A firm may have multinational presence but still lack global strategic management. Electrolux, for example, the Swedish industrial group and appliances manufacturer, is reliant on its home country for only 17 percent of revenues and 20 percent of its employees. Traditionally it has put local management in charge of its manufacturing and sales operations in some 50 countries around the world. During the 1980s Electrolux had made around 100 acquisitions on both sides of the Atlantic, vastly expanding its core household appliances businesses and adding a growing number of smaller and disparate activities until it has today two dozen fully different product lines. The diversity of product lines and the nature of the appliances industry, which many contend remains fragmented by different national preferences, had led to an extremely decentralized management approach.

However, Europe's progress toward economic integration, as well as the managerial challenges of coordinating activities in widely diverse markets, has led the company to reassess its strategy, organization, and relationship to subordinate units. The basic strategy is to become a major competitor in every country market where it is active, and this entails building cross-national synergies through production economies of scale (aimed at international cost leadership) and the use of common components for products tailored as before to national markets. The highly decentralized structure will be turned into a set of interdependent but flexible "networks," with product development, manufacturing, and supply all spanning international borders. Finally, relations with subordinate units will be strengthened through "corporate parenting," under which the issues such as quality, just-in-time supply, inventory control, and accounts receivable of each unit will be monitored much more closely by corporate headquarters. Through such actions, Electrolux will have adopted a global orientation.

ESTABLISHED PATTERNS OF GLOBAL STRATEGY

Let us begin the delineation of global strategies by viewing the patterns established by multinational firms, which have already established operations abroad. Based on the product life cycle model discussed in Chapter 1, Vernon posits the existence of three types of internationally involved firms.[2] The first is the innovative multinational corporation (MNC) with a highly developed capacity for global scanning, and with multiple markets having equal opportunity to stimulate the firm towards innovation. Such a firm would presumably innovate in response to opportunity or threat in any of the many markets in which it operates. The innovation itself may be undertaken in the specific market where the opportunity or threat arises or, for reasons associated with economies of scale or existing production capabilities, in a site far removed from the target market. Whichever the case, the innovation can rapidly be applied to any or all of the firm's markets. In any event, the global scanner is in an advantageous position in relation to its competitors who lack such scanning capabilities. Under these circumstances, the product life cycle concept does not fully hold due to the enhanced position of foreign markets as stimuli to innovation, and due to the fact that production is not necessarily undertaken in the market that first stimulated the innovation. However, this type of MNC is, at present, more hypothetical than real.

A second type of MNC develops and produces a line of standardized products for relatively homogeneous, worldwide demand: typical of many commodity markets, but also increasingly typical of certain manufactures such as aircraft, computers, and automobiles. The recent introduction of "world cars" reflects this pattern in manufactures, which provides advantages in production and marketing economies. It is a development not fully consistent with the product life cycle model in that it presupposes the simultaneous introduction of new products worldwide. The basic innovation will typically be developed in the home country, to assure effective integration of activities at headquarters; however, certain developmental activities and the production of some basic components might well be undertaken in various locations abroad. The widely dispersed production of components in numerous plants in various countries is not consistent with the original product life cycle model, but it provides economies of scale, low-cost sourcing, and similar cost advantages. While some firms might choose to compete via economies reaped through world models, others in the same industry of course might see greater benefits in designing products more specifically for individual markets.

A third type of innovative MNC continues its focus primarily on the home market, and permits its foreign subsidiaries to adopt the innovations at their discretion. This practice is the closest of the three to the original concept of the product life cycle model, but even here the time interval of foreign diffusion of the innovation is shortened. Moreover, the oligopolistic advantages of the firm are somewhat weakened by such an approach. In addition, should an innovation possibility emerge among any of the foreign subsidiaries, exploitation of those opportunities might be constrained by the risk-taking propensity of the foreign subsidiary's management or by potentially low resource slacks of the subsidiary.

Strategic Advantages of Multinational Corporations

Vernon and Wells have differentiated MNC strategies on the basis of whether they are aimed at exploiting a technological lead, a strong trade name, advantages of scale, or a scanning capability.[3] These are not mutually exclusive, nor are they necessarily incompatible with the product life cycle model. They are, in addition, strategies which generically are fully appropriate for firms which are not multinational in nature.

Technological Lead

Firms that exploit a technological lead abroad do not need to have manufacturing bases abroad, in contrast to the pattern posited by the product life cycle model. Boeing, Lockheed, and other aircraft manufacturers typically rely on exports rather than on foreign production facilities, yet are very heavily involved in global strategies. We owe our soft contact lenses and ball-point pens to innovations first made in Czechoslovakia and Hungary, respectively, but the innovators chose to license their technology rather than go abroad with it. Given rapid technological developments abroad, especially in Western Europe and Japan, this latter pattern suggests an extremely attractive opportunity for many U.S. firms — that of in-licensing foreign technologies for exploitation in the huge American market.

Strong Trade Name

The exploitation of a strong trade name is an oligopolistic strategy that has the potential to give the firm a strong competitive advantage over national competitors in foreign markets. Especially today, under the conditions of rapid and continuous international communication flows, and the penetration of many areas by American cultural patterns, a strong trade name can lead to quick entry into foreign markets. Coca-Cola, for example, has 26 percent of its assets outside the United States, but derives approximately 75 percent of its total operating profits from foreign markets. Conditions may change fairly rapidly, however, as suggested by the fact that "Made in Japan" had a highly derogatory connotation not many years ago.

Advantages of Scale

In many basic global industries, such as oil, copper, aluminum, and heavy chemicals, neither technology nor trade names provide significant competitive advantages. Instead, it is advantages of scale that typically differentiate the firms. Vertical integration, multiple markets and sources, high entry costs and defensive pricing strategies are all aspects of such industries which are greatly enhanced by global strategies rather than strategies restricted to individual national markets.

Scanning Competencies

The MNC's scanning capabilities, based on its worldwide presence, are a significant asset. Many of the larger MNCs operate in more than 50 countries, and the efficiency of the MNC in searching the world for low-cost sourcing, new technologies, and new marketing opportunities is of great importance. Global scanning capabilities also provide an enhanced opportunity for closely monitoring similar behavior on the part of its major competitors.

THE NEED FOR A GLOBAL STRATEGY

Note however that MNC activities abroad do not necessarily presume a global strategy. Indeed, many multinationals today are less global in their strategies than some firms with no significant operations abroad. Such MNCs may have many subsidiaries scattered throughout the world, but each subsidiary is treated as a separate entity, serving the individual market in which it is located. In many cases, such a decentralized or "portfolio" approach to foreign investment results in substantial suboptimization. Such a national market approach rather than global orientation might well be justified in industries where economies are insignificant, research and development is closely tied to particular markets, and product specifications vary significantly across country boundaries. But consider the case of a British subsidiary in 1984, when the British pound hit an all-time low due to rumors that Nigeria might leave the OPEC cartel. For the manager of the British subsidiary, the fall of the pound might not seem important if the subsidiary has no substantial international links except technical ownership by an American conglomerate. For headquarters, however, the development reflects a sudden deterioration of the British subsidiary's performance, when the pounds are repatriated and translated into U.S. dollars. One cannot escape international linkages, no matter how remote they might at first appear. And in fully considering those linkages through assuming a global strategy, at least at the headquarters level, corporate managers are in a better position to make the correct strategic decisions.

Economic and Political Imperatives

Doz distinguishes among three generic strategies of MNCs according to their response to either economic imperatives, or political imperatives, or both.[4] Economic realities of many industries, such as the availability of economies of scale or low-cost sourcing from abroad, suggest a strategy of worldwide integration and product rationalization based, for example, on the production of various components in different countries. On the other hand, many governments increasingly require foreign-based firms located in their countries to adapt their policies more to the benefit of the individual country. This is the political imperative, which is the basis of a second, or "national responsiveness" strategy. The nationally responsive strategy, at the extreme, is incompatible with a global strategic orientation. The third strategy delineated by Doz is the "administrative coordination" strategy, which is a compromise between the other two. Here the MNC accepts the inevitable conflict between economic and political imperatives, and looks for structural and administrative adjustments instead of strategic solutions. Such an administrative solution allows no real strategy in itself, except to negotiate each strategic decision on its own merits instead of coordinating decisions as a mutually reinforcing set of strategic plans.

According to Doz, each of these strategies might be appropriate, depending on the markets being served, the competition being faced, and the technology being used by the firm. For some products, such as telecommunications equipment, the technology and economies of production mandate global rationalization, but national political imperatives are sufficiently strong to prevent it. In other industries, such as automobiles, economic imperatives mandate global rationalization, and this is fully possible in the absence of strong political imperatives. Thus Ford has announced its Brazilian "world truck," which will have a European cab and panels, a North American chassis, a diesel engine developed by Ford's agricultural group, and it will be assembled in Brazil for the domestic and North American markets. Third, there are those businesses, such as computers, whose markets are partly government-controlled and partly internationally competitive. In such industries, where both economic and political imperatives are critical, the MNC faces its most difficult choice. All three types of strategies may be found among the firms in such industries, according to the relative strengths of each. The smaller firms, for example, might well yield more quickly to government pressures, and in so doing gain a competitive advantage to help offset their relative disadvantage in economies. Thus it was Honeywell, not IBM, who joined forces with the French state-owned computer companies.

Competition

Porter, focussing on competitive rather than economic or political imperatives, has defined global industries as those in which the strategic positions of competitors in major geographic or national markets are fundamentally affected by their overall global positions.[5] Thus, IBM's strategic position in France or Germany is significantly improved by the technology and marketing skills developed elsewhere in the company. To analyze competition in a global industry, it is necessary to examine industry economics and competitors in the various markets jointly rather than individually.

Porter identifies four generic strategies found in global industries.

1. The "broad line global" strategy is one through which firms compete worldwide in the full product line of the industry. This is the approach Caterpillar Tractor Company has taken in the construction equipment industry. The strategy requires substantial resources and a long-term horizon, significant economies of scale or scope, product differentiation, or an overall low-cost position.

2. The "global focus" strategy targets a particular segment of the industry for competing worldwide, and is aimed similarly at creating product differentiation or a low-cost position. Coles Cranes and Jones Cranes, both of Great Britain, have used this approach in the construction equipment industry, concentrating on cranes and leaving to others the manufacturing and marketing of bulldozers, excavators, and similar heavy equipment.

3. The "national focus" strategy is one which takes advantage of differences in national markets. This strategy is one through which the firm consciously selects one or two major markets out of many, and by focussing its efforts on them, the firm is potentially able to outcompete global firms in those specific markets. Thus Kockums has been highly successful in the Scandinavian markets for certain lines of construction equipment.

4. One may adopt a "protected niche" strategy by seeking out countries where government restraints exclude global competition to a

large extent; for example, by requiring a high proportion of local content in the product and by protection against foreign competition through high tariff barriers.

GLOBAL INDUSTRIES AND STRATEGY

The aircraft manufacturing industry is a global industry, mainly due to the huge capital requirements and the subsequent need for global markets to assure sufficient scales through which to amortize the investment costs. So too is the semiconductor industry, whose high capital and research and development investments must be made under conditions of short product lives and substantial swings in demand that put a premium on swift decision-making and flexibility. Marketing, design, and production must be done worldwide. Worldwide marketing is needed in order to recover the huge investment outlays in capital and research and development. Design must be dispersed because chipmaking increasingly requires that the entire system of which the chip will be a part should be taken into account when the chip itself is designed; and this in turn gives an advantage to chip-makers that are geographically close to their customers. Moreover, under conditions of intense competition, a global manufacturing and marketing perspective allows products to be manufactured in the lowest-cost countries, updated quickly with technological improvements, and marketed powerfully from the center.

An increasingly prevalent approach to implementing the more ambitious strategies in global industries is the creation of "transnational coalitions," or cooperative agreements between firms in the industry of different home countries. The telecommunications industry, for example, has experienced a very rapid increase of collaborative ventures in recent years, as technologies become rapidly outdated, markets become reshaped virtually overnight, and firms seek linkages with other firms in order to strengthen their competitive position, expand geographically into new markets, and diversify into new product lines. These developments, spurred in general by the convergence of what was once two industries (computers and communications), have fostered linkages among firms which until quite recently operated in completely different markets.

These collaborative linkages assume a wide range of forms—from relatively informal agreements between companies to unite in support of common technical standards, through joint ventures in research, product development or marketing, to outright acquisition. Such linkages were enouraged in the United States by deregulation and the subsequent, increasingly intense competition. In Europe the computer markets are fairly competitive, although the telecommunications markets are still largely monopolistic due to national standards and restrictions, preferences given to nationalized firms, and the high degree of duplication of product lines among Europe's leading companies. Thus, Europe's two largest electronics companies, Philips (Holland) and Siemens (West Germany), are conducting joint research to develop a new type of computer memory chip. The two companies are investing more than $425 million in the project, including $140 million in grants from the Dutch and German governments. Lacking homogeneous and large markets in Europe, this is one way to compete against American and Japanese companies, which have access to larger markets and more abundant sources of venture capital. In addition, the European Economic Community has launched ESPRIT, a five-year, $1.5 billion plan to support information-technology research in Europe. But many European companies individually are linking with either U.S. or Japanese firms to stimulate their research and marketing capabilities. Olivetti (Italy) has recently linked forces with more than 20 U.S. companies, to gain access to advanced technologies and also to world markets. Through such links the American companies in turn gain access to European technologies and markets.

In addition to ESPRIT, a number of other government-supported, collaborative research programs have been initiated in Europe. In 1987 the second five-year Framework Program was launched to help coordinate research and technological development. The European Space Agency (ESA) has a budget supported by every European Community member except Greece and Luxembourg. Eureka, one of the most successful initiatives (having had over 200 projects launched to date), brings together European companies for collaboration in (precompetitive) new technologies. Jessl is a joint-European submicron silicon project to enhance technological progress for large scale integrated circuits. Race entails joint research and development in advanced communication technology, and Brite fosters joint research in industrial technologies and advanced materials. These are only a few of the government-backed projects in Europe aimed at increasing the competitiveness of European companies in international markets.

ADOPTING GLOBAL STRATEGIES

At the present, many multinationals still do not have a global strategy. Until recently, for example, Ford's European operations were a unit in itself, reporting to the International Division in Dearborn but not at all integrated with Ford's other activities. The International Division has now been discarded, a change designed to acknowledge the evolving relationships among the company's operations worldwide, and to enhance the coordination of the company's major activities. Ford has made progress in designing a "world car," but for the time being it is impossible to offer the same vehicle to every world market. Customer tastes vary substantially across major markets. Moreover, most Latin American countries have local content laws which increase investment outlays and require each model to be kept in production longer, meaning that they cannot be replaced at the same pace as similar models in North America or Europe. Ford is thus focussing its efforts on making as many components as interchangeable as possible.

Ford is also building a $500 million export-oriented factory in Mexico, taking advantage of low-cost labor in Mexico and Japanese technology (from Toyo Kogyu, which is 25 percent owned by Ford). The impetus for that decision stemmed in part from GM's decision to build cars in California using Japanese technology, and in part from Mexican government requirements that foreign auto makers in Mexico reduce the number of models which they make (in order to become price-competitive on world markets) unless they export over half the output and are self-sufficient in foreign exchange.

Caterpillar Tractor Company is another multinational that is just now adopting a global perspective. This may sound surprising for a firm that holds a 50 percent share of the U.S. market and a 35 percent share worldwide in the construction equipment business, but the firm faced three straight years of losses in the early 1980s after 50 years of continuous profitability. It faces also an increasing threat from low-cost foreign competitors — mainly Komatsu of Japan, which has surged rapidly to become number two in the industry worldwide and is now specifically targeting the United States market for penetration (partly by merging with the construction machinery operations of Dresser Industries). Large overcapacity in the industry had led to severe price discounting, while the strong American dollar during the early 1980s virtually wiped out many of Caterpillar's export markets. In response to competitive pressures, Caterpillar has reduced overall employment by some 30,000 since 1979, has won significant concessions in basic pay scales (at the expense of a seven month strike by the United Auto Workers during 1982–83), and has pressured its suppliers to cut prices and speed deliveries (the latter aimed at increasing inventory turnover 50 percent by 1986). Caterpillar's strategy also includes increased sourcing from foreign firms, which is a new element in Caterpillar's approach. German and Japanese companies now supply crankshafts once made exclusively in the United States, and the company is switching much of its U.S. lift-truck manufacturing to South Korea and Norway. Caterpillar has also contracted with a German company to make hydraulic excavators under the Caterpillar name to be marketed in Europe.

Recognizing Potential Through Global Strategy

To be sure, many industries seem to be lacking the prerequisites for a global strategy on the part of firms. In areas where economies of scale are too modest, research and development tied too closely to particular markets, products differ significantly across country boundaries, lead times are short or transportation costs and government barriers are high, it is easy to assume that global strategies make no sense.

State-owned firms are heavily geared to their own national activities, and they are rarely among the competitive, fast-growing multinationals. Such firms are typically not profit maximizers, but rather tend towards serving other purposes, such as maintaining employment at home and providing useful social services at small profits or subsidized losses. Yet in the past decade or so an increasing number of European state-owned firms have gone international and adopted global policies, and quite successfully so. Such firms often have built-in markets and monopoly powers at home, and do not need to earn profits if other national goals are considered more important. Many see in this trend a distinct competitive threat because the rules of the game are somewhat altered.[6] But even those state-owned firms that stay at home gain tremendously by adopting global strategies in their search for new technologies, whether related to product or process.

Traditionally, service firms (i.e. legal, medical, or accounting services, etc.) have been strategically oriented around purely domestic and largely regional markets. Today, the implementation of licensing requirements for these firms has contributed towards their transformation into national industries. However, many legal, medical, and accounting firms are now expanding abroad through affiliates located in other countries and staffed with nationals. Particulary in the medical field, one must keep in constant touch with research developments abroad. Evidence of the growing importance of service industries internationally is the focus on the needs of this sector in the current GATT negotiations.

How about the small local restaurant, which many would contend can easily ignore international developments? Many have become quite successful by specializing in "foreign technologies." One need only to visit a university town to note the many restaurants that specialize in various international cuisines. Some restaurants, such as McDonald's, Kentucky Fried Chicken, Wendy's, and Wienerwald, have been tremendously successful in their expansion abroad. In 1987, for example, nearly 30 percent of McDonald's total sales came from foreign operations. The adoption of a global strategy has brought great benefits to these firms.

SUMMARY

Out of about 9 million U.S. firms, all but 10,000 or so stay at home. Some become internationally active through exporting and importing; many public organizations become involved in selling services to foreigners, for example university enrollment of foreign students. Such activities are generally peripheral to the perceived major thrusts of the company or organization, but this need not preclude the adoption of a global strategy. For many small- and medium-sized businesses, the changed competitive environment suggests that a global search for critical inputs or expanded markets can lead to significant competitive advantages.

In the past, multinational expansion was based not so much on global perspectives than on incremental changes in the company's philosophy. Henry Ford built his first foreign car in Canada in 1906. Moving perhaps two miles from Detroit to Windsor, Ontario, to do this did not represent a massive strategic change, but by 1920 Fords were being assembled in over twenty countries, mainly to save freight charges. By 1930, Ford had manufacturing plants in at least five countries, and General Motors followed the initiative of Ford by establishing facilities in Britain and Germany.

Historically, the typical pattern for such firms was to begin with exports and then gradually to move to direct investment abroad. Technological leadership and economies of scale provided by the huge American market meant that exports from the United States were quite competitive abroad. But, as suggested by the product life cycle model discussed in Chapter 1, the success of American products abroad tended to whet the competitive appetites of foreign producers in their domestic markets, and competition stiffened. To offset the disadvantages of transportation costs and extended distribution networks, as well as to get closer to the pulse of the market, American firms began to replace exports with investment abroad to serve the foreign markets.

Often, this move was forced by other countries' policies, which were aimed at helping domestic firms become competitive by creating tariff and nontariff barriers to imports. In the late 19th century, for example, Canada enacted high tariffs on imports to protect its domestic producers. Rather than abandon the market, U.S. producers simply invested in Canadian plants and began to manufacture there, since Canada is not perceived, like most of the world, to be substantially different from the United States. One consequence of this is that around 50 percent of Canada's manufacturing capacity is foreign owned today, and overwhelmingly by U.S. firms. This is a continual source of friction between the two governments, but it is also a source of the living standards in Canada, which are substantially higher than they would have been without such foreign investment.

In these cases, no company emerged as a full blown multinational overnight. The typical pattern was one of evolution, often over decades, with frequent international involvement from the firm's early history through exports and imports. Then for one reason or another, as noted earlier, the firm gradually made direct investments and became more directly involved in other countries. Such activities were typically seen as minor affairs at the outset, and the first export orders hardly merited top management attention. But when a third or more of sales, and a greater amount of profits began to be generated abroad, attitudes began to change.

This change in philosophy and increased commitment to international operations were not necessarily the consequences of formal analytical planning processes. On the contrary, quite often the real strategy tended to evolve, as internal decisions and external events flowed together to create a new, widely shared consensus for action among key members of the top management team. Such a process, on which Quinn's concept of logical incrementalism is based,[7] might be by accident or design. In any case, the corporate philosophy often became oriented to the world rather than to the national environment, and some firms even perceived that global optimization of the MNC's position was necessary.

Today, the totally global view is still relatively rare, but firms no longer have the luxury of letting a world view develop, as if by accident, over a period of a decade or more. Changed environmental conditions demand a conscious approach to internationalization, and such an approach is as essential to those firms that do not go abroad as it is to those multinationals with foreign operations. Competitiveness in some industries may not require a foreign presence at all, but it will require increasingly a global view of factor and product markets as well as of general competitive developments.

DISCUSSION QUESTIONS

1. What general environmental changes have made the adoption of global strategies more essential?
2. The product life cycle model is probably less descriptive today than 20 years ago, but it still serves as a basis for some viable corporate strategies. What might such strategies be?
3. In what regards may a firm be multinational in nature yet lack a global perspective?
4. What are the characteristics of a global industry?
5. What are the four basic competitive strategies for global industries, as delineated by Porter?
6. How is the global outlook reflected in recent strategic decisions at the Ford and Caterpillar companies?

NOTES

1. An excellent discussion of these issues is found in: "Managing America's Business," *The Economist* (December 22, 1984), 91–112.
2. Raymond Vernon, "The Product Cycle Hypothesis in a New International Environment," in *Strategic Management of Multinational Corporations: The Essentials*, eds., Heidi Vernon Wortzel and Lawrence H. Wortzel (New York: John Wiley and Sons, 1985), 16–27.

3. Raymond Vernon and Louis T. Wells, Jr., *Manager in the International Economy*, 4th Ed. (Englewood Cliffs, N.J.: Prentice-Hall, 1981), 6–22.

4. Yves L. Doz, "Strategic Management in Multinational Companies," *Sloan Management Review* (Winter, 1980), 27–46.

5. Michael E. Porter, *Competitive Strategy: Techniques for Analyzing Industries and Competitors* (New York: The Free Press, 1980), 294–295.

6. Kenneth D. Walters and R. Joseph Monsen, "State-Owned Business Abroad: New Competitive Threat," *Harvard Business Review* (March–April, 1979), 160–170.

7. James Brian Quinn, *Strategies For Change: Logical Incrementalism* (Homewood, Ill.: Irwin, 1980), 51–59.

FURTHER READING

1. Grosse, Robert and Duane Kujawa. *International Business* (Homewood, Ill.: Irwin, 1988).

2. Kefalas, A. G. *Global Business Strategy* (Cincinnati: South-Western Publishing Co., 1990).

3. Markusen, James R. and James R. Melvin. *The Theory of International Trade* (Cambridge: Harper and Row, 1988).

4. Mazzolini, Renato. "The International Strategy of State-Owned Firms: An Organizational Process and Politics Perspective." *Strategic Management Journal*, April–June, 1980, 101–118.

5. Onkvisit, Sak and John J. Shaw. "An Examination of the International Product Life Cycle and Its Application within Marketing." *Columbia Journal of World Business*, Fall, 1983, 73–78.

6. Porter, Michael E. *Competition in Global Industries* (Boston: Harvard Business School Press, 1986).

7. Walters, Kenneth D. and R. Joseph Monsen. "Managing the Nationalized Company." *California Management Review*, Summer, 1983, 16–26.

CHAPTER 4

▼

Strategy Formulation

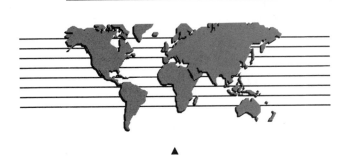

▲

Long range strategic planning has become commonplace for most successful companies, and those that have adopted a global orientation in their strategic planning by focussing on worldwide rather than merely national or regional opportunities, markets, and resources, have done particularly well. The global planning process, similar to that which focusses on more restricted regions, includes an assessment of the external environment and of the firm's internal capabilities. Based on that assessment, corporate objectives are set that realistically aim at exploiting external opportunities, minimizing the impact of potential threats, and building on internal capabilities. Planning is somewhat more complicated for global strategies, however, due to unique problems associated with such factors as geographical diversification, country (political) and foreign exchange risk analysis, and methods of entering foreign markets or gaining access to foreign inputs.

Under today's competitive conditions, it is also clear that companies not presently engaged in international operations can reap significant benefits by adopting a global strategic planning perspective. One benefit, but perhaps not even the major one, is that the firm can thereby monitor growth opportunities in overseas markets, which might offer improved horizons for expansion and exploitation of the firm's existing product lines and the firm's research and development, marketing, and management technology. Conversely, the firm might be able to significantly upgrade these capabilities through the acquisition of foreign products, technologies, and skills. More to the point, however, even where such opportunities do not exist, awareness of trends in other markets is essential because they may hold portent for domestic markets, signalling, for example, future market trends, entry of foreign competition and other changes that might require a reexamination of the current product/market portfolio of the firm.[1]

Internationally active companies need to constantly evaluate the degree and nature of their involvement in international markets. Thus those firms that now rely on exports might reassess their strategies, especially in view of the volatile currency fluctuations of recent years. Those firms with fully owned subsidiaries abroad might reconsider their reluctance to engage in joint ventures. And generally, a reassessment of geographical coverage of specific product lines might be advisable.

It will not suffice merely to monitor developments in individual country markets. What happens in Spain or Portugal, or indeed in the entire European Community, will depend to a great extent on changes brought about by the entry of these two countries to the Common Market. What happens in Chile will depend to a great extent on how the entire Latin American debt crisis is resolved. What happens in Egypt will depend to a great extent on developments in the entire Middle East.

At the same time, global strategic planning must include forecasts that are country specific. The nature of these forecasts will clearly differ according to which approach the individual firm takes to a particular market. If a firm's link to a country is only through exports or through a search for new technologies the firm is potentially interested in, its forecasting and other market study needs will be very different in nature from those of the firm that has a wholly owned subsidiary or joint venture operations abroad.

This chapter explores some of the international dimensions of strategic planning and control, including a section on political risk analysis. Political risk factors are the overriding environmental ingredient in developing plausible alternative scenarios regarding the futures of individual countries, and explicit recognition of this is central to effective strategic planning for world markets.[2]

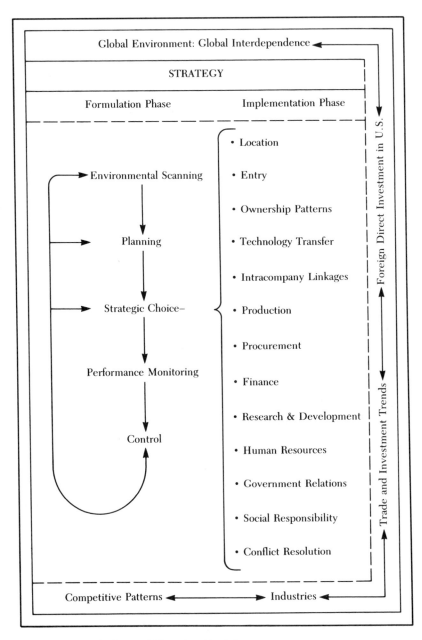

FIGURE 4-1 A General Planning Model

PLANNING

Planning by globally oriented firms is an extension of conventional planning techniques used by domestically oriented firms, but it is much more complex because the plans must necessarily deal with far more complicated environments. Currencies fluctuate in value, political environments are exceedingly turbulent, rules are changed in the middle of the game, sources of supply are cut off, and much basic information is either highly unreliable, or not available at all. These situations are faced by purely domestic firms also, but only by exception. For the firm involved globally, they are the rule. As difficult as planning is for the globally oriented firm, it is still quite essential in order to assure the synergies available through the proper integration of the firm's widely distributed operations.

Predicting Future Variables

To plan effectively, one must first have a fairly accurate picture of what the critical environmental conditions will be in the future. This may be the most difficult step of all, and few people really are good at spotting problems in advance. Few anticipated the introduction of floating currencies in the early 1970s; fewer still anticipated the OPEC actions. Currently, the Third World is in an extreme state of indebtedness and the outcome of this crisis is unknown. But the problem will apparently persist, and there the planning process begins, at least in the Western world. For planning inherently entails the concept that the future can also, in certain ways, be changed by design. Not all cultures accept this Faustian concept, and it is difficult to get affiliate managers deeply involved in planning if they believe that the future lies solely in the hands of Fate.

Long-term planning is increasingly based on the use of scenarios, which is a technique for describing several more or less likely environmental conditions in the future. For a high-tech firm, such planning might focus on probable technological breakthroughs over the next twenty years. For a firm in the extractive industries, the focus might be on the projected reliability and development of supply sources, as well as the emergence of possible substitutes for the mineral in question. In both cases, potential political and general economic trends are considered. Each scenario is given a quantitative probability ranking, and each is then considered in light of the firm's competitive situation and its basic competencies. Long-run changes in strategy are then considered in order to adapt the corporate capabilities and goals and activities to projected changes in the environment.

Medium-term planning, as for the domestic firm, is much more directed towards the implementation of strategy already decided upon. If it has been decided to enter the European or Latin American markets, or to significantly change the nature of operations already being undertaken there, then new requirements for finance and facilities, for personnel and for operations, for marketing and procurement, must be carefully assessed by all relevant departments and branches. These are important decisions, for they involve long-term commitments. Here both quantitative and nonquantitative methods are used, with the early emphasis perhaps placed on projected capital requirements and market potential. The process is exactly that used by purely domestic firms, but the options and constraints are typically much more complex.

In listing alternative actions by the MNC in response to projected environmental developments, options are not as clear-cut as for the domestic firm. It is not simply a question of choosing alternative sites based on the expected rates of return. Exchange risk, political risk, limitations on the repatriation of profits, the possible effects of Spain's entry to the European Community: all of these are issues that make the international planning alternatives much more complex than those of the local firm.

Evaluation and selection of the alternatives is similarly complex. Planning, for example, must explicitly address the issue of the product life cycle in international business. Thus, the firm might well anticipate that early exports to West Germany might lead to investments in foreign manufacturing facilities there. These facilities will at least initially depend on imported components from the home base, but perhaps later the home base will be importing manufactures from its foreign affiliate. Operating modes, too, are not static. If the firm today has licensing affiliates or industrial cooperation partners abroad, it must plan for the day when those contractual arrangements legally expire.

Issues of little significance in domestic planning loom large for the international planner. At home perhaps there are reliable suppliers of high-quality components, and the simple decision is made to buy instead of make. Abroad, suppliers might not be available, and operations of a different sort are introduced. Logistical problems of every type emerge in countries lacking adequate infrastructural support. Inventory supplies might have to be kept at significantly higher levels than preferred at home, due to the uncertainties involved. These issues may seem trivial at first but if they are ignored during the planning stages, then serious delays will occur in bringing the foreign operations on stream. The planning premises can be very different when the firm is involved in international operations.

The policy framework of any firm acts to limit planning alternatives. If a firm has the policy of insisting on nothing but fully owned subsidiaries abroad, then the planning task is made easier by the simple elimination of options that include partners. At the same time, however, such policies severely limit international opportunities. The sole ownership policy makes sense at home, but it precludes entry into Japan or Mexico, two very significant markets. Hence it is common to find MNCs examining even their most basic policies from time to time, in their own best interests, when looking at international options.

Resource Allocation

Resource allocation lies at the heart of planning. Assume that the Nigerian affiliate cannot easily obtain certain valves critical to its petrochemical operations. The valves could be produced cheaply in the British branch which makes auto components, but the firm lacks expertise in corrosion resistant processes. It would take years to build such expertise internally, but no company with the expertise is a candidate for acquisition. Still, the MNC may wish to push into the new area anyway. The reason is that if it really looks good, side bets are useful. It would be unlikely that the firm would invest $500 million in such a project, but it may well allocate a few million for research and development, both on the technical and marketing sides, for this potentially intriguing market. Hence, one aspect of resource allocation is to make some low-cost side bets in promising areas. Another is to focus the big money in known areas where the company has tremendous expertise in every functional aspect.

There is no handbook on how to do all of this, in spite of some relatively sophisticated models now available. Suppliers, ever anxious for profits, may offer new types of capital equipment. Foreign governments, ever anxious to gain income and employment, may offer intriguing tax holidays and other incentives. Out of many such ideas, the junior people look, evaluate, and report. Most projects are abandoned after short study, while others survive to undergo more extensive scrutiny. Quite a few die because they are too small. It is common for a major company to have a policy of not spending time on anything that does not promise a reasonably-sized market, simply because such things are not worth top management time. A peculiar result of this is that smaller, local firms often flourish and do multimillion dollar businesses in items that aren't worth it for the big companies. No one is perfect, and what looked like a minor market may turn out to be huge, and a new MNC is born.

Location

Once a global orientation suggests that there are excellent opportunities abroad, who goes where? Actually, the decision regarding location of foreign activities often depends as much on what the company is, and what its distinctive competencies are, as on the specific options abroad. Firms have comparative advantages, as do countries, and the wise manager plays from strength. That strength may lie in a differentiated product, such as Polaroid's; in marketing expertise, such as Coca-Cola's; in servicing and distribution networks, such as Caterpillar Tractor's; in manufacturing efficiency, such as Deere's; or in a number of other critical organizational aspects. There seem, however, to be at least five basic types of corporate strengths, as follows.

1. The market oriented firm has its major strengths in its marketing capabilities. It may be brilliant at developing brand franchises, or it may know exactly how to move down the marketing channel. Such firms are obviously successful at production and other business functions, but selling and market penetration are the stronger points. Major automobile companies are of this type. Many auto companies have failed because they could not sell what they could make, however efficiently; and the perceptive company somehow manages to have the right product at the right price in the right places. At times this can more than compensate for a relatively inefficient production operation compared to the market leaders, as General Motors demonstrated to Ford during the 1930s.

The locational problem here is to find, and then further develop, good markets. Countries that have high per capita incomes are the most alluring to many such firms, which is one reason why by far most of the world's trade is conducted among the relatively rich, industrialized countries. Countries with very large populations but lower per capita incomes might be viewed favorably by firms that sell low-priced, mass consumption items. Careful consideration of markets will be a major issue in scanning world environments for this type of firm. If the market can be tapped, the rest of the productive process falls into place.

Some otherwise promising markets may be unavailable for a number of reasons. Some countries, typically those with central planning systems, do not allow direct foreign investment, and those firms that have a company policy of "fully owned subsidiaries or nothing" are effectively shut out of those markets. In addition, many countries in the Third World are critically short of foreign exchange, and those markets are effectively shut off to exporters except those which supply critically needed inputs or which are willing to enter some sort of modern bartering techniques. Other countries may simply insist on too many onerous restrictions to make the firm's activities there profitable. Japan would be a huge market for many consumer goods marketers, but entry into that country is difficult. And for many consumer goods, the markets of communist countries are completely shut off.

2. Raw materials oriented firms produce, refine, or otherwise process and sell raw materials. Oil exploration and development firms are classic examples, as are firms mining copper, bauxite, or any other mineral. Historically, this was the first substantial area of foreign direct investment. For many such firms, the locational decision is simple: you go to where the raw material is. Such firms may spend many hundreds of millions of dollars on preliminary work to find out what the best possibilities are, and then try to work out deals with the countries that control the potential deposits. There can be many options available in this approach, since countries may offer different incentives and barriers. A major factor in assessing a location is to determine which mix of problems, incentives, and accessibility of raw materials leads to the optimal location.

Raw materials oriented firms are found all over the world, often in countries that are unattractive for any other type of investment. But if the oil or copper or gold is there, some materials oriented firm will be trying to get in and exploit the situation. One very important strategic thrust of such companies in recent years, given the increased political turbulence, is to diversify their sourcing capabilities.

3. Cost reducers typically operate in very competitive markets, often where price is determined by impersonal supply and demand factors. If you get your costs down, you can prosper even in the most mature of industries. Producers of textiles, toys, consumer electronics items, and many other light manufactures are of this type, as are producers of such items as refined aluminum ingots, gasoline, and other processed raw materials.

These companies go where costs are low. Often they are not as large as the well-known multinationals, which is a major reason why their markets are so competitive. Some seek out cheap labor, and are known derogatorily as runaway plants. Thus a firm manufacturing electronics components for television sets will move out of the United States to Taiwan or Mexico, where labor costs are low, or a textile firm will set up shop in Haiti or Hong Kong. To many this represents a final stage of the product life cycle, when firms manufacture abroad only, and import the manufactures into the home market. Many countries have low-cost labor, and many are willing to allow foreigners in to utilize it. Forty cents an hour might not be viewed as adequate by an American or a Japanese, but if the option in Haiti is making twenty cents a day as an agricultural laborer, or worse yet being unemployed, such pay can look very attractive to a local. When bigger firms move to cheap labor, they do not advertise the fact much, given the inevitable criticism that will come from unions and workers back home. But often this is the only choice, if the product is indeed labor intensive.

A more socially acceptable method of cost reduction is to reduce some cost other than labor. Thus aluminum smelters are found in Ghana and Norway, not because of low labor costs but because electric power is very cheap in both these countries. Since the major cost element in aluminum smelting is electricity, firms will move to low-cost power sources. Thus U.S. firms, which have tended to dominate the industry worldwide, have quickly moved into Australia, Brazil and Canada in response to energy cost developments in recent years.

4. Technologically-based firms typically seek new markets worldwide in view of the rapid obsolescence of many new technologies and the very high research and development costs that require large markets for rapid amortization. The strength of such firms might be based on a single product or process, such as Land's Polaroid camera or Head's metal skis. Probably more typical today are a number of rapidly changing technologies which have numerous applications, such as electronics, telecommunications, industrial materials, production automation, robotics, biotechnology, and artificial intelligence. These technologies have tremendous potential, not only for creating new industries but also for revitalizing the old ones. The exploitation of these new technologies depends often on vast and complex networks of collaboration among the leading firms, and equity and non-equity joint ventures have increased significantly in number. Such collaborative agreements may focus on research and development activities, production, marketing, or a combination of these. While in some cases the collaboration is motivated by the need to pool resources and to share costs and risks, stronger motivations are to gain access to technology developed by the partners and to gain preferential access to foreign markets. One consequence of the interfirm links in high-technology areas is that most of such activities take place in the developed, industrialized countries.

5. Firms that are brain renters sell their human skills, such as engineering advice or accounting knowledge. Characteristically, they employ large staffs of highly skilled and highly paid professionals. These companies will establish themselves wherever the local market needs their expertise. As countries become wealthier and their economies more complex, the demand for financial services increases. Firms locate offices in these countries to fill the growing need for personnel skilled in such areas as public accounting, brokerage, and banking. Small and poor countries often plan major irrigation or power projects, and require the valuable services of engineering consulting firms. During the last decade engineering firms have found huge markets in the Middle Eastern countries, and some engineering industries, like those in Italy, South Korea, Japan, and India, have sent thousands of construction crews to that part of the world.

In many cases, a firm may be in a foreign country for only a single project, so the direct investment can be minimal. In other situations, however, a firm may set up offices and stay permanently, as do major banks in cities around the world where their services are needed. Many firms never go abroad; instead, the clients come to them. For example, virtually every American state university is banned by law from establishing foreign branches. But foreign students flock to such schools and to most private colleges and universities. Over 300,000 foreign students spend about $3.5 billion a year in the United States. Other countries with fine university systems, such as Canada, Britain, France, and West Germany, also sell their educational services to foreigners.

This discussion suggests how a firm begins its locational analysis, focussing on the firm's distinctive competencies and goals. Given this, which countries appear the most attractive? Consideration of these points will quickly suggest many places to avoid. A market oriented consumer goods firm is not likely to begin abroad in a small poor country, but in a large wealthier market, such as Western Europe. An oil field developer will ignore all places where finding oil is unlikely. A labor cost reducer will quickly eliminate from consideration all countries with high labor costs.

ENVIRONMENTAL SCANNING

After the initial analysis to determine potential locations, a firm must then choose among its options, and at this point turns to environmental scanning. To begin with, it is important to find out what cannot be done. Japan's market looks great, but Japanese law is very restrictive towards direct foreign investment. Brazil's market is the largest in Latin America, but there are severe profit repatriation laws. Some countries which seem to offer very interesting oil possibilities prohibit the granting of concessions to foreign private firms. Going to any communist country involves particularly restrictive constraints. Firms seeking foreign options have need of really good local lawyers very early in the game.

Entry control is obvious, but other legal questions may be equally important. A market oriented firm may have built its strength on the brilliance of its television advertising, but in quite a few countries such advertising is not allowed. Another firm may have its power based on brand names and franchises, but in countries with strict price controls on consumer goods, such branding can lead to disaster. The very popular brand cannot legally raise its price, even though local inflation is 50 percent a year, so losses mount. Meanwhile, a local competitor simply stops making its brand and starts another that, being new, can sell for much higher prices. Such a consumer goods oriented firm must have a very keen knowledge of local laws before it plunges in. One might expect that a well-managed, large company would easily foresee such difficulties, but quite often they do not, and trouble is certain. Foreign disinvestment now amounts to many billions of dollars per year, as MNCs bail out of low-profit or even loss situations. Analysis of such situations often suggests that some minor point in local law turned out to be deadly for the company.

Environmental scanning can be as intricate or as simple as seems necessary. One easy way to do it is to watch competitors and go where they go, on the assumption that they must know what they are doing or that following them abroad will help counter whatever perceived advantage they might reap by locating abroad. Such thinking may seem incredibly simplistic, but quite a few large MNCs actually began their international activity in such a manner.

At the other extreme, a company can examine the foreign environment in great detail, looking carefully at all relevant educational, legal, political, sociological, and economic factors. The literature now contains many excellent patterns of analysis for such work. Much data about all industrialized countries exist, often down to very micro levels (such as the income in British census tracts per family). Less developed countries usually have some macrodata, although reliability of the data is often a problem, and really useful information may not be available. Indeed, one major cost for any firm going abroad is getting usable and reliable information and data for the countries in which it is interested. Moreover, critical concerns, such as the exchange rate for the country's currency, or the local political and legal constraints, can change very rapidly. A country that looked really good in 1981 might be out of the question in 1990 (as in the case of several Latin American countries). What a company emphasizes in environmental scanning is linked closely to its strengths and weaknesses. A firm that has ample sources of capital outside the country being considered is not likely to worry much about the money market in that country. But if the firm's production depends critically on relatively cheap and reliable sources of electric power, this point will be explored in considerable detail. In some countries highly skilled labor is simply unavailable, thus precluding entry by multinationals in search of such labor. In addition, firms seeking low-wage labor sometimes find to their dismay that in some countries the labor productivity is also low, proportional to the wages. If the multinational depends on reliable suppliers of components, planners will spend considerable time looking at local firms and analyzing how well they might be able to supply needed inputs.

Figure 4–2 suggests the general pattern of this environmental scanning, including its linkages to the firm and its needs. All inputs will be considered, and an effort will be made to determine just what the bottlenecks might be. The international environment will also be considered, in terms of foreign exchange rates, currency convertibility, and the country's foreign policy, particularly in countries in sensitive areas, or those with nearby dangerous enemies. And the local environment will be linked to these critical firm problems.

This process often eliminates from consideration quite a few countries, and can also suggest some order of priorities. Thus for a consumer goods manufacturer, Canada may look the best, but Britain, France, and West Germany also are possible good bets. An expansion path involving continuous penetration into various foreign markets might be prepared at this point.

An extremely important part of this environmental assessment is what one's competitors are doing. Very few big firms are monopolies, and in oligopoly, one is always analyzing what competitors are doing. Perhaps one of the large U.S. firms begins to make direct investments in Europe. Its four or five major rivals, hearing of this through the grapevine, the trade press, and other sources, wonder just what is up. If the competitor is on to something, it had best be investigated. Otherwise, the competitor's move could lead to his pulling ahead, growing

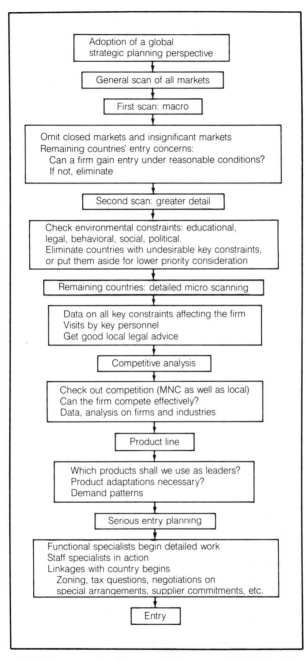

FIGURE 4-2 The Process of Environmental Scanning for a Marketing-Based Corporation

faster, and becoming more profitable. Frequently one sees the pattern of one major firm beginning to make major foreign commitments, followed fairly closely by its key competitors. Firms simply cannot afford to be left behind.

Assessment of the foreign competitive situation also is important when considering any foreign environment. How many local rivals are there, and how good are they? If the rivals are very efficient, and their products excellent, and their marketing superb, then the situation is much different than if there are no competitors, or if the firms in the country are inept and inefficient. A firm scanning alternative possibilities might well avoid a country, at least temporarily, that offers strong domestic or other foreign competition. This is especially true if the market is relatively small or saturated.

Penetrating a Foreign Market

Major firms may have literally hundreds of products and many product lines. One way to penetrate foreign markets is to begin with exports, then move production into the best markets with the most generally acceptable product. Later, lesser markets can be penetrated, and other product lines can be introduced in markets where the MNC has already established itself with its more readily acceptable products. As new products are developed at home, tested, and found successful, they can later be introduced in foreign markets. But leading with products selected on the basis of their competitiveness alleviates such tasks as finding reliable suppliers and establishing competitive distribution and servicing networks.

It may take a firm many decades to complete this total penetration process, and no company has yet been able to introduce all of its products to all markets. Procter & Gamble often begins its foreign expansion by introducing Tide, having found out that this detergent is very attractive to customers everywhere. After developing the initial market through exports, this company begins to manufacture the product abroad. Then other product lines can be introduced, taking advantage of the market established by Tide. Since Procter & Gamble has hundreds of products, all carefully tested in the United States, they have a long way to go before all products are in all markets. In some smaller markets, of course, some of the products may be impractical to produce or even to market, so they are not available. Also, local customs may make some lines poor sellers, and conversely, relatively marginal products in the United States could be very popular in other cultures. Figuring out just what works can occupy key managers for decades, and then the process begins anew when what was once a marginal market becomes ready for entry, or when a lucrative market disappears, perhaps as a result of political revolution. Continuous environmental turbulence is part of the international game.

Major MNCs have a significant advantage over local firms as this penetration process unfolds. Procter & Gamble has many products ready for introduction abroad, and the company already knows much about markets and consumers. Foreign markets will be somewhat different, but the research and development costs are already incurred and only marginal expenditures may be necessary to adapt the product (e.g., its packaging) to any given local foreign market. Hence the company has an ongoing possibility of steady expansion all over the world. Local firms cannot compete on such terms. Even if they have a few good products and an excellent knowledge of local markets, they find it impossible to match Procter & Gamble's diversity and know-how. This is one major reason why large companies can rather easily penetrate into many foreign markets quite rapidly.

It is obvious that the variables which must be taken into consideration by the globally oriented firm are greater in both number and complexity than for the domestically oriented firm. One must include in planning the global strategy such items as exchange rates, the political environment and market growth rates in multiple national markets, national inflation rates and cross-country comparisons. Because none of these factors is static, the forecasting of trends is imperative.

Forecasting

Hawkins and Walter have identified three types of forecasting that MNCs tend to use in planning, although the extent to which they apply to firms less directly involved in foreign markets might vary.[3] The first is the forecasting of macroeconomic performance of the foreign markets and host countries in which an MNC operates. These forecasts generally focus on the expected sizes of various markets for specific products and on the availabilities of input factors as influenced by real incomes, incomes per capita, degrees of industrialization, supplies and costs of labor, and availabilities and costs of raw materials or primary products.

A second type of forecasting enables us to predict exchange rates, exchange controls, balances of payments, and inflation rates. These factors are critical in long-range planning, mainly because of their impact on returns on invested capital. They are also useful for short-term planning due to their influence on transfer prices, lending and borrowing among affiliated subsidiaries, and similar transactions which, in turn, alter reported profits, tax liabilities, and the ability to transfer profits among countries.

A third type of forecasting allows us to predict the firm's market share and the market shares of its major competitors. It is especially important to follow the competitor's performance, because, as noted in our earlier discussion of the theory of foreign investment, it is mainly oligopolistic competitors that are the major actors in international markets. And indeed, that is one basic reason why firms must adopt a global strategy rather than one which focusses mainly on one or two individual markets.

These three types of forecasting used in planning deal essentially with the economic and competitive environment. In addition, complementary assessment needs to be taken of the political environment, which is typically much more difficult to quantify. Political, or "country risk," assessment is still much more of an art than a science, yet it is extremely important to corporate plans in many parts of the world.

Country Risk Assessment

MNCs are especially vulnerable to a wide range of risks associated with government or societal actions and policies which adversely affect foreign business operations and investments. The more obvious societal actions in this regard include both civil and foreign wars, revolutions, terrorism, and other forms of general civil unrest. Here we are primarily concerned with specific government policies that adversely affect the business climate, and note that there has been an alarming increase in the introduction of such policies during the last decade.

Political risk includes both the political orientation of a given government and political instability. It is the second of these which poses the greater problem. MNCs are flexible enough to adjust for example to the inevitable distrust of private enterprise prevalent in communist countries. It is much more difficult to adjust to the uncertainty involved when a country faces internal antagonistic divisions, possible overthrow of the government, and subsequently unpredictable government policies. Quite often, in such cases, the economic and social fabric of the country are also in disarray, so that there are many problems adversely affecting MNC operations in addition to political turmoil. Very frequently the quality of the leadership's economic management is a prime determinant of the unrest. An example of this can be found in Latin America, where the political orientation towards private enterprise is often difficult to predict. Here some countries have suffered from particularly incompetent leadership, while others have benefitted from relatively sound economic management.

Political risks may be distinguished on a macro and micro level.[4] The former includes government actions and policies affecting all foreign enterprises in a given country, such as rampant inflation and general restrictions on the repatriation of profits. Micro level political risks include government actions and policies directed only at selected sectors of foreign business, such as selective indigenization, discriminatory taxes, local content laws, and all industry-specific regulations. The distinction is important, because it stresses that in many cases individual MNCs may be affected quite differently. For example, the indebtedness crisis in Latin America has forced virtually every country in the region to introduce policies of import substitution (i.e., producing at home what had previously been imported) and export promotion. This poses significant problems for MNCs whose affiliates depend on the supply of components from the home country. Conversely, the introduction of subsidies and other export incentives has been a boon to those MNCs whose Latin American affiliates serve mainly as an export base.

Also important is the distinction between asset protection risks and operational profitability risks.[5] For example wars, civil riots, and various forms of expropriation are associated with risks involving asset protection. Typically, these risks are the ones that are most dramatic and highly publicized. Of much greater importance, however, are the government policy changes that adversely affect operational profitability.

Expropriation

Between 1960 and 1979, there were reports of 1,660 takeovers of foreign enterprises by 79 developing countries.[6] This does not include takeovers caused by indigenization laws ("creeping expropriation"), through which, in Mexico for example, MNCs have had to cede majority ownership to nationals. Although there are exceptions (e.g., France under

73

its current Socialist government), the risks of expropriation or nationalization are typically associated with the relatively poor, relatively unstable, and relatively non-Western states, who are suspicious of Western culture and Western MNCs.

The vulnerability of individual firms to expropriation varies according to the industrial sector, size, composition of ownership, nature of the technology involved, and the degree of both vertical and horizontal integration.[7] Firms in the extractive, agricultural, and infrastructural industries are especially vulnerable to expropriation due to the overriding importance of these sectors to many less developed countries. If a country depends on the export of one or two primary commodities for perhaps 70 percent of its export earnings, it does not want output or prices to be determined by foreign interests.

Firms with a low profile and relatively small investment in the host country are relatively safe from expropriation, due mainly to a simple cost/benefit analysis by the government. To seize relatively small operations would not benefit the country substantially in economic terms, but the costs are great in that virtually any act of expropriation brings on the country the wrath of the international trade and investment community. Foreign banks for example withhold funds and refuse to extend future credits, and international organizations such as the IMF (International Monetary Fund) and the World Bank often follow suit. Expropriation is seldom conducted indiscriminately.

Firms that enter joint ventures with domestic private firms are relatively safe from expropriation, perhaps because they have a local voice with vested interests in the project. However, joint ventures with government-owned partners appear to be even more risky than fully owned subsidiaries. The fact that the partner is owned by the government is in itself an indication that there is strong government interest in the sector.

Firms that have advanced proprietary technology and are leaders in their field seldom get expropriated as long as they keep the technology in-house, for the government will not be able to duplicate the technology if it seizes the physical assets. At the other extreme, firms with low technology (e.g., food processing) are relatively safe because the country is already capable of competing in those lines and would gain little through expropriation. In the middle technology ranges, however, the government might see good reason to expropriate manageable firms that provide technological advancement.

These findings, based on research by Bradley, have obvious strategic implications for MNCs. A well coordinated and relatively centralized approach is required to reduce the risk of expropriation: operations affected include production, logistics, marketing, finance, research and development, exports, and technology transfer. The key is to keep the local affiliate dependent on the parent in each or any of these operations.

For example, the MNC can protect itself by integrating either vertically or horizontally. If the parent controls either the supply channels for crucial inputs (e.g., firm-specific technology components available only from the parent) or the market outlets and distribution channels, it will do the country little good to expropriate. Similarly, the MNC might choose to produce five different components for the same end product in five different countries. This reduces both the risk and impact of expropriation if it should occur. Many countries might be interested in expropriating an automobile plant, simply for the prestige of having one's own auto industry. Few would be interested in expropriating an auto axle plant, because the axles are useless with no cars to put them in, and because no MNC would agree to source components from such a government.

Other obvious strategies that might be pursued include keeping technology in-house and research and development at home. Small multiple-site operations might be preferred if the absence of economies of scale permit. Local stakeholders in the enterprise should be nurtured, including suppliers, customers, and local banks as well as employees and managing partners. The very risk of expropriation itself, even if it never materializes, can basically determine the nature of a firm's involvement in any given country. If expropriation should result, all is not lost. The MNC might then opt for licensing or management contracts, handling exports on a commission basis, or agreeing to supply the necessary components or raw materials. Ownership is not a necessary condition for profitable operations, however preferable it might be.

Operational Profitability Risks

As dramatic an event as expropriation is, there are far more prevalent risks that the MNC faces. Local content laws may force the MNC to rely on domestic suppliers instead of on intracorporate transfers. Severe constraints may be placed on the importing of components or raw materials from the home country. Profit repatriation laws may make it impossible to remit more than a token amount of earnings to the parent. Export markets may be substantially constricted by unilateral government decisions. Exchange controls and delay of payments may make the financing of affiliate operations untenable. Sources of raw materials supplies may be completely cut off or drastically curtailed. Contracts to build turnkey plants may be abruptly and unilaterally cancelled. Contractual agreements underlying the MNC's decision to invest in the first place may be subject to renegotiation by government fiat. Price and wage controls may basically erode the projected profitability of operations. All these risks are essentially country-specific, although in some cases (e.g., the Andean Market) they occur on a larger, regional basis also, thus limiting the ability of the MNC to reduce risk by diversifying locations within the given region.

The increase of such risks during the last decade has led some MNCs to considerably strengthen their environmental analysis function, although it appears that for many the function still remains informal, irregular, and seldom systematically integrated into the strategic decision-making process. All too often the focus has been on the major events, such as war and expropriations, rather than on the continuous, incremental government interventions which are much more difficult to assess. Financial risk can be measured with existing, highly sophisticated quantitative models; measuring economic risk is somewhat more difficult, but firms have learned to live with it. Political risk analysis however, requires a great deal of subjectivity, and no tool has yet been found to handle it satisfactorily.

Economic indicators of risk in a very broad context include the general performance of the economy (growth of GNP, inflation rate, exchange rate), the balance of payments (reserves, trade balance, current account balance, capital flows), and the external debt (absolute amount, debt ratio to GNP, debt service ratio). These items can be measured fairly well, but they are just the tip of the iceberg. The problem is, even if such figures alone were sufficient to serve as quantitative indicators (and there are literally hundreds of other factors that may be more important), it remains highly ambiguous how to translate the risk assessments into specific corporate policies. One reason is, that the weight of each variable must vary according to the total configuration of each individual country. Otherwise, less than a decade ago Iran would have ranked as a much safer investment risk than Canada.

Firms use a combination of approaches in analyzing foreign political climates. One is the "grand tour" approach, through which an executive (or staff) team visits the country in question to hold conferences with government and business leaders. Another is the "old hands" approach, through which the MNC seeks consultation with persons (e.g., former diplomats) having expertise on the country. Delphi methods involve an iterative process whereby a number of experts rank the country along specified relevant dimensions and arrive at an overall consensus. Computerized quantitative models are becoming more and more in vogue, through which numerical rankings place countries in different risk categories. None of these approaches suffices in itself, and all are highly dependent on the weight given to specific variables, which is a subjective decision. Specialized publications may be used, and the number of such services has proliferated along with the increase of risk itself; but they are seldom industry-specific. Firms rely also on input from their customers and suppliers in the foreign country, as well as on their own field managers. In-house monitoring is undertaken to reveal, for example, delays or modifications in the financing patterns of suppliers and customers. Attitudes of official agencies are monitored, such as the IMF, central banks, or export credit agencies.

And, if all else fails, there is insurance. But it is expensive. Political risk insurance is available, but it is exceedingly narrow in coverage and deals only with such major events as war, rebellion, and insurrection. Also available are: expropriation insurance, inconvertibility insurance, contract repudiation insurance, license cancellation insurance, wrongful calling of guarantee insurance, commercial credit insurance, and marine cargo insurance. The insurance business thrives; however, the risks affect different companies in different ways.

All countries have some element of risk to the foreign investor. But taking risk is what business is all about, or so it is said. Nevertheless, the risk that the MNC faces is immeasurably greater than that faced by the purely domestic firm, for discrimination against foreign investment is virtually a universal trait. It may take the shape of a mere preference to buy from local firms, or it may be associated with the more serious tactics that we have discussed. If the foreign investment is a major one relative to overall enterprise activities; or if the foreign operations are significantly integrated into the firm's overall production and marketing capabilities, creating greater interdependency; or if risk conditions change substantially in a given country during a relatively short period of time; then the greater the need to assess risk and the more complex the monitoring of risk will be. Whatever the case, it is clear that risk assessment is of strategic importance, and that it must be an ongoing process rather than just an ad hoc project preceding the initial investment decision.

CONTROL

Typically, control is an administrative function more closely associated with the implementation of strategy than with the formulation of strategy. We prefer to discuss it here, however, because the control of international business activities requires, in certain basic ways, a change in perspective. At the same time, we defer our treatment of evaluation until later, although the evaluation of managerial performance overseas is a critical aspect of control, just as it is in purely domestic operations. One can, of course, justifiably argue that, at least conceptually, control in the MNC is much the same as for local companies, and the control strategies tend to take the same forms whether or not the firm is multinational. Firms set goals and quantifiable limits on activities; they check how things are going through numerous feedback loops from various sensing spots; and they then correct deviations through the appropriate managerial or technical actions. They also use advance controls, such as not allowing branch managers to spend more than one thousand dollars for capital equipment without approval from higher authorities, or having two people sign checks to make them valid. They spend much time and money auditing activities in various ways, which is another means of spotting intolerable deviations. To this point, nothing much is different, although those involved in control know how difficult it is to keep things in line, especially for the MNC, whose activities are typically very diversified, dispersed, and complex.

MNCs have, however, four major new control areas, which parallel their multinational status. One relates to foreign exchange risks. We shall later note some of the concerns in this area, where a movement in exchange rates may negate a year's operating profits. MNCs employ continuous monitoring, risk limits, exchange rate forecasting, and other techniques designed to control this risk, in addition to the typical hedging strategies.

A second major new control area for MNCs is linked to the fact that the firm operates in multiple environments. As these environments differ, the firm adjusts, and as it adjusts, control systems can change. For example, accounting and tax standards vary greatly among countries, and one result is that routine controls at home may have to be changed to meet new legal needs. Perhaps one country imposes an inventory tax, and another does not. If the tax is payable on inventories as of March 15 each year, one obvious control procedure is to minimize inventories on this date in the country concerned, while in the nontax country, this control is irrelevant. Since countries often have different types of taxes, with different implications for operations, MNCs have to analyze each situation to see what needs to be done.

Economic variations also lead to a variety of control practices. A country where inflation is routinely 100 percent per year, or higher, requires quite different inventory policies, among many other things, than a country where the inflation rate is 5 percent. Firms failing to make such adjustments and maintaining the control standards of their home country may find that they are operating very inefficiently indeed; but it takes years of experience and a flexible managerial cadre to develop relevant and appropriate controls.

Differences in social overhead capital can force changes in control procedures. A manager accustomed to routinely calling in certain daily cash results can be very frustrated in a country where the telephones fail to work half the time, or where it takes five days to place an international call. Electric power failures can foul up both equipment and inventory that needs cooling or heating, so extra controls may be required and backup systems provided to make sure that critical temperatures are maintained.

Educational levels of the work force can also force control system changes. If many workers are illiterate, then written forms don't work very well, and if a country lacks skilled clerks, technicians, and accountants, it is more difficult to administer a good control system than in places where such labor is in good supply.

A third major area of new controls for MNCs is in the risk assessment field. We addressed that issue earlier in this chapter, and suggested how terribly difficult it is to forecast such risks accurately. If there are indications of serious increases in political risk in any given country or region, then the entire control system may be modified to minimize the risk. Inventories of critical technology components might be sharply reduced, funds might be quickly brought out of the country, and other inventory controls might be dramatically modified.

In these first three special cases of the MNC, there is nothing new in control philosophy or technique. As usual, good business management practices work well everywhere. The critical difference lies in the areas controlled and the kinds of controls applied in a given situation, and MNCs have somewhat different, and quite a bit more complex control requirements than most local firms.

A fourth new area of control is associated with a very complex issue we discuss in detail later: the basic conflict between host governments and the MNC as to which of these two should control certain key aspects of MNC affiliated activities. This issue of control arises because the objectives of the two are not fully compatible, and it is an issue not normally associated with control in its more common organizational connotation, i.e., from the viewpoint of the relations between top and lower levels of management.

Centralization and Decentralization

Doz distinguishes between the economic versus political imperatives of foreign investment.[8] From this viewpoint, the integration of global activities to increase overall efficiency, which requires tighter central control, improves the international *economic* competitiveness of the MNC. A national responsiveness strategy, however, which entails giving more leeway to foreign affiliates so they may more effectively respond to local environmental conditions, improves the *political* competitiveness of the MNC. Even this second, relatively decentralized approach, however, requires central coordination of some functions, including finance, research and development (since it is too costly to duplicate), export marketing (to avoid intracorporate frictions), and the transfer of technology to affiliates.

Because effective performance requires both integration and differentiation, one rarely finds either extreme centralization or extreme decentralization. MNCs typically centralize some decisions and decentralize others, depending on a number of factors, as discussed below. In this context, the MNC simply lives with the conflict (between the requirements of integration and differentiation), and seeks structural and administrative adjustments instead of strategic solutions to the centralization/decentralization dilemma. That is, according to Doz the strategy is to have no set strategy regarding the degree of control, but instead to make a series of ad hoc and limited adjustments in response to the specific developments which occur. As new uncertainties arise, the MNC will centralize or decentralize, according to the nature of the problem and the perceived importance of either economic or political environmental changes. At times, greater global rationalization will prevail; at other times, localized national responsiveness will prevail; in many cases, an ambiguous blend of the two will result. In brief, this strategy trades off internal economic efficiency for external political flexibility, both of which are components of the overall competitiveness of the MNC.

The extent of corporate control over affiliate activities depends on many factors. One of these factors is obviously the mode of operations abroad. Licensing or industrial cooperation agreements for example may involve some quality control or control over marketing channels, but clearly less control overall than do fully owned subsidiaries or majority-owned joint ventures.

The extent to which foreign operations are integrated into global operations is also a key determinant of the degree of corporate control. If the foreign operations for example serve mainly as a source of components or raw materials vital to the overall success of the MNC, central control will be relatively tight. If the operations abroad are essentially limited to relatively insignificant export sales through independent distributors, then such operations will be decentralized to a great extent. A high level of intracorporate movement of goods and services (between headquarters and the affiliates or among affiliates) requires greater coordination and therefore more centralized control.

Technology and Industry as Determinants of Control

The nature of the technology involved and the nature of the industry are also determinants of the extent of central control. We shall later suggest that firms competing on the basis of product technology are more highly centralized than firms competing on the basis of process technology. On the one hand, the segmentability of process technologies often makes them more amenable to decentralization, even when product uniformity is required. On the other hand, firms whose competitiveness is based on unique product technology are quite naturally prone to guard closely the technologies involved, leading to relatively high degrees of centralization.

The degree of centralization of course varies within single firms depending on the functions involved. Finance and planning are typically highly centralized. Many MNCs resemble financial holding companies, where local managers make most decisions, but where financial controls, including budgetary planning and rates of return, are carefully controlled from the center. Questions relating to the firm's legitimacy and survival are also centralized, since the costs of being wrong can be huge. Research and development is typically centralized because of the economies involved and because in certain industries such work is central to the firm's survival. The sourcing of materials, quality control, and critical marketing decisions may also tend to be centralized.

Other relevant factors include the relative importance of the foreign market and the headquarters' confidence in the affiliate's management, as well as the experience of the MNC abroad and general changes in the environment. European managerial cadres are among the very best, and an operation in Sweden or West Germany might well rely on local managerial control over all but the most critical of decisions. In many countries of the Third World, however, such managerial competence is not available, and the MNC would monitor and control such operations from the home base much more closely.

Political Determinants

The political sensitivity of operations is also a determinant of the degree to which operations are decentralized. Both the auto and telecommunications industries are based on technologies and economies of scale that strongly encourage global integration of corporate activities. But the relative political sensitivity of the telecommunications industry has made it one in which global integration has been less acceptable than in the auto industry. In such a case, the balancing of economic and political imperatives is an extremely delicate task, for the simultaneous needs to integrate and to differentiate are in basic conflict here.

Stage of Internationalization as a Determinant

Finally, the maturity of the MNC itself has some effect on the relative degree of control over foreign operations. As noted earlier, when a firm first expands abroad, its overseas operations are typically insignificant, decentralized, and poorly integrated with overall corporate activities; its initial concern is for a specific case at hand without consideration of a wider application. When foreign sales increase, when sufficient international experience has been gained, when foreign markets are increasingly diversified, and when top management is ready to commit itself to a global strategy, then integration and some degree of centralization occur.

SUMMARY

The formulation of strategy for the globally oriented firm is a complex undertaking, for it poses problems of coordination across widely varying environments. However universal the functions of planning and control might be, their effective implementation in an international context requires a relatively sophisticated consideration of variables often of less significance in the purely domestic context. Environmental scanning, macro- and microeconomic forecasting, country risk assessment, and the complexity of control mechanisms assume greater weight as the firm takes on a more global orientation.

DISCUSSION QUESTIONS

1. To what extent are the planning and control functions of administration different in the international context compared to purely domestic operations?

2. In formulating global corporate strategy, why does it not suffice to study intensely only the country targeted, even if there are strong indications that that is where the firm wishes to invest? For example, why study trends and developments in France, if one plans to go to Spain?

3. Country risk assessment depends heavily on the subjective assessment of factors that are not equally relevant to firms competing in different industries. Discuss.

4. What different approaches to risk assessment might be taken by a firm relying solely on exports compared to a firm that plans a direct investment abroad in a manufacturing plant?

NOTES

1. Yoram Wind and Susan Douglas, "International Portfolio Analysis and Strategy: The Challenge of the 80s," in *Strategic Planning: Concepts and Implementation*, eds., John K. Ryans, Jr., and William L. Shanklin (New York: Random House, 1985), 301–318.

2. John K. Ryans, Jr., and William L. Shanklin, eds., *Strategic Planning: Concepts and Implementation* (New York: Random House, 1985), 279.

3. Robert G. Hawkins and Ingo Walter, "Planning Multinational Operations,"

in *Handbook of Organizational Design*, eds., Paul C. Nystrom and William H. Starbuck (New York: Oxford University Press, 1981), 253–267.

4. Stefan H. Robock, "Political Risk: Identification and Assessment," *Columbia Journal of World Business* (July–August, 1971), 6–20.

5. Charles W. Hofer and Terry P. Haller, "Globescan: A Way To Better International Risk Assessment," *Journal of Business Strategy* (Fall, 1980), 42–55.

6. "Insuring Against Risk Abroad," *Business Week* (September 14, 1981), 59.

7. David G. Bradley, "Managing Against Expropriation, *Harvard Business Review* (July–August, 1977), 75–83.

8. Yves L. Doz, "Strategic Management in Multinational Companies," *Sloan Management Review* (Winter, 1980), 27–46.

FURTHER READINGS

1. Banker, Pravin. "You're the Best Judge of Foreign Risks." *Harvard Business Review*, March–April, 1983, 157–165.

2. Moyer, Reed. *International Business: Issues and Concepts*. New York: John Wiley and Sons, 1984.

3. Robinson, Richard D. *Internationalization of Business*. Chicago: Dryden Press, 1984.

4. Simon, Jeffrey D. "Political Risk Assessment: Past Trends and Future Prospects." *Columbia Journal of World Business*, Fall, 1982, 62–71.

CHAPTER 5

▼

Strategy Implementation: Location, Entry, and Ownership Patterns

▲

Some corporate decisions and policies are more important than others, in that they can determine the future of the firm for decades or even a century. Hence the decision to adopt a global strategy will, if carried to its logical conclusion, totally change the nature of what was formerly a domestically oriented firm. And especially if the firm decides to expand abroad, new knowledge will have to be acquired; new specialists will be needed; line managers will now need new skills, in addition to their old ones; and new relationships with outsiders will have to be nurtured. After a decade or so, the firm will look very different from what it was.

Such a critical strategy is a core strategy, and this chapter and the next briefly develop the major critical strategic areas that are directly affected by international activities. Specifically, we address here the issues of locational, entry, and ownership patterns, and in Chapter 6 the issues of technology transfer and intracompany linkages. These items are treated individually, but it is clear that they are fully interdependent. Thus, the method of entry will, to a large extent, determine location, the means of technology transfer, and the structure of intrafirm as well as interfirm linkages.

The discussion is based primarily on the experience of relatively large multinational corporations operating throughout the world, but we do not wish to suggest that all truly efficient firms are the multinational ones. Such is not the case. Often the costs of administration, management, and control are substantially greater for the MNC compared to local firms, and very real other advantages can be gained by staying small and specialized. Hundreds of thousands of small local firms compete very effectively against multinational giants, especially in developed countries having large numbers of highly skilled people and in industries in which economies of scale are not a highly significant factor. Small local firms, very knowledgeable about local labor markets and local suppliers, can in many cases operate more efficiently than distantly managed large firms. Small firms do supply quality products at competitive prices, and they do thrive locally when the market is sufficiently large. Moreover, small firms may indeed become more globally oriented in their strategy than many multinationals are today, which would give the smaller firm an even greater advantage.

In addition, many giant firms have done quite poorly. One can point to those that have folded completely, and to those that have come close to folding. Among the latter the reader will be familiar with the case of International Harvester, whose financial difficulties have forced it to shed both its construction equipment and agricultural equipment groups (as well as its group for turbines, which was much smaller). Chrysler, American Motors, and Massey-Ferguson have all come very close to going under in recent years, and were kept afloat temporarily by government financial help (by the U.S., French, and Canadian governments, respectively).

But industries learn from their mistakes in international competition, and much of their experience abroad is fully relevant to the small firms, which can get heavily involved in international business through activities like exporting and importing, transferring technology in or out, and joint ventures. Ultimately, the critical strategic decision is just how globally oriented the firm is willing to become. This is the decision that will influence the company's performance for decades to come.

LOCATIONAL STRATEGIES

We note in Chapter 4 that locational decisions depend very much on what the individual firm is looking for (e.g., markets for consumer goods vs. sources of raw materials). We further suggest that firms make detailed environmental assessments on macro as well as micro levels; on political and social as well as economic developments; and especially on industry and competitive conditions in various countries and regions. The results of these assessments determine in part which countries are most desirable for specific industries or firms. However, top management still typically has options as to which countries it chooses to enter. Each country has its own unique configuration of incentives and disincentives for foreign investment. Almost always there are some special entry controls applying only to foreign firms, and often special negotiations with government officials are called for in order to precisely determine the conditions of entry.

It should first be noted that around 80 percent of all foreign investment by U.S. multinational firms is in other developed countries, mainly in Canada and Europe. Only around 20 percent of their foreign investment has been in the less developed countries, and of that 20 percent a substantial amount of the investment has been in extractive rather than manufacturing activities. In the centrally planned (communist) countries, direct investment has typically not been allowed at all, although during the 1970s a few countries, notably Hungary, Romania, Poland, Bulgaria, and Yugoslavia, enacted joint venture legislation (under restrictive conditions which have failed to entice much foreign investment). However, following the political and economic realignments of the region in 1989, several countries (notably Poland and Hungary) are now actively seeking direct foreign investment as a part of their economic reform programs.

The reason why U.S. investment abroad is so overwhelmingly concentrated in the rich, industrialized countries is typically believed to be because of the size of the markets. This is clearly a dominant factor, but not the only one. Just as germane, in many cases, are the conditions under which technology transfer occurs; for it is essentially through the transfer of technology (including managerial know-how) that the multinational expands abroad. Moreover, the aggregate size of markets may be misleading. For example, many U.S. firms have located at least one major subsidiary in some country that is a member of the European

Economic Community, in order to gain access to the markets of the entire Community. But this is not possible in the telecommunications field because the individual state members of the EEC still employ different technical standards and regulations (which is a major reason why European companies are in the main not competitive in that particular industry outside their own home markets).

Aside from these general factors, other issues come into play. Some multinationals flatly refuse to consider investments where possible in the centrally planned (communist) countries. Such a policy is frequently not ideologically based, but a simple recognition that in such countries the firm's managerial flexibility is extremely constrained. Multinationals also typically avoid countries with much political turbulence, since the costs of being wrong on political risk assessment are too high. Firms may additionally avoid countries because of possibilities of retaliation by other countries. The Arab states have boycott provisions against all firms making direct investments in Israel, and a firm investing in Israel can thus expect to be cut off from lucrative Middle Eastern markets. Investments in the Union of South Africa can bring retaliation from other African countries or even from U.S. consumer groups who perceive, rightly or wrongly, that direct investment in South Africa implicitly supports that government's policy of apartheid. In such cases, managers must determine whether such potential retaliation is worth the investment. Quite a few multinationals are in fact active in South Africa, and the decision of location in such cases had to be based in part on the consideration of the potentially disruptive consequences for the firm's activities in other parts of the world.

Multinationals may also have policies that preclude certain types of investments. Japan, for example, normally requires joint ventures as a condition for accepting foreign investment, joint ventures that prevent the foreign firm from keeping majority control over its investment. Many firms will not consider such organizational arrangements, and Japan and countries having similar requirements are excluded from the beginning in the consideration of options. Later discussion of joint ventures will suggest why some firms refuse to accept such a form of entry, when other firms have found joint ventures very attractive.

Multinational investment abroad gives the host country definite gains, and often very substantial ones. Skilled and unskilled workers gain employment, tax revenues rise, local people learn new skills, local suppliers may gain large orders, and hard currency earnings may also increase. Especially under today's global economic and financial conditions, national, regional, and local development commissions virtually everywhere in the world are trying to lure foreign capital, skills, and technology. Since most banks are increasingly reluctant to increase their exposure abroad, the MNC's traditional role as the most significant foreign source of economic growth has been strengthened.

Consequently, incentives of all types are being offered to MNCs, even by countries that until quite recently viewed MNCs with hostility, since, to many less developed countries, MNCs are the most visible symbol of an international system that seems intent on keeping the less developed in a position of dependency. These incentives include tax holidays, accelerated depreciation, rent-free land and buildings, outright grants, low-interest loans, loan guarantees, subsidized energy or transportation rates, infrastructural improvements such as better road access, and free professional training.

To be sure, there are often performance requirements or concomitant disincentives to qualifying for such benefits. Industries which governments wish to develop are also those they wish to control. Performance requirements typically include job creation quotas, export minimums to generate foreign exchange, local value-added minimums, domestic market share maximums, and obligatory local participation in ownership (and sometimes in management).[1] For example, import substitution and export generation policies are very common in Latin America today. The catastrophic foreign debts incurred by this region have most likely been a major reason for generating these policies. Import substitution policies require the foreign affiliates of the MNC to begin making in-house (or purchasing from domestic suppliers) those components that they previously imported from the home country. Export incentives can be either positive, such as the government's granting of tax rebates based on export volumes; or negative, such as limiting the value of imports to a percentage of the value of exports. Minimum production volume requirements can have the same effect as export quotas if the domestic market is relatively small, forcing the MNC to export a larger proportion of production for economic reasons.

These incentives and disincentives often make operations abroad less amenable to integration on a global basis; essentially they may alter a company's strategy for the region. They affect, for example, a firm's make-or-buy decision, intracorporate transfer policies (e.g., between subsidiaries or between headquarters and the subsidiaries), both horizontal and vertical sourcing arrangements, and so on. In effect, they can weaken the MNC's mandate for global efficiency by encouraging the firm to suboptimize. This is a basic conflict between host countries and the MNC that we will refer back to later.

There are also other types of government control on MNC activities; they include wage and price controls, labor regulations, local content requirements, restrictions on profit repatriation and other remittances, tax controls, and controls on technology transfer. But negotiations about the most onerous local rules are often possible, especially if the MNC has strong bargaining power because of the real or perceived advantages that it brings to the country in question.

Once the decision to enter a country has been made and the country approves, the question of where to locate within the country is relevant. Industrialized northern Italy, for example, bears little resemblance to the poverty stricken south of the country. Even smaller countries can show extreme diversity within their borders. At the outset, typical locational factors apply, such as the availability of transportation, electric power, key inputs, potentially large markets, port facilities, communications, and similar infrastructural factors. As is often the case in international business, the same locational models used at home apply abroad.

But there may be special factors that require top policy decisions. Many European countries have depressed industrial areas, and there are special tax breaks and subsidies for local and foreign firms that agree to locate in these areas. Even in West Germany, which has one of the soundest industrialized economies, such incentives are available to firms willing to locate either in Berlin or along the border between East and West Germany. Should the MNC take advantage of such subsidies? Often the answer is yes, but there may be strings attached to such offers which the MNC might not be willing to accept, so the legislation or enticements must be scanned carefully. The usual reason for offering subsidies is that something is wrong. Otherwise, local firms in the area would not have moved away or be in deep decline. Perhaps the pressures causing local firms to avoid locating there do not apply to MNCs, given the latter's ability to tap outside resources. In Britain, declining coal deposits or unrest among the miners may cause firms dependent on coal to move; but an MNC with its production processes geared to oil would have no such dependency and could take advantage of government largesse. Possibilities of gaining other concessions by moving into such an area are also present. Perhaps the government will be cooperative on interpretation of some obscure tax law, if the MNC moves into a high-unemployment area.

Examination of all these factors takes time and therefore money, and the MNC may feel that it is not worth it. Or it may eagerly seek such subsidies. In either case, locational decisions will be affected, and resulting decisions about trade unions, transportation costs, access to markets, and many other factors will be affected.

Often, unstated but important locational considerations can also affect the eligibility of a specific location. Firms accustomed to tractable trade unions may seek to avoid heavily unionized areas. Japanese firms in the United States appear to follow this policy often. Voting patterns may matter, as when a firm avoids areas that are heavily socialist in a nominally capitalist country. The MNC may feel that in such an area the local government might be overly restrictive.

Firms may avoid extremely congested areas, or they may feel that their business requires them to be there. In many countries it is quite common to find one city that is the political, economic, social, cultural and business center for the whole country, and everyone wants to be there at once. The results may be high rents, extreme congestion leading to lost productivity, jammed communications, and port congestion. Locating a factory in such an area may offer access to good labor, but other costs may outweigh the advantages: as always, there are trade-offs. But a bank or accounting firm may feel that it has to locate in such an area, because that is where most of its clients are located.

Firms may also intentionally avoid building one large, single plant in a country because a strike or another disaster could seriously disrupt system production. Better to build five scattered plants with perhaps 500 employees each than one large one that could cease production at any time. With scattered plants, the locational decisions assume an added dimension beyond those of a single plant location, and factors such as transportation and communications networks become quite relevant.

Plants and other fixed investments are large-scale, long-term ventures; and once the decision to invest is made, the MNC can be committed for a long time. When bargaining with a country over entry conditions, it may be relatively easy for the MNC to obtain concessions; but once the plant is built, the bargaining power shifts in favor of the country it is built in. Many less developed countries (LDCs) are insisting on rewriting contracts signed years ago, for example; and some countries have enacted indigenization laws, which force MNCs to cede majority ownership of their foreign affiliates to host country nationals. This may lead to short-run gains by the host countries at the expense of scaring away future investment in the country by MNCs. These are some of the factors that MNCs consider in their careful evaluation of optional locations. Most of this work is invisible to outsiders, and we see only what happens after the fact, when the facility is built or perhaps when the first contracts are signed. But every major firm spends a significant amount of time and money evaluating these issues, and quite often they become top management preoccupations.

ENTRY AND OWNERSHIP STRATEGIES

There are numerous entry and ownership strategies available to the MNC once it decides on which markets to enter. The most common of these include fully owned (100 percent) subsidiaries; joint ventures; industrial cooperation agreements; licensing; turnkey projects; and traditional exporting and importing activities. These will be discussed further, but a few general observations are in order here.

1. These forms are not mutually exclusive. Licensing, for example, can be associated with any of the other forms, and the same holds true for exports and imports. There is, therefore, no necessarily clear delineation among the forms. However, there are conceptual advantages to treating them separately.

2. Various options are associated with differing degrees of risk and return, each having its own specific configuration of advantages and disadvantages. Some forms are more amenable to specific industries than to others, depending in part on the nature of the technology involved and the intensity of competition.

3. In recent years, there has been a shift among American MNCs away from an earlier predilection for fully owned foreign affiliates and towards more cooperative forms of direct investment. This is partly a consequence of host country policies, such as indigenization laws. It is also partially a consequence of competitive pressures. European and Japanese firms for example, have traditionally viewed joint ventures more favorably than American MNCs, and often the U.S. firm must follow suit in order to maintain its bargaining power during negotiations. Economic conditions have also played a role in this shift of focus, for the alternatives to fully owned subsidiaries typically require fewer financial and other commitments by the parent firm.

4. The *relative* share of American firms in total foreign investment by MNCs has decreased significantly during the last decade or so. Numerous

reasons for this include the relative strengthening of the European and Japanese currencies during the 1970s; the rapid closing of the technological gap in many industries that had earlier favored American firms; and the increased competitiveness of European and Japanese MNCs.[2]

5. Whatever form it takes, foreign direct investment by MNCs is likely to become an increasingly important means of channeling funds from one country to another during the nineties. The relative importance of MNCs in stimulating growth abroad has been augmented by the reluctance of many private banks to increase their exposure in various parts of the world due to the debt crisis. But foreign investment is also to some extent counter-cyclical. That is, firms are motivated to invest abroad during times of slow growth or stagnant markets at home. And under the conditions that have prevailed during the early part of the eighties, there has been intense competition among MNCs to penetrate third markets.

Fully Owned Subsidiaries

Direct investment abroad in the form of fully owned affiliates has traditionally been viewed primarily as an international movement of capital. However, it is much more than that. It differs from other kinds of international capital movements in that the capital transfers are accompanied by managerial control, technology flows, and access to input and output markets otherwise unattainable (or at least not readily attainable) to the recipient country. It is important to note that this package of resource transfers across national borders takes place *within* the enterprise. This is partly because fully owned subsidiaries abroad are viewed by many to be the most efficient means of transferring technology and the form of direct investment most amenable to integration into the total global activities of the MNC.

Direct investment in the form of fully owned affiliates has also been viewed as a consequence of imperfect markets and monopolistic competition. It is perceived by many, especially in less developed countries, as a means of stifling local economic development by driving out the smaller, less efficient, domestic firms. A contrasting argument presented by some economists is that the main impact of fully owned foreign affiliates has clearly been to widen the area of competition to include those protected producers who were not previously significant competitors in the international markets.[3]

Labor unions based in the home country of the parent firm frequently charge that fully owned foreign subsidiaries serve markets previously served by exports, and thus tend to "export jobs." This is an industry-specific issue, holding true in some cases and not in others. Foreign affiliates of MNCs foster economic growth in the host countries, increasing those countries' capacity to trade. Expansion occurs in both the size and diversity of production and markets. In aggregate therefore, although factor movements displace trade in some cases, statistical data suggest that the growth effect of fully owned subsidiaries on trade is greater than their substitution effects.[4]

These differences in perspective are highly relevant, because local viewpoints have strong influence on the political climate under which investment decisions are made. Clearly, they have also affected the legal environment, for in many countries subsidiaries fully owned by the MNC are no longer permissible. Countries barring fully owned subsidiaries gain, perhaps, the psychological benefit of thinking that they now have more control over foreign operations in their countries. It may also have great political appeal domestically, but it comes at the expense of foregoing investment in critical sectors by the many MNCs whose policy is full ownership or none.

The reasons why some MNCs insist on full ownership are typically associated with control and managerial efficiency. Local partners typically tend to take a provincial view of things, such as insisting on high cash dividends, whereas the MNC is trying to practice worldwide cash flow management. Critical decisions about expansion or new product development can be delayed as a minority of stockholders quibble about the potential profitability of such moves. With total ownership, such problems are generally avoided.

Fully owned subsidiaries may be started from scratch or by acquiring firms already established in the host country. Acquisition may lead to significant benefits if the acquired firm has complementary product lines or established distribution and servicing networks. These were two factors that highly influenced J. I. Case's decision to acquire International Harvester's agricultural equipment group in late 1984. Case's product line was very much reinforced and broadened, and its number of dealers was thereby tripled, bringing its network close to the size of Deere's, the industry leader.

Very rapid growth of fully or majority owned subsidiaries abroad has occurred since the end of the Second World War. However, two significant trends emerged during the seventies. First, the flow of financial capital to the less developed countries grew much more rapidly than the flow of direct foreign investment by multinationals in the form of fully or majority owned subsidiaries. Second, different multinational forms of investment (other than fully or majority owned subsidiaries) began to play an increasingly important role in the less developed countries. These alternative forms of investment include such things as joint international business ventures in which foreign-held equity does not exceed 50 percent; and various international contractual arrangements that involve at least an element of investment from the foreign firm's viewpoint, but which may involve no equity participation by that firm whatsoever (i.e., licensing agreements, management contracts, subcontracting, and the like).[5] One potential consequence of these trends is that small- and medium-sized firms, lacking large resource bases (in managerial personnel as well as in capital), might become more active in global competition, offering their particular expertise rather than a bundled package of investment.

Industrial Cooperation

There is no universally accepted definition of industrial cooperation, but all would agree that it is based on long-term, interfirm relationships going beyond the straightforward sale or purchase of goods and services, and that it includes complementary operations in production, the development and transfer of technology, and marketing. Its most common forms include licensing, turnkey projects, subcontracting, coproduction, specialization, and joint ventures, although each of these can be found also in isolation. Industrial cooperation is a generic term connoting a wide range of related economic activities that emerged during the 1970s and that represent interfirm linkages qualitatively distinct from those of the past.

Although the individual activities on which industrial cooperation is based have long been practiced, it is the totality of the interfirm relationship that has become increasingly important. The concept of industrial cooperation, in fact, was not really developed until the early 1970s, when it became the major mechanism of interfirm linkages between Western corporations and the government-owned enterprises of Eastern Europe. Indeed, in discussing industrial cooperation one must distinguish between interfirm linkages in an East–West context, in a North–South context (meaning between developed and less developed countries), and in a West–West context (i.e., among the developed countries).

In an East–West context, industrial cooperation was (and still is) predominantly based on the transfer of Western technology to the enterprises of Eastern Europe. The primary motive of the Western firms was to gain access to the huge Eastern European markets, from which they were otherwise barred by law (generally precluding any direct investment) and policy (all foreign trade being exclusively conducted by the state). A secondary Western motive was to source low-cost components from the East to improve the firm's competitive position in Western markets. The primary motive of the Eastern enterprises was to modernize their industries and thus to become more competitive in Eastern, Third World, and hopefully also Western markets.

In virtually all cases, East–West industrial cooperation assumed high strategic priority and required ad hoc decisions at the highest corporate levels. New corporate planning units were created to develop the new and potentially huge markets. New forms of financial planning were introduced, as payment was typically received in kind (i.e., products) instead of in currency. Public relations activities had to be intensified due to the political sensitivity of East–West trade. Manufacturing decisions often became more centralized in order to assure coordination between the activities in Eastern Europe and the activities of Western European affiliates. Personnel problems took on added importance, because very few in the West had any understanding of the administrative and economic environment in the centrally planned economies. Marketing problems arose due to unreliable delivery or unacceptable low-quality goods and components received from the Eastern partners. Virtually every aspect of the cooperation assumed strategic importance, catching many by surprise.

If properly planned and structured, as some cooperation agreements were, the cooperation provided substantial gains for all parties involved. But many of the problems were unexpected, and problems usually resolved by lower management levels in a purely Western context became issues which had to be addressed at the highest corporate levels. For example, assume a Polish enterprise cooperating with a Western firm has to rely on another domestic supplier of gaskets for diesel engines. The supplier of gaskets, a state-owned firm in which incentives are based on quantity rather than quality of production, delivers gaskets fully unusable. What does the firm do? In the West, one would find a better supplier. In Poland, there is no other supplier. Either the gaskets must be imported for hard currency, which is not available in Poland, or production stops due to the bottleneck in supplies. This kind of difficulty causes downtime also in the Western European affiliates of the Western partner, who are depending on diesels from Poland to put in their trucks or tractors. Western European distributors affiliated with the Western partner begin to lose market share. And all for the want of a horseshoe nail.

The question of a lousy gasket is not typically thought of as a top level management issue, but in this case it was. The basic problem is that communist states have no markets in the Western sense, and middle managers from the West have grown up in places where markets are critical. When something happens and a market is required to solve the problem, the middle manager is helpless, and top managers must become involved. Such seemingly trivial questions can cause major projects to stall for years, and indeed this is what has happened all too often in an East–West context.

There have been some exceptionally successful cooperation agreements, such as International Harvester's construction equipment project in Poland. Others, such as Massey Ferguson's agricultural tractor project in Poland, never really get off the ground. It often seems as if cooperation agreements in an East–West context work best when the product involved does not require complex inputs from the local economy. If the export is to be natural gas, or some chemical using local raw materials, cooperation can work out very well. Since such cooperation agreements may be the only way to enter potentially huge markets in communist countries, MNCs are willing to consider them.

The problems noted above are not characteristic of industrial cooperation with less developed countries, but there cooperation also takes on strategic importance. Cooperation in Latin America, for example, is viewed by those countries as a major means of gaining at least some degree of managerial control over MNC activities. Thus fully owned subsidiaries in some countries are no longer possible, in-house production must replace component imports, larger shares of the production must be exported, and so on. All this requires MNC management to reassess their strategic plans for Latin America; it also makes it more difficult to integrate Latin American activities into the global operations of the MNC.

Industrial cooperation among firms in the industrialized Western countries has increased very rapidly as well. In the older and mature industries, such as auto, farm machinery, and construction equipment, such collaboration serves essentially two purposes: to take up spare capacity, or to escape the costs of introducing new models by producing a proven success. In high-technology industries, such as telecommunications, the reasons for cooperation are somewhat different: to break into new markets essentially protected by governments and/or tight oligopolies. Problems necessarily arise through such collaboration, but it has been one widespread response to the overcapacity and intense competition in many industries today.

Cooperation among firms in the industrialized countries, unlike cooperation in an East–West or North–South context, is undertaken mainly by firms that directly compete against each other in broad product lines. For example, two construction equipment producers might compete fiercely in numerous classes of bulldozers, cranes, excavators, and off-highway loaders. But one might agree to market and service for the other a specific model of materials handling equipment. The producer of the equipment would thus gain new markets, and the other firm would gain economies of scope by widening the product line handled by its distributors.

There are many forms of such cooperative agreements. Production-sharing or risk-sharing contracts are common in the extractive industries, due to the high capital requirements of investment. Management or technical assistance contracts are frequently used in manufacturing and tourism. Contract manufacturing is widespread. All of these fall outside the category of joint venture, but all are, in common with joint ventures, based on the mutuality of interests.

Industrial cooperation, like joint ventures, must be closely monitored by top management. When a firm's cooperation partner also has agreements with other firms, several dangers appear. One is the risk of leakage of the firm's proprietary technology through the partner to third firms, however unintended. Projects can also become downgraded, or even abandoned, as other alliances become more important to the partner. Moreover, industrial cooperation may in some cases weaken rather than strengthen the firm. An example of this would be when the firm which previously made an entire product completely turns over to the partner the production of a critical component, thus losing its own ability to produce the entire product again. This is precisely what happened to British Aerospace, which now makes wings for Airbus Industrie but lacks the staff, experience, and money to build a large airliner on its own.[6]

Another example of the type of problem that can occur in a joint venture is afforded by the situation that arose during the collaboration between Renault and International Harvester in the agricultural equipment sector.[7] The two companies were studying ways of cooperating in the joint purchase and supply of tractor components and parts, with the aim of achieving better economies of scale and lower production costs. They were also considering collaboration in the joint production of new tractor components in Europe. An agreement was signed, but fortunately the cooperation had not yet been put into implementation when International Harvester shortly thereafter sold its agricultural equipment operations to J. I. Case. Case had the option of picking up International Harvester's European operations. Had implementation begun and Case then decided not to pick up the option, Renault would have been left in an awkward position.

Joint Ventures

Joint ventures may be either of an equity or nonequity nature. The nonequity joint venture, unfamiliar to many because it is not highly visible, is a contractual arrangement used heavily in such areas as engineering and construction, consulting services, and the extractive industries. In the extractive industries, mainly due to the huge capital investments required and to the length of the projects, different types of joint ventures may be utilized in the exploration; developmental; exploitation or drilling; production; processing and refining; marketing; or downstream processing phases.[8]

An international equity joint venture arises when an MNC invests in a business enterprise with a local partner in the target country. The MNC may hold a majority, minority, or equal share of the equity, all based on the initial (and sometimes subsequent), relative contributions of the partners to the venture. The MNC for example may contribute mostly technology in return for the local partner's manufacturing capacity, access to low-cost labor, or marketing channels. But the venture may be strictly a marketing venture, a manufacturing venture, or a research and development venture; commonly it includes all of these. The joint venture typically allows the MNC to quickly enter into new markets, since the partner is already established and knows local customs, laws, and suppliers.

Unlike wholly owned subsidiaries, in joint ventures there is no single authority to make decisions when conflicts of interest arise. One often finds that majority ownership is preferred over minority ownership because it implies managerial control, and that the 50-50 arrangement is the least preferred since it provides an extremely inefficient basis for decision making. That may be partially true, but it is also somewhat misleading. Joint ventures are organized to facilitate consensus among the owners and to develop cooperation in areas of mutual interest. Where such mutuality of interests is not fostered, the basis of the joint venture erodes. To executives, therefore, the sharing of management is a much more fundamental characteristic of joint ventures than the sharing of equity.[9] That is why practitioners do not consider as joint ventures those arrangements in which one partner has an overwhelmingly dominant stake, such as 90 percent. For a two-partner joint venture, it is frequently stated that the minority partner must have at least a 25 percent stake; for those cases in which there are three or four partners, a 10 percent stake will suffice.

How then are decision making and control implemented? Typically, the majority partner has jurisdiction over operational management and short-term matters, but at the very least the partners share in the setting of long-term business objectives and in the generation and approval of long-term strategies. Even in those countries where law precludes the MNC's having a majority stake, the MNC is often given, either contractually or by implicit understanding, control over operational management. That concession by the foreign partner typically stems from his recognition of the managerial competence of the MNC. Nevertheless, such arrangements provide insufficient control by the MNC, which will characteristically refuse to transfer its most advanced technologies under minority stake conditions. MNCs must be especially cautious in protecting their proprietary technology when the foreign partner is a government-owned rather than private enterprise. Joint ventures with government partners have been found to be particularly vulnerable to expropriation.[10]

Control problems are inherent to joint ventures, but if an MNC seeks entry into Japan or Mexico, to name two important countries which bar fully owned subsidiaries, there is little choice other than the nonequity arrangements discussed below. In joint ventures the interests of local partners must be taken into consideration. From a strategic viewpoint, this makes it extremely difficult for the MNC to fully integrate any joint venture operation into the rest of its global activities. For example, jurisdictional disputes arise in regard to export markets. The MNC may feel that the Canadian market, which it has long served, is not a proper market for the joint venture's marketing activities; the MNC's partner may feel quite the contrary. Sales to third country markets can be a continuous source of conflict. In view of such problems, MNCs dependent on a very narrow product line typically have much less tolerance for joint ventures than do firms that have relatively broad product lines, and are thus capable of engaging in joint ventures affecting a relatively small portion of their overall operations.[11] The more diversified firm is clearly less exposed to risk in taking on a joint venture partner.

Thus, major disadvantages of joint ventures are frequently associated with the lack of full control over the joint activities by either partner, and with managerial disagreements between the partners, as discussed above. Swift decision making is necessary, especially in sectors where competition is intense, yet the flexibility of the partners in this regard is seriously constrained when managerial dissension emerges. On the other hand, contractual clauses in the joint venture agreements may to some extent alleviate such concerns. Even when the partners disagree on basic objectives, for example, as when one partner seeks long-run market share and the other seeks short-run profits and immediate returns, resolution of the conflicts may be facilitated through a variety of means, such as provisions for royalties, technical assistance fees, and auxiliary component or product sales. These help smooth cyclical fluctuations in the profitability of the joint venture operations, and also offer some protection against potential government controls on the repatriation of profits, freezing of foreign exchange, or even, in extreme cases, against the threat of expropriation.[12]

Compared to the fully owned subsidiaries discussed previously, however, joint ventures have several advantages. Many small- and medium-sized firms lack adequate financial and managerial resources to establish or acquire outright their own international sales and service networks, let alone any productive facilities abroad. The cash requirements for joint ventures are significantly lower, especially since capitalization of technology (know-how or patents) is generally accepted as a partial or even total contribution to the foreign firm's equity share of the venture. In addition, front-end payments for the transfer of technology and ongoing royalties (based on a small percentage of either sales or production) can more than offset the initial cash requirements of the foreign partner, and these inflows complement the normal participation in income from the venture. In regard to managerial resources, it requires much high level managerial effort to negotiate the joint venture and to set in motion the basic technology transfer. Still, joint ventures typically result in much less drain on the firm's managerial resources than the establishment and subsequent operation of fully owned facilities abroad. Other advantages of joint ventures include readier access to a market and to market information, reciprocal flows of technology from the partner, and in some cases (mainly in the Third World) greater patent or copyright protection and remuneration than are provided through pure licensing agreements.[13]

Some industries are especially amenable to joint ventures. A highly complex network of manufacturing joint ventures for example can be found in the commercial vehicle and auto component industries. Figures 5–1 and 5–2 illustrate some, but not all, of the joint venture links in the European truck manufacturing and auto component industries in 1982. Legislation concerning such areas as safety, pollution control, and energy efficiency has pushed the firms in these industries in the same general direction, which is one reason why joint efforts make sense. Perhaps more importantly, it makes sense to share the cost of developing and producing relatively low-volume but high-cost components between several companies at a time when the two industries are seriously short of investment cash. Thus, one trend in the truck manufacturing industry is towards joint ventures between component suppliers and truck makers (e.g., between Iveco and Rockwell for axle production and between Leyland and Commins for diesel engines). At least in this industry, when strong companies have linked up with relatively weak ones (e.g., Daimler with FBW), the motivation of the stronger firm has typically been to gain access to the partner's distribution network. Establishing a dealer and service point network from scratch in a new market is tremendously expensive, but no truck manufacturer can afford to be without an efficient network of that type.

Not all joint ventures succeed of course, and major reasons for their failure have included inadequate market analysis, product defects, and higher costs than anticipated. These problems are in turn often traceable mainly to insufficient attention, interest, and support from top management, marketing, engineering, and production staffs. Major remedies involve providing better screening for foreign ventures, revamping the organization of joint venture responsibilities, improving communications between the partners, and especially strengthening liaison between domestic product divisions and the joint venture operations.[14]

The strategic choice on whether to use joint ventures as an entry strategy, and then whether to aim at majority or minority participation, will depend to a great extent on the degree of control that the firm

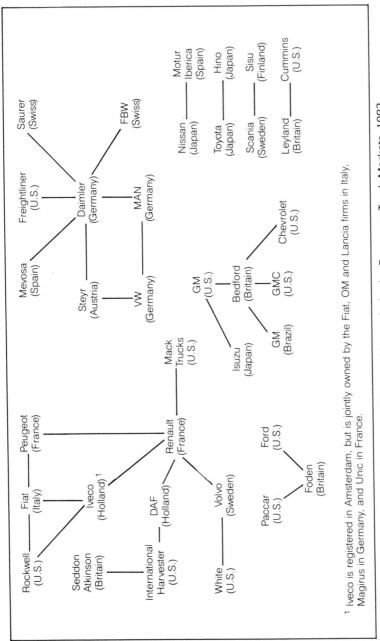

FIGURE 5–1 Joint Venture Networks in the European Truck Markets, 1982
SOURCE: Adapted from the *Financial Times*, London (November 15, 1982).

[1] Iveco is registered in Amsterdam, but is jointly owned by the Fiat, OM and Lancia firms in Italy, Magirus in Germany, and Unic in France.

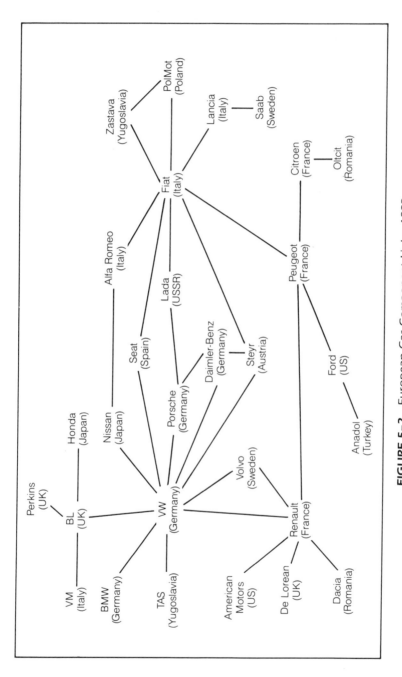

FIGURE 5-2 European Car Component Links, 1982
SOURCE: Adapted from the *Financial Times*, London (Oct. 19, 1982).

insists on keeping to itself. If proprietary technology is a major competitive strength of the firm, the firm may not wish to transfer such technology. Note, however, that attitudes regarding this approach change over time as environmental conditions change. For example, in late 1984 IBM forged its first joint venture in Europe, with Elsag (Italy), in the area of technological collaboration. At the same time, a proposed joint venture between IBM and British Telecommunications was blocked by the British government on anticompetitive grounds. Some companies refuse to consider joint ventures because it is perceived that joint ventures often make more difficult the global rationalization of production, marketing, finance, and transfer pricing. Suboptimization may result.

On the other hand, joint ventures may, under certain conditions, provide an excellent means of diversifying product lines, substantially expanding one's distribution and servicing networks, and gaining components and technology from the partner. They may also serve to cut losses by reducing production costs and eliminating excess capacity, two motivations of Ford and Volkswagen in forming their joint venture in Brazil. Especially under the conditions of rapidly changing technology and intense competition at present, American firms might do well to search for joint venture partners to establish operations either at home or abroad.

Licensing

International licensing involves the transfer of industrial property rights (patents, trademarks, and/or proprietary know-how) from a licensor in one country to a licensee in a second country. Industrial property rights are seldom sold outright. Typically, the licensor allows the licensee to use the rights for a specified period of time in return for a royalty compensation.

The fee may be based on some percentage of sales, a flat rate, or possibly a sliding scale of revenues. A simple example of licensing is when a British publisher sells to a French publisher the French language rights for a book whose copyright the British firm owns. Patent rights are generally more complex, for typically the seller imposes many conditions on the sale. For example, the seller may prohibit the buyer from marketing the product in markets already served by the seller. The sale may also call for ongoing consultations between technicians of the two firms for quality control or product development purposes. Variations are common, and each agreement will reflect firm-specific and product-specific issues.

There are a number of conditions under which licensing seems appropriate.[15] Licensing is especially suitable, for example, during the mature stage of the product life cycle, when competition is intense, margins decline, and production is relatively standardized. It is a viable means of penetrating foreign markets when there are constraints on direct investment or direct investment income (through profit repatriation laws limiting the amount of profits which may be taken out of a country). Licensing is also a feasible response to some countries' import-substitution policies, which may make direct investment less desirable. The propensity to use licensing is generally inversely related to the size of the licensor within a given industry. That is because small firms typically lack the financial and managerial resources necessary for direct investment abroad. Some licensing firms can be very small indeed. One small press with gross revenues of about $20,000 per year actually sold two licenses for foreign book rights in recent years from the United States.

Companies that spend relatively more on research and development as a percentage of sales tend to license more than others. Relatively rapid technological change in an industry induces a significant use of licensing. The larger firms which opt for a significant amount of licensing are typically those with diversified product lines. This is possibly because the greater the diversification, the thinner are financial and managerial resources stretched and the greater the firm's need for external support from licensees.

While the issues noted above are usually firm- or sector-specific, some generalizations may be made concerning the advantages of licensing. It does provide a relatively quick, low-cost, low-risk means of penetrating new markets. Especially for firms not already heavily involved in international operations, it allows the firm to explore new markets and to become identified with locally established firms. It provides additional revenues from "shelf" technology, that is, from products whose research and development costs have possibly already been amortized.

Disadvantages, however, are also clear. Licensing returns, however attractive, must be viewed in the light of the long-run problem of the licensor losing a competitive edge to its licensee. One's partner of today may become the main competitor once the licensing agreement expires. Having transferred the rights, the licensor sometimes creates his own competition. Problems arise also in areas like quality control and marketing jurisdiction. More than one licensor has shut himself out of lucrative markets by giving the licensee marketing rights in certain regions. Such an opportunity cost can be especially irksome when the licensee fails to exploit the market potential himself.

International licensing is most commonly found in combination with other international activities of the firm. Indeed, the majority of licensing agreements by American firms are with their own foreign subsidiaries.[16] That notwithstanding, there are research and development firms whose main business is to develop new ideas for sale at home and abroad. While licensing is thus typically used to support other international operations of the MNC, this is not necessarily the case.

The semiconductor industry is one in which licensing is fairly common. In recent years the cost of entry into the industry has significantly increased, due to the increased complexity of semiconductor devices; this in turn increases the demand for licenses for those already in the industry, as well as for new entrants. Competition is intense, especially since there are several different semiconductor technologies in use, which in turn reduces the value of individual patents. Because of the rapid development of technology and the rapid introduction of new products, the rate of technical innovation and product obsolescence is high. The result is that a product's lifetime is typically around five years, which makes rapid licensing more important to help spread the costs of research and development. And one fascinating occurrence in the industry has been very rarely heard of in most other industries: the providing of technology by one firm to another, even to a competitor, for no money. This happens because customers require it. In this industry, customers usually insist on an alternate source of supply for any new product before they will design that product into what they make. Consequently, semiconductor manufacturers often solicit one or more of their competitors to commit to manufacture a new product and thereby serve as a second source. Such actions are taken relatively early in the production of the new product, in order to gain orders and thereby lock in customers to that specific design. In gaining the commitment of the competitor, however, the original producer of the new product often has to transfer numerous logic and circuit diagrams. Ideally, the innovative firm would find a competitor that is not particularly strong. That is often not possible, however, because the potential customer (i.e., manufacturer of finished goods) insists that the secondary source be in good health.[17]

Turnkey Projects

Some firms may be able to provide complete facilities for another country, train the workers and managers, and then go home. The entire project is a package bought and paid for by someone in the recipient country. Such projects are common in heavy construction. A Third World country may contract for a dam and irrigation facilities. A worldwide contractor bids and wins the project, sends large numbers of foreign technicians, workers, and managers to the site, builds the project, and turns it over to the host government. Often such projects take years to complete, so the foreigners are in the country for extended periods.

Such activities are not possible for all firms, but many international contracting firms follow this strategy exclusively, and their talents and resources are structured to take on such vast works. The world market for turnkey projects is large, and the larger projects can run to billions of dollars each.

On occasion, a manufacturer may take on such a project if it offers good profit potential. Thus several major television manufacturers built a major television production facility in Algeria. This country wanted no foreign direct investment in the sector, but it did want an indigenous industry, and it was willing to pay for it. Such possibilities arise from time to time for many firms, and one critical policy question is whether or not to enter into such agreements.

During the early 1980s, there was an increase in the sales of used factories in the form of turnkey projects. Second-hand plants, deemed obsolete in the United States and other industrialized countries because of small size, environmental problems or high energy or labor requirements, were being sold to Third World countries hoping to reduce the level of their imports of manufactured products. Both partners to such arrangements benefit, the one by getting rid of surplus equipment and the other by getting the plant at a bargain price.

Franchising

Franchising, most frequently found in fast-food outlets, has become a rapidly growing phenomenon in many countries after its introduction and development in the United States. Franchising amounts to collaboration between a company that wishes to exploit its trademark and an independent individual who enters a contract with the franchisor. The independent franchisee accepts the working principles of the franchisor, and often enters a commitment to buy certain inputs from the franchisor.

A major advantage for the firm that acts as franchisor is that it gains rapid business growth and a faster establishment of its trademark, all at relatively little capital expense. The franchisee benefits, in turn, from a business, and sometimes from a clientele, that are already established; at the same time, the franchisee legally keeps a great deal of its independence. The franchisee also benefits considerably from the franchisor's reputation when approaching banks for financial support.

Typically, the franchisee pays a front-end lump sum to the franchisor, in addition to ongoing royalty payments. The royalty fees may be based on turnover or on a percentage of the cost of basic supplies. The royalty is intended to cover the cost of any further training, advice, administrative backup, and local and national advertising. One potential threat to the franchisor is that the franchisee might not live up to the quality (mainly in regard to service, but also in regard to product) standards of the franchisor, thus doing damage to numerous outlets rather than merely to the single outlet in question. There typically are, however, general (though expensive) provisions for disenfranchising. A main risk for the franchisee is below expected support by the franchisor.

Export/Import

Exporting and importing are the more traditional components of international business, and they certainly do not normally involve the corporate commitment required of the more complex forms of international operations. However, for smaller firms it is often the only feasible choice. The intricacies of documentation and foreign currency conversion can be turned over to expert outsiders such as EMCs (export management companies), who specialize in getting foreign sales for others and in getting products to foreign buyers. Or the firm can have its own export department and perform such technical tasks itself. Major banks and other specialists are happy to provide (for a price) such services as currency conversion, letters of credit, and related financial arrangements.

Exporting can lead to problems of finding the right distributors in various countries, which is an art and science all to itself. Countries often have very strict rules about dropping distributors, and a poor choice here can lead to sluggish sales for decades. Firms, particularly those that are relatively new to international operations, often stumble into poor contracts through ignorance of the country or its markets.

Firms may also make extensive direct investments in marketing facilities, such as warehouses, transportation facilities, and sales offices, without making direct manufacturing investments abroad. Japanese firms in particular do this in the United States, and since marketing costs are large, such investments can be multibillion dollar expenditures in their own right. All sorts of variations are possible. A firm could have a warehouse joint venture with its local distributor, yet not be perceived as being a direct investor in the country. The foreign firm could even own all or part of the distributor, or the advertising agencies used, or other pieces of the marketing system.

Many firms perceived as domestic may have international ties through importing. Large retail chains may buy huge amounts of goods from foreign firms, and their buyers may frequent such countries as Hong Kong, Taiwan, and South Korea, looking for good bargains in textiles, toys, or consumer electronic goods. In Western Europe, due to the development of the Common Market, EEC firms buy goods from other European countries so easily that it hardly seems to be international business. Canadian department stores are heavily stocked with products manufactured in the United States. And it is very common for any MNC to export its production to another branch of the same firm, as when Brazilian auto engines are exported to Canada for installation in cars manufactured there by the same MNC. Much of world trade is intracorporate trade.

The volume of world trade has been increasing about 10 percent per year in real terms since 1946, meaning that it doubles every seven years or so. Even the most provincial citizen of the most isolated part of his or her country is related to the world through imports and exports.

In manufacturing, exporting and importing are clearly not limited to smaller firms. Several giant firms have decided to maintain a local base and export, instead of making direct investments abroad. If your product is as good as those of the Boeing Aircraft Company, you may make it work. Japanese auto companies also have used this strategy until very recently. A real problem here is that if local competition is strong (economically or politically), you may face new tariff barriers and other constraints that eventually force you to make direct investments abroad. Thus a major danger of relying totally on exporting is that the firm might be cut off from lucrative markets.

Pressures of this sort induce direct investment. The only viable move for the Japanese is to make direct investments in the United States if they wish to retain their approximately 30 percent share of the U.S. auto market. Such investments can total many billions of dollars, and of course they lead to all of the multinational problems we have discussed, but the option, in general terms, is potential stagnation for the firm. So the investments take place. Similar pressures on U.S. auto firms, starting as far back as 1915, led them to invest abroad and become MNCs. The export game may only work well for smaller firms in special situations, or for bigger firms whose product is so superior that foreigners must have it in any case. Some armaments manufacturers are in this position, as are a few very high technology companies that choose to stay home. But for most companies, export of the final product is a transitional strategy that cannot be sustained in the long run.

It is also common for MNCs and other large companies to rely heavily on local specialist firms and buy from them for import, without trying to take them over. Given industrial and environmental constraints, it is cheaper and more efficient. Thus there are thousands of very efficient firms in Hong Kong that are locally owned, but whose output is largely exported, typically through the large orders placed by major foreign firms. A small textile firm may be selling half its output to J. C. Penneys or Sears and Roebuck in the United States, or Marks and Spencer in Britain. The brand names will be American or British, and the local Hong Kong firm has very low marketing costs as a result. But Sears is not interested in buying the company, since it lacks the expertise to manage it properly. This anonymous supplier structure is also common domestically, and it usually works well for all concerned.

SUMMARY

Direct investment abroad is the traditional base of multinational corporate activity. However, it is only one of many alternatives for the MNC. We have discussed some of the more common options, including fully owned subsidiaries, joint ventures, industrial cooperation agreements, licensing, turnkey projects, and the more historical importing and exporting. In the increasingly stringent environment for direct investment, firms can no longer afford a policy which automatically rules out all options other than that of fully owned subsidiaries. Unwritten policies as well as explicit laws have made fully owned subsidiaries impossible in many parts of the world, and less viable than before in others. The closing of the technological gap that existed during the years immediately following the end of the Second World War has led to a sharp increase in international competition, and that competition is partly based on the flexibility of firms in adjusting to the specific requirements of the host country. Market saturation at home and economic stagnation virtually everywhere are forcing firms to take a more discriminating look at alternative methods of doing business abroad.

Whatever form the international activities assume, it requires a strategic decision at the highest levels. Those decisions influence the future form, size, and structure of the firm. Some forms of international involvement offer fast growth possibilities for smaller companies; others are more useful for corporate giants. Typically, given the variety of constraints imposed by different countries, a mixture of forms has evolved. An MNC may license in some countries, export to others, import from some, make direct investments in a few key markets, pursue joint ventures in Latin America, and engage in industrial cooperation in Eastern Europe. The specific forms depend on both the MNC's evaluation of options and environmental constraints. Even for smaller firms these choices must be made, either deliberately or implicitly. It is common to discover in huge firms that both types of decision making occurred in the past, and that the modern structure of the company is a function of almost forgotten historic decisions made by men now long dead. But they *do* matter, and they can matter a great deal.

DISCUSSION QUESTIONS

1. What are the basic determinants for choosing a location when the firm expands abroad?

2. What advantages and disadvantages are associated with the various entry modes of international operations?

3. What political considerations have contributed to the very rapid increase of industrial cooperation agreements in recent years?

4. How is decision making typically handled in joint venture operations?

5. In the long run, the sharing of management is more critical to the success of joint ventures than to the sharing of equity. Defend or refute this proposition.

NOTES

1. Robert Weigand, "International Investments: Weighing the Incentives," *Harvard Business Review* (July–August, 1983), 146–152.

2. Lawrence G. Franko, "Multinationals: The End of U.S. Dominance," *Harvard Business Review* (November–December, 1978), 93–101.

3. Charles P. Kindleberger, "The Theory of Direct Investment," in *International Trade and Finance: Readings,* eds., Baldwin and Richardson (Boston: Little, Brown and Company, 1974), 267–285.

4. Franklin R. Root, *International Trade and Investment,* 5th Ed. (Cincinnati: South-Western Publishing Company, 1984), 477–482.

5. Charles Oman, *New Forms of International Investment in Developing Countries* (Paris: Organization for Economic Cooperation and Development, 1984), 36–37.

6. "Co-operative Capitalist Plots," *The Economist* (February 11, 1984), 63.

7. Paul Betts, "Renault and Harvester in Tractor Pact," *Financial Times* (October 9, 1984), 24.

8. Robert J. Radway, "Overview of Foreign Joint Ventures," *The Business Lawyer* (May, 1983), 1040–1048.

9. Allen R. Janger, *Organization of International Joint Ventures* (New York: The Conference Board, 1980), 7–8.

10. David G. Bradley, "Managing Against Expropriation," *Harvard Business Review* (July–August, 1977), 75–83.

11. Lawrence G. Franko, "Joint Venture Divorce in the Multinational Company," *Columbia Journal of World Business* (May–June, 1971), 13–22.

12. Farok J. Contractor, "Strategies for Structuring Joint Ventures: A Negotiations Planning Paradigm," *Columbia Journal of World Business* (Summer, 1984), 30–39.

13. F. Kingston Berlew, "The Joint Venture — A Way Into Foreign Markets," *Harvard Business Review* (July–August, 1984), 48–54.

14. Thomas P. Collier, "Succeeding With a Joint Venture," *Les Nouvelles* (March, 1981), 27–30.

15. Farok J. Contractor, "The Role of Licensing in International Strategy," *Columbia Journal of World Business* (Winter, 1981), 73–81.

16. Franklin R. Root, "Entering International Markets," in *Handbook of International Business*, ed., Ingo Walter (New York: John Wiley and Sons, 1982), 31: 3–22.

17. Alan H. MacPherson, "Licensing and Semiconductor Industry," *Les Nouvelles* (September, 1982), 180–183.

FURTHER READING

1. Contractor, Farok J. and Lorange, Peter. *Cooperative Strategies in International Business* (Lexington: D.C. Heath and Co., 1988).

2. Hladik, Karen J. *International Joint Ventures* (Lexington: D.C. Heath and Co., 1985).

3. Robock, Stefan H., and Kenneth Simmonds. *International Business and Multinational Enterprises*, 3rd Ed. (Homewood, Ill.: Irwin, 1983).

4. Rutenberg, David P. *Multinational Management*. (Boston: Little, Brown and Co., 1982).

5. Vernon, Raymond, and Louis T. Wells, Jr. *Manager in the International Economy*, 4th ed. (Englewood Cliffs, N.J.: Prentice-Hall, 1981).

CHAPTER 6

▼

Strategy Implementation: Technology Transfer and Intracompany Linkages

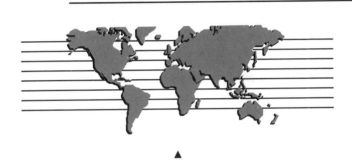

▲

The locational, entry, and ownership patterns discussed in the preceding chapter determine to a large extent the nature of intrafirm linkages through which the transfer of technology is implemented. Here we enter an area of multinational activity that is often controversial, for while the transfer of technology is typically welcomed by the recipient country, the intrafirm linkages through which it is implemented are often not. The two cannot be divorced, however, for generally the transfer of technology requires close association between the headquarter's unit and its affiliates abroad.

TECHNOLOGY TRANSFER

No matter what the mode of entry into foreign markets, success in the international arena for most industries depends heavily on the efficient and effective transfer of technology. Indeed, perhaps the greatest contribution that the globally oriented firm has made to development on a worldwide basis has been its stimulus to innovation and growth through the mechanism of technology transfer. In this regard, two major developments have been noticeable in the last decade or so. First, the need for technology transfer is growing considerably as a consequence of the drive for economic growth and development over large parts of the globe. Second, the potential recipients of the technology are imposing far stricter conditions on its transfer than earlier, and frequently resist the classic modes of transfer. Both of these developments present substantial challenges to the globally oriented firm.

Different Forms of Technology Transfer

Before we discuss those issues, however, it is helpful to make three sets of distinctions basic to the technology transfer process:

1. between embodied and disembodied technology
2. among material, design, and capacity transfers
3. between process and product technologies

An understanding of these distinctions should help explain why technology transfer is successful in some cases, but not in others.

Embodied vs. Disembodied Technology

Embodied technology is essentially hardware, a piece of equipment whose transfer typically poses few problems. An engine made in one country, for example, will generally function in another (although adjustments must sometimes be made in connection with climatic conditions). Disembodied technology, such as that typically transferred through licensing, is software, and it poses many more problems when transferred abroad due to basic differences in microlevel infrastructures (e.g., the plant-level operational procedures), the ability of the recipients to easily absorb and diffuse the technology, and other general environmental conditions.

Material, Design, and Capacity Transfers

Material transfer refers to the import of a product; design transfer to the import of facilities, such as a turnkey plant, to make the product; and capacity transfer to the import of the knowledge of how to make similar plants without further recourse to foreign suppliers. It is capacity transfer which is the most complex of these, and which entails the ability of the recipient country or firm to absorb and diffuse an imported technology by indigenous effort. It is important to note here that a progressively greater contribution is generally required of the indigenous technological resources as one moves up the scale from material to design to capacity transfers of technology.[1]

Process vs. Product Technologies

The distinction between process and product technologies is more directly associated with the nature of the technology itself than with the transfer mechanisms. Firms engaged in manufacturing may be viewed as competing either on the basis of product technology or on the basis of process technology.[2] Product technology involves the development of new and unique products that have few close substitutes. This is typical, for example, in the pharmaceutical industry and high technology fields, and of individual products when they first appear, such as Polaroid cameras. Here the firm's competitive advantage is derived from its ownership of the product rather than from its ability to produce the product cheaply, although low-cost production is also possible. The exercise of this property right over the product yields monopoly profits for the innovating firm, thus compensating it for its research and development expenditures.

Process technology, in contrast, is associated with the firm's ability to produce and market a given product efficiently. This includes ways of organizing production; altering the structural characteristics of the product so as to lower costs; motivating consumers to purchase the products; and servicing the product once it has been sold. A firm with an advantage in process technology will be able to either produce the same or similar product as its competitors at lower cost or produce a better product at the same cost as incurred by its competitors. There is not a country in the world, for example, which cannot produce construction equipment. But no company in the world has the process technology of Caterpillar Tractor Company, which is one reason why that firm commands a very significant share of the United States and, indeed, world markets.

The distinction between product technology and process technology has fundamental implications for the strategic structuring of intracompany relations. Firms that compete on the basis of product technology tend to be centralized, vertically integrated, and unlikely to transfer technology to outsiders. Firms that compete on the basis of process technology tend to be relatively decentralized, horizontally integrated, and more willing to share technology and control with outsiders. In the context of our discussion above, firms competing on the basis of product technology would strongly insist on fully owned subsidiaries abroad, thus precluding their entry into countries where fully owned subsidiaries are not permissible. Firms competing on the basis of process technology are much more willing to enter into joint venture, industrial cooperation, and licensing arrangements. Another logical consequence of the distinction between the two types of technology is that foreign affiliates will have a great deal more autonomy if their parent competes on the basis of process in contrast to product technologies.

Licensing as a Key Mechanism of Technology Transfer

The licensing of the multinational corporation's (MNC's) technology is relevant here, whether to an overseas affiliate or, through an arm's length transaction, to an independent third party. Whether or not the MNC licenses its technology, and under what conditions, may well be critical strategic questions. These questions, as well as the possession of state of the art technologies, directly affect the MNC's bargaining position. A company like IBM will be able to withhold its technology from others by refusing to license, but still gain entry into the Japanese market without a partner, which is a rare capability. Other firms may have a policy of licensing only to fully owned affiliates abroad, avoiding joint ventures. In recent years, however, licensing appears to have substantially increased in importance for the majority of MNCs.

As noted above, MNCs rarely use licensing as a primary means of entry into foreign markets. Instead, it tends to be used mainly in a secondary or supportive role in association with other foreign market development strategies. Thus, a large proportion of licensing agreements are found in connection with intracorporate trade between the headquarters and foreign affiliates of a single company. Even when that is not the case, licensing is often used as a residual strategy when other, more preferable means of penetrating foreign markets are not feasible.[3] For example, when foreign laws prohibit fully owned subsidiaries or indeed direct investment in any form by foreign corporations; or when foreign markets are considered too small to justify direct investment or extensive export campaigns.

There are conditions, however, under which the use of licensing as a primary means of market entry makes sense. Often, for example, the research and development unit of an MNC develops technology relatively far removed from the mainstream of the firm's activities. In such cases no competitive threat arises from licensing the technology, nor does the firm need to develop internally the infrastructural support that in-house production would require. In other cases, countries have imposed new restrictions on the importing of components or otherwise forced the MNC's subsidiaries abroad to produce in-house what previously had been imported from the home country (e.g., through exchange controls or local content laws). In such cases licensing is one method of sustaining foreign operations which otherwise would have to be substantially scaled down, if not divested completely.

Licensing is frequently an excellent means of market penetration in the sense that it opens up foreign markets to associated sales of plants, equipment, component parts, raw material inputs, or service contracts. These can all be very profitable, depending on the nature of the technology involved and the competitive configuration of the industry. Such licensing agreements also often lead to reciprocal licensing arrangements, a two-way cooperative sharing of technological and innovative improvements with the partner firm, which can broaden the technological and product base of the MNC.

When dealing with licensees based in less developed countries and when the MNC has no direct managerial control over the licensing affiliate, a front-end, lump-sum payment is often preferred instead of ongoing royalties based on the volume of production or sales. This is in part because the licensee often has an unrealistic (i.e., overly optimistic) assessment of his capabilities of efficiently absorbing the licensed technology. Indeed, one serious concern of the licensor must be whether it has sufficient personnel to deploy to the licensee's country when the inevitable problems of technology absorption arise.

The Environment of Technology Transfer

Why inevitable? That has much to do with the environment in general, which can be either hostile to the process of technology transfer itself, or quite favorable for the transfer process. But it also has a lot to do with the distinctions made above in regard to embodied and disembodied technology, material and design and capacity transfers, and product and process technologies. Note, in this regard, that eventual technical success of any given firm is by no means in itself a guarantee of commercial success. Perhaps the best example of this distinction is found in the centrally planned economies, which have fostered technological progress by a heavy commitment of resources to the development of technology, by establishing a quite adequate technical and scientific base, and by training vast numbers of highly skilled manpower. But they also suffer from serious technological lag compared to the West, because their organizational, managerial, and institutional framework has created an environment unfavorable for the absorption and diffusion of new technologies. There are many reasons for this, but one of the most critical is the lack of proper incentives at the enterprise level to innovate, which hinders the application of new technologies to the productive systems. Indeed, in the centrally planned economies one often finds extremely strong *dis*incentives to innovation and technological progress, especially since the introduction of new technologies disrupts present operations (by design), and thus interferes with the meeting of planned targets.

This occurs in the less-developed countries as well, where often, as also in the case of centrally planned economies, one does not view technology as an ongoing flow. Technology is a way of doing things, not a piece of equipment. But many seem to believe the opposite. The feeling is, one can buy a piece of equipment and ignore the (necessary) infrastructural changes and linkages under which the new equipment is effective.

This attitude is shown most notably in some types of turnkey projects. An oil-rich country decides it wants to manufacture its own television sets, but it does not want to allow foreign MNCs to operate within its borders. So it buys a turnkey television production plant, pays the contractor to train workers, and when the job is done, the country has its plant. So far, so good, but television production and development is an ongoing process. Unless the country is very lucky, whatever new developments occur outside the country will be unnoticed in this new plant. So in 1995 the plant continues to churn out 1980 vintage television sets and no one, except the citizens of that country, will want to buy them. The country is suspicious of foreigners and does not allow its own technicians to go abroad to visit the numerous trade shows and technical meetings where ideas are exchanged. The country's technicians may not read English or German, and have little access to new ideas. And contact with MNCs is discouraged, so salesmen from components firms with new products, or capital equipment makers with new machinery, will not be met. In short, the country bought a can of knowledge and then cut off information flows.

With competition like this, it is easy to see how MNCs can compete so effectively. But other governments, equally convinced that there is a can of R & D to buy, will propose other projects, all equally disastrous in the long run.

Also note here the close relationship between all information flows and R & D, which is one reason many countries are reluctant to allow their technicians to travel widely. With the flow of technology comes a flow of culture, and the engineers may bring home, if indeed they don't defect, some rather dangerous social ideas. When they do, as is often the case, this makes such governments even more reluctant to allow free information flows. But frequently the cost is technological stagnation, and perhaps in another ten years, when it dawns on the country's leaders that the rest of the world is moving far ahead, they reluctantly contact the MNC to buy some technology in the form of a cooperation agreement, or yet one more turnkey project that will change the domestic world. Those MNC managers, who perceive themselves to be highly conservative, sow revolutionary ideas wherever they go.

To be sure, the transfer of technology to developed Western countries takes place in a climate of mutual understanding, presents no insoluble problems of remuneration and payment, and typically poses no problems of technical assistance and guarantees. The recipients of the technology are technologically literate and the environment conducive to the efficient and effective transfer, absorption, and diffusion of the technology. In the case of technology transfer to less developed countries, however, difficult problems arise. There are substantial gaps in technical training, and the social and administrative infrastructure and milieu are not fully compatible with the requirements of transferring modern technologies. Some less developed countries, such as Brazil and Mexico, have sufficiently competent managers and technicians; but due to the present debt crisis, they lack sufficient funds to import the needed technology. Others, mainly several OPEC members, have sufficient funds but insufficient managerial and technical competence to make proper use of imported technology. The vast majority of less-developed countries, however, have neither the funds nor the cadres to substantially reap the benefits of technology transfer.[4]

The large-scale resistance to fully owned subsidiaries as a means of technology transfer reduces in many cases the effectiveness of such transfers. This is generally because the successful transfer of technology requires a sustained and close enterprise-to-enterprise relationship between the transferor and recipient. A great deal of coordination is required throughout, and areas that require attention in this respect include the aspects of project feasibility studies; the proper choice of product mix and product design; plant design and erection; start-up operations; production and quality control systems; other managerial supporting concerns (such as marketing); the updating of the technology involved, and further product or process development. Every single managerial function is involved, including raw materials sourcing as well as production, and personnel as well as marketing. Operations personnel must be informed and educated on technological developments in the industry; the choice of channels through which technology is most readily transferred; the fabrication and supply of equipment; and quality control over raw materials and processes as well as products.

Each of these items individually is tremendously complex, and the interrelationship of the various components of the technology package is seldom fully appreciated by less developed recipients. Particularly in the case of highly sophisticated technologies, there are very frequently problems associated with the capability of the recipient to fully absorb the technology. Technical training and the transfer of show-how as well as of know-how often require a much more extended effort on the part of both enterprises than at first anticipated, and delays in bringing the projects on stream protract the transferor's technical involvement.

Yet many countries insist on unbundling the technology package (seeking the least expensive source of each of its components among numerous suppliers) and on imposing increasingly strict rules on the transfer of technology. In general, the less developed countries perceive three basic problems with the traditional modes of transfer.

1. The market for technology is imperfect, giving the supplier of technology oligopolistic or monopolistic bargaining powers during negotiations.

2. The technology which is transferred is often considered to be inappropriate to the needs and conditions of the recipient country.

3. The cost of technology transfer is held to be excessive.

It is not the place here to explore the merits of such arguments, but the point is made that these perceptions have forced the MNCs in many cases to make strategic adjustments in their approach to the entire issue of technology transfer.

It is not only less developed countries which sometimes regulate the inflow of technology. During the second half of the 1970s and the first half of 1980s, Canada screened all foreign investment through its Foreign Investment Review Agency in order to assure that the foreign investment was likely to be of significant benefit to the country. That sounds reasonable enough, but implementation of the process caused increased friction between Canada and many MNCs that invest in the country. Ownership in itself is not an issue in the case of Canada, at least according to official pronouncements. Instead, proposals are assessed in terms of their effect on: the level and nature of economic activity in Canada; the degree and significance of participation by Canadians in the business; productivity, industrial efficiency, and technological development; product innovation and product variety; competition with the sector; and compatibility of the transaction with national and provincial policies.

One problem which arises from all this is the effect on the MNC's ability to take a global view. The maintaining of product uniformity, for example, is often necessary to assure the interchangeability of parts and equipment, which in turn is essential for an efficient servicing network. However sound it may be for individual countries to insist that technology transfer be of significant benefit to the country, technological imperatives often preclude adaptation to local priorities, whatever they might be.

All this is not to deny that a relatively small number of less developed countries have indeed made significant progress in industrialization in the last decade or two. These countries have embarked on a determined effort to develop indigenous capacities in such industries as petrochemicals, steel, transport equipment, and numerous light engineering goods. Their basic strategy has been one of import substitution, which relies on imports of intermediate goods and components, and they also encouraged licensing agreements to satisfy the resulting need to produce exportables. The ability to purchase licenses as an alternative to having affiliates fully owned by foreign companies is partly the result of intensified competition in international markets by the technology suppliers. If Japanese and European firms are willing to engage in joint ventures or licensing arrangements rather than insisting on fully owned subsidiaries, U.S. firms must adapt for competitive reasons.

Nevertheless, some MNCs continue to assume a strong bargaining stance, particularly when involved in negotiations with countries considered to be of high political risk. Here the MNCs frequently hold back from transferring the total technology package, and prefer instead to keep under tight control a critical component without which the rest is useless. Thus an electronics firm may produce in a Third World country, but one key component is made solely in the home country and imported by the affiliate abroad. This gizmo is encased in plastic, and efforts to open it trigger a self-destructing process.

Should a revolution occur, and the triumphant radicals attempt to nationalize the plant, it may run for a few weeks using components in stock, but eventually it closes down for good. The workers own the plant perhaps, but there is no production. The key component essential for the entire operation is available from no one, certainly not from the firm that was expropriated. Other firms may produce similar components, but the original producer had made certain that those components of competitors are incompatible with the firm-specific technology that the state has taken over.

An unnoticed aftermath to such events occurs two to five years later. The now sober and poorer revolutionaries arrange to pay compensation for the expropriated plant, make a deal with the MNC, and get the plant back into production. Often the management contract or whatever deal is worked out is more lucrative to the MNC than owning the plant was. And that key component, now significantly modified and improved, still gets imported from the home country. Again the critical importance of information flows and ongoing technological progress is demonstrated.

Recipient countries do not like such activity, but they do not have sufficient bargaining power to stop it. Less developed countries in particular feel a sense of powerlessness in this regard, and this has been one significant source of their frequently violent criticism of the MNCs. They can ban the investment, but then they lose the income and employment. They can expropriate foreign assets in their territory, but then they end up with little else other than an empty building and the wrath of the international investment community, on whom the future flow of credits depends. They can demand technology sharing, but then they end up with outdated technology off the shelf rather than the most modern and competitive of technologies. Actually, that outdated technology is often the most appropriate, because modern technologies, developed mainly in the industrialized countries where wages are high, tend to be labor-saving in nature, while the less developed countries, with their high levels of unemployment, need technologies that create rather than save jobs.

What the less developed countries probably cannot do is to see to a successful conclusion their political efforts, through the United Nations Conference on Trade and Development, to force the transfer of technology from the rich to the poor. They would have this done, moreover, at the cost of transfer rather than at the cost of the research and development activities, for they view technology as the common heritage of mankind. The problem is, if the development of innovation and technology is not profitable for the company, it will no longer be of strategic concern to the company. Technological progress would be stifled for lack of incentives, and the less developed countries would suffer along with all.

Again, our discussion of international economic and trade issues borders on the political. This is inevitable, and it also has profound implications for the technology transfer strategies of individual companies. The political environment has made no longer tenable the traditional pattern of MNC activities, entailing globally integrated production abroad in fully owned subsidiaries and under management dominated by the home country. Instead, MNC producers will be gradually replaced, at least in the Third World, by MNC suppliers of inputs such as technology, skills, and market information, and the traditional investment package will therefore be largely unbundled.[5] In other words, agents in the less developed countries will selectively acquire individual components of an investment package from numerous firms, using domestic sources where possible but also relying heavily on competition among MNCs to assure more favorable terms for the necessary transfers from abroad. Essential aspects of this unbundling process include the forced spin-off of ownership-based control, the forced transfer of functions (such as marketing or the processing of raw materials), and the transfer of know-how, skills, and technology in general.

All this suggests a compelling need for flexible corporate policies to conform to host countries' perceived needs. The new arrangements also might well suggest both lower risk and higher profit for the firms willing and able to adapt to such conditions. It is difficult to generalize, however, because when one talks of less developed countries, one refers to around 140 different nations, whose circumstances, needs, and policies differ substantially. In such diverse environmental conditions, it is an extremely complex task for the globally oriented firm to rationalize its policies across country lines.

The problem of shaping a global technology transfer strategy is greatly exacerbated by the need to develop technologies which are appropriate to the individual recipient countries. The appropriateness of technology is not simply an issue of labor-creating versus labor-saving technology. The importing country may have very high priorities which include the replacement of imported raw materials by domestically available materials of a different quality; less energy intensive production processes; or the altering of processes to more efficiently handle economies of smaller scale. All of this typically requires substantial alteration of the capital and technology package transferred by the MNC. According to the severity of local conditions, the package must be designed to meet specific needs, which vary greatly from country to country.

STRUCTURING OF INTRACOMPANY LINKAGES

All organizations inevitably face conflict of interest between the whole and the parts. For the multinational corporation, however, this bifurcation of interests is especially acute. The need for rationalizing functional operations across national frontiers is a far more complex problem than that of rationalizing in a purely domestic context. One obvious reason for this is that there exist strong political and economic pressures to integrate the activities of overseas units into the economy and national life of the host countries. Such pressures directly influence the structuring of intracompany linkages.

The basic forms of MNC involvement abroad are associated with vertical and horizontal integration of enterprise activities, the former being either backward (to inputs) or forward (to markets). An example of vertical integration is the extraction of raw materials in less developed countries by the MNC, which are then processed for in-house use or for marketing. Horizontal integration essentially implies the establishment of numerous subsidiaries in various countries, each accounting for specific regional markets or for the manufacturing of specific components or products which are then distributed by the worldwide system.

The structuring of intracompany linkages is most assuredly dependent on the entry and ownership strategies discussed above. For example, the nature of strategic linkages with (and among) fully owned foreign subsidiaries is quite different from the nature of such linkages with joint venture, industrial cooperation, and licensing affiliates. The discussion which follows applies generally to fully or majority owned units abroad.

The Evolution of Structure

Organizations are continually in flux, and once an organizational design is determined, that design itself unleashes pressure for change. This is because the solution to any single organizational structural problem inevitably creates new problems, as discussed below. Nevertheless, in international firms, one can detect a rather steady structural evolution towards the global view. The various structures presented in Figures 6–1 through 6–5 indicate some of the more common organizational solutions discussed below.

The Export Manager   A growing, local, domestically oriented firm will occasionally receive inquiries from abroad which lead to export orders. This company, if such orders continue to come in, will eventually assign an export manager to handle foreign orders, as shown in Figure 6–1. Foreign orders are a novelty at first, but if sales abroad rapidly increase relative to domestic sales, the export manager, in the opinion of some, begins to overstep his or her bounds. For example, he or she may tell the production people that sales would increase even more if they would make certain adjustments to the product to be more in keeping with foreign tastes and requirements. The finance people may become irked at delays in changing foreign money to dollars, and may not understand the many new shipping and other forms they are now expected to master. At this point the firm is still very domestically oriented, and the export manager lacks sufficient clout as an advocate of the international operations. This first phase of international activity,

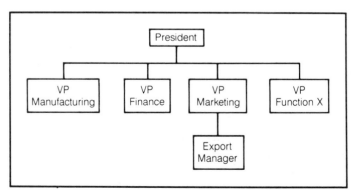

FIGURE 6-1   International Organizational Structures: Beginnings

if the firm's products continue to sell abroad, leads to further structural adjustment.

The International Division   As the volume of international business grows and becomes relatively more important the firm typically establishes an international division, as shown in Figure 6–2. The structure of the international division is highly centralized, and may be found in conjunction with either functional or product divisions. However, the international division structure typically appears to be a transitional structure, although it can still be found today in some highly successful multinationals. It places international operations at the same organizational level as the functional or product group divisions, but the international operations are still less autonomous than these divisions. This situation exists because the international division depends considerably more on the cooperation of other divisions than they depend on it. At least during the early stages of internationalization, the product division managers, for example, continue to concentrate on the domestic market and give low priority to international operations. Conflicts arise, and jurisdictional disputes become common. Eventually, the faster growth of foreign over domestic markets leads to a replacement of the international division structure with a structure that more closely integrates the domestic activities of the MNC with its foreign operations.

The Functional Structure   Exactly how that integration proceeds depends on the nature of both products and markets. Three organiza-

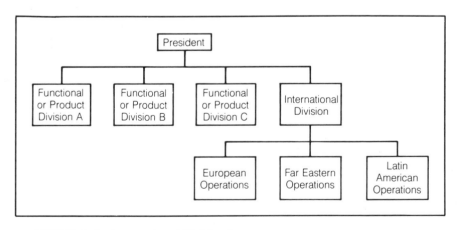

FIGURE 6–2 International Division Structure

tional dimensions are important determinants of organization design: functions, products, and geography. Figure 6–3 shows a functional structure, which is a highly efficient form for promoting functional specialization (e.g., divisions for marketing, finance, production, research and development, and so on). This structural form still exists in certain industries today, such as extractive raw materials. The reason for this is that for many such industries, the technological, production, and marketing systems are essentially the same throughout the world, and thus need not be restructured to suit different environments. If the company's products and markets are largely homogeneous, a functional structure is often appropriate, especially for small- and medium-sized firms. But when the scale and complexity of international operations increase, this functional structure is typically abandoned. Moreover, in many industries, a firm's expansion into new markets and/or product lines make the functionally oriented structure inefficient because of the growing complexity of production and marketing requirements, and because of the need to more closely coordinate activities across the functional areas. Rapid decision making is often impaired because decisions involving multiple functions must be carried to the very top of the organization before they are resolved.

The Product Group Structure   Thus, often a multidivisional product group structure emerges, as in Figure 6–4. Here, functional responsibilities are delegated to the product division general managers. The product group divisions are relatively autonomous, with coordination

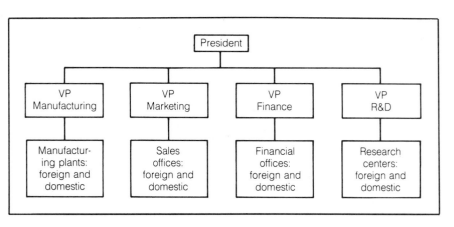

FIGURE 6–3 International Functional Structure

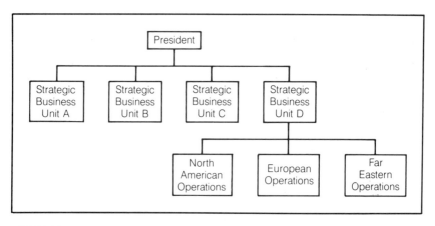

FIGURE 6-4 Worldwide Product Group Structure

and control from the central offices concentrated in finance and also, perhaps, special staff functions, such as planning or research and development. The managers of the product groups, or what are often referred to as strategic business units (although SBUs are not necessarily restricted to product groups), typically deal exclusively with single businesses, and they are therefore quite knowledgeable about both product and environmental specifics. Disadvantages of the product group structure include difficulties in gaining economies of scale in certain functional areas and problems associated with the coordination of company-wide activities within each region. For example, it often makes little sense to have completely separate facilities in any individual foreign country for each of the product groups.

The Geographical Structure　Some of these problems can be alleviated by the forming of geographical area structures, as indicated in Figure 6-5. The geographical structure (e.g., vice presidents for North America, Latin America, Europe and the Far East) permits greater emphasis on specific market requirements, and can be found in firms with standardized product lines for which marketing, rather than production or technology, is the critical variable. This is an ideal mechanism for achieving regional coordination, but it fails to encourage worldwide coordination of either functional or product line activities. Moreover, a major disadvantage of this structure is its slowness to adjust to central

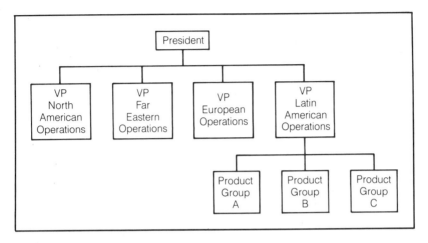

FIGURE 6-5   Geographical Area Structure of International Organizations

management directives. That is, strategic management changes emanating from the center take longer to implement.

The Matrix Structure   There are trade-offs in each of these structures, for each has characteristic advantages and disadvantages. As noted earlier, the solution to any one organizational problem creates new problems. In order to address this issue, many firms have experimented with matrix structures, in which there is no longer the hierarchy of power and unity of control typical of the more traditional structures. Instead, there is a dual or multiple chain of command, in which middle management reports directly to several superiors. Here, policy formulation is often the result of negotiation between units, and the emphasis is on contractual rather than hierarchical management. Such a structure requires managers who can cope with ambiguity and conflict; decision making is often slow. Nevertheless, some companies have been relatively successful in their aim to create a structure that simultaneously addresses the issues of function, product line, and geographical area.

The Subsidiary Structure   Less common among U.S. companies, but found frequently in Europe, is the national subsidiary structure, through which corporate headquarters acts, in effect, as a holding company for largely autonomous foreign subsidiaries. There is an obvious disadvantage here associated with the tendency to suboptimize, but the structure might well be appropriate to European firms when their individual foreign operations are as large as, or perhaps even larger than, their home base operations.

Beyond Formal Structure

To be sure, organizational charts are misleading in that they omit consideration of many crucial organizational flows. Who communicates with whom is an important aspect of power relations within the company. Social interactions and interpersonal relationships are not revealed in the organizational charts. The fact that Smith gets along with Brown poorly but with Black reasonably well can make a major difference in the direction of the firm. The charts also do not reveal internal political activities, which are inevitable in large organizations. But the general idea that top people should be in charge of and responsible for all significant activities within their area, including those in foreign countries, is clear.

The communication and interpersonal problems noted above are compounded for the multinational, which by expanding abroad creates its own in-house Tower of Babel. Although English is a world language, communication with persons of widely differing linguistic and cultural backgrounds poses a serious problem. Even if the foreign managers are relatively fluent in the English language, connotations associated with facial expressions or body language may lead to misinterpretations. Not every brilliant manager can speak English, nor can many key government officials, administrators, religious leaders, suppliers, or customers. Translation of critical information is necessary.

This may not seem very important, until a major tractor and heavy equipment manufacturer, proud of its distinguished record in after-sales service, discovers that it has perhaps 200,000 pages of technical manuals that field maintenance personnel must have. This firm works in 42 major languages, and technical translation costs can run around $150 per page, depending on the language. The manuals have to be printed, too, so someone must find an Arabic typesetter. Costs are substantial, and the company's very able engineers and technical writers generate hundreds of new pages daily.

What began here as a simple translation problem somehow ends up with a top management policy decision, given the costs of the project. One possible policy option would be to teach English to all field maintenance personnel (who work for others, such as distributors and customers), and then print all the manuals in this one language. But how does one convince these people to learn English; how does one teach them all; how long does it take; and how much would this cost? Here, a question that is handled at relatively low management levels at home becomes a concern of top management, given the international differences. Thus, the question of centralization versus decentralization of decision making takes on new dimensions in an international context.

Decentralization typically refers to the hierarchical levels at which decisions are made. Thus, centralization connotes decision making at relatively high levels in the organization, whereas decentralization connotes the delegation of decision making to lower levels of executive authority. These are relative terms, however, and are not to be viewed as absolute concepts. Decision making is quite often, in fact, incremental in nature, and critical decisions usually require input from persons at a number of different hierarchical levels. While one level may technically have the authority to make specific decisions, influence on the decision-making process comes from many levels.

Flexibility is often forced upon any firm that expands abroad. But total flexibility is anarchy, and some policies have to be consistant. Given the endless minor and major environmental differences in various countries, just how much flexibility should be allowed? A classic manifestation of this problem is demonstrated by astute observers who talk about company problems with various managers in a given country, and then go to corporate headquarters to talk about the same problems with the top managers. The inevitable reaction is that those guys (in the field or at home) just don't understand the problem! The field manager is forever trying to explain to headquarters why he or she is doing such strange things, while the headquarters personnel are baffled as to why those people out in the field don't seem to grasp the corporate way of doing things.

Large multinational companies in the past have tended to adopt structures which stress the integration of all world-wide units (such as IBM) or the opposite, even to the extent of encouraging internal competition among the separate units. Increasingly, firms today seem to prefer a hybrid approach rather than the extremes of centralization or decentralization. 3M, for example, has established a joint marketing group for its previously separate and widely diverse consumer product businesses. Matsushita, a consumer electronics conglomerate, has established a centralized research and development program to replace the previously fragmented efforts of many of its divisions. At the other extreme, IBM is relaxing its central grip on parts of its organization. Such changes in corporate structure are generally aimed at providing greater flexibility to respond to increasingly competitive markets. In other words, firms are quickly discovering the dysfunctional consequences of rigid organizational structure, and trying to replace those structures by qualitative improvements in the adaptability of the firm to more complex environments and more intense competition. The focus of such changes varies for each corporation, because successful adaptation depends on the nature of the critical links among the various subunits of the firm. For some the critical links may be associated with technology transfer or component sourcing, while for others the critical links may be associated with distribution networks or other marketing dimensions. The key is to improve the management of interdependencies among subunits, and this in turn suggests that the nature of headquarters/subsidiary relationships varies according to specific functions and to the specific circumstances of the geographical location of the subunits.

The question, essentially, is one of determining which policies should be centralized, and which decentralized. Distant managers, faced with problems often quite different from those faced in the home country market, cannot be supervised very closely, for sheer lack of physical contact. The usual solution is to decentralize virtually all matters that are considered to be local in nature, while centralizing key financial questions rather tightly. Selection of key personnel is often centralized as well, since who makes decisions can be critical to the long-term future of the firm.

One major factor which encourages centralization of the financial function is the rather chaotic state of the international monetary system at present. But the very rapid improvements in transportation and communications have served to encourage the centralization of other functions as well. Few places are more than minutes away by telex or telephone, and communications costs are relatively low today, compared with the past. Moreover, few places are more than thirty hours away from anywhere by jet airplane, so managers and key technical personnel can be on the spot should conditions so warrant. Thus, any branch anywhere can be in relatively continuous contact with headquarters, and it is common today for MNCs to have worldwide daily cash-flow, profit, and sales data on all relevant currencies. A major aspect of the global philosophy noted earlier is that the MNC can optimize its financial position in dozens of currencies and thousands of banks almost instantly. Thanks to virtually instantaneous communication, such financial planning and control is quite feasible.

Tight and sound financial controls can compensate for, and therefore make possible, decentralization in many other areas. Any branch that gets into cash trouble can be spotted quickly, and remedies applied. But to prevent suboptimization, the branches must cooperate with headquarters in the implementation of global financial control. Suppose that the firm's exchange rate experts are convinced that the English pound will decline in value rather quickly relative to other major currencies. The British manager may be doing very well, not only making profits but piling up large cash inflows which she intends to use for domestic expansion. From her point of view, hanging on to the pounds makes sense. But if the MNC holds many pounds, and if their value declines, the MNC will have suffered a major exchange loss. Financial managers at headquarters, noting global events, can ask (order) the British manager to transfer those pounds into German marks or dollars. The Briton will scream, but she will make the transfer.

Assume the pound does drop by 10 percent shortly after £100 million was transferred at two dollars to the pound. One has $200 million safely invested in certificates of deposit earning perhaps 14 percent interest. Had one waited, those 100 million pounds would have been converted at the new rate of $1.80 to the pound, and the company would be out $20 million in exchange loss. Such losses are rather painful, and they may be hard to explain to the board of directors. By taking the global view and forcing a local manager to act in the corporation's best interest, the company may have made as much profit as the whole English affiliate made in operating profits that year.

Welcome to the world of international finance. Just how the financial experts forecast an exchange rate decline is a subject for an international finance class, but the point here is that a globally optimizing firm, with good financial data and controls, can do much better than any local firm. The local British companies generally don't have any dollar options within their companies, and local U.S. firms don't deal in pounds. They also lack the option of intracorporate transfers of funds among affiliates, using surpluses generated in one country to invest in promising markets elsewhere.

In this case, the MNC reacted to turbulence in the international monetary environment, a common event in our world of floating exchange rates. But similar possibilities exist in other critical areas. Astute MNCs do political risk assessment for numerous countries, and the staff of one such firm might report to management that a certain country appears to be heading towards revolution and a government that will probably nationalize major foreign firms. Top management might decide to reduce its exposure there. All liquid capital can be withdrawn, new investments stopped, existing investments possibly sold for cash to locals or other MNCs who are not as astute, and key personnel transferred to other countries. Inventories of goods in process and raw materials can be minimized.

The revolution arrives, and firms are nationalized. But somehow the new revolutionary government gets a run-down plant, no inventories of key parts, and no skilled personnel to operate what's left. The firm may well have taken losses, but they will have been minimized. While all this was going on, the local manager, having his own biases, remained firmly convinced that the conservatives would handle the radicals. Again, the global viewpoint is critical to the management of firms involved internationally. Those local revolutionaries might have been evil incarnate or the saviors of their civilization: to the multinational, such concerns are of little importance except when they directly touch on the firm's own code of behavior. What is important are actions that endanger the performance of the firm. It is for this reason that many local people all over the world are very suspicious of multinationals, which they might view as foreign devils caring very little about really important provincial issues. And they are right, for typically, the multinational cannot be concerned with such isssues.

The legal environment abroad is also a direct determinant of intracompany linkages. Any multinational corporation is comprised of a number of branches and affiliates, located throughout the world. A branch in a small country may be a very minor part of the company, but in that country the branch may be, by law, an independent corporation, which requires a president and a board of directors. To the multinational, the local manager is really a middle manager, but to the local population he or she is an important person indeed. He or she may by law have certain powers that extend considerably beyond his or her nominal powers reflected in the multinational's organization chart. In one case in Europe, this minor official, under local law, literally had the power to sell the entire company for cash and keep the cash him or herself! Fortunately for the multinational, top management had selected a highly responsible person to head the foreign operations there. In any event, the legal considerations provide a framework of basic options which may then be further developed through intracorporate links related to functional product group, and geographical concerns. This example suggests one type of linkage between various branches which must be structured strategically by top managers. One obvious constraint here is the necessity of meeting local legal requirements for forming a corporation; thus, the MNC may become deeply involved in the realm of local laws and taxes. Most countries have a variety of legal organizational forms, each with different tax consequences, and it takes a good local lawyer to work out the optimum local, legal structure. In some cases, organizational branches in several countries may be grouped organizationally, but they cannot be so easily grouped legally.

As the MNC expands, various branches deal with each other in a variety of ways. One strong determinant of the extent to which operations may be decentralized, therefore, is the degree of interdependency, integration, or overlap among the diversified organizational components. Clearly, less decentralization is possible if there is a great degree of interaction among the units, and especially if a decision made by one unit affects the operations of other units. The West German plant may be supplying components to the French subsidiary, or, in larger organizations, the European group may be supplying finished products or components to the North American group. Such a situation calls for high-level coordination not only of product standardization, but also of matters such as pricing, quality control, scheduling, and so on.

The question of open or closed supply systems arises here as well, since the North American group may feel that it can buy local components at less cost than it can buy them from within the company. But the arrangement through which internal purchases are required may mean that economies of scale are achieved in Europe, thus making the MNC as a whole more competitive than it otherwise would have been. Explicit corporate policies are necessary in such cases to avoid suboptimization and to resolve the inherent bifurcation of interests.

Similarly, questions of which public accounting firm might do the audits for the various countries might arise, or which banks should be used by the various branches. Policy here will clearly depend on many internal company factors, plus some local environmental constraints. This can lead to odd situations, as when one major public accounting firm does all the audits except in a few countries where, by law, other

137

companies are required, or perhaps some public audit system is used. A strong major local bank might get much business in a given country for political or other reasons, even though most of the firm's banking is handled through a few major multinational banks. Companies have complex histories, and examination of such intrafirm situations may reveal that situations no longer prevalent have determined such patterns, and that policy adjustments have not been made to reflect current conditions.

Planning for global production can involve the close coordination of many branches, a common pattern for many MNCs. But other MNCs operate as loose holding companies, in which each local branch operates with very considerable autonomy. Such differences reflect both operating philosophies and practical realities. A firm may have a French branch which is very profitable and managed by able French citizens. This company manufactures products which serve the bulk of the European markets, and they are not exported to the United States or Canada, which may in itself be a company policy. But the strong-minded French managers prefer to do it their way, and they do perform very well. When headquarters interferes too much, huge battles rage, and key employees threaten to resign. Rather than endlessly fight such trans-Atlantic battles, top headquarter management may well decide to let the French management go their own way, subject to a few key financial constraints and constraints on what markets may be entered. The system works fine, and the MNC profits handsomely. Why change?

Such relative autonomy is impossible for the branch that is essentially a component or raw material supplier to other branches of the company. Here, quite detailed controls might exist for quality, costs, delivery times, budgets, and similar matters. Local managers have very little autonomy. Nor do they need much. Between these two extreme possibilities, innumerable alternatives can be found in the complex MNC world. But it is typically true that interbranch control costs for an MNC are higher than for a purely domestic firm. Communications (including translation) and transportation costs are higher, and both geographical and cultural distance can make it difficult to impose tight controls. Consequently, linkages can become quite loose, except for some financial controls.

One financial problem that inevitably gets much top management attention is intracorporate transfer pricing. When a branch sells its outputs to another branch of the company in another country, what price should be charged? This decision seems simple enough until one realizes that "proper" pricing can shift tax burdens quite dramatically from one country to another. Local tax collectors are aware of the "games" played with intracorporate transfer pricing and controversy is certain.

Consider a pharmaceutical company that produces a patented drug in one branch in a foreign country. The country was happy enough to get this plant years ago, but now the government has changed, and the new administration, quite hostile to foreign business within its country, has raised the corporate income tax to 90 percent. This branch will not make much money under any circumstances.

Or will it? Suppose that after all normal costs, the branch has a net profit in a given year of $1 million. But one cost remains, which is the charge the parent company makes for the license to produce the patented drug. The drug had development costs of over $100 million a few years ago, and various branches and the parent company must be charged a fee to recoup this expense. The home office can send a bill for $990,000 to this branch, which is a legitimate (?) expense. Now this year's profits are $10,000, of which the government gets $9,000. The MNC has neatly evaded taxes of $990,000 by this method. If this technique seems too crude, the MNC could simply require the branch to buy its raw chemicals from the home country, and then set prices which wipe out the branch's profits.

The country in question complains bitterly about such tactics, but if the government decides to really get tough about the issue, the firm may well withdraw. Now the country's citizens have to buy an expensive imported drug or do without. Such pricing techniques can also be used to obtain funds from countries with blocked currencies which cannot be readily converted to dollars. Such countries often allow companies to use foreign currency to buy licenses, critical components, and other research-related items.

Note that if all this is done, the home company reaps larger profits. Headquarters of course may well be sited in a country which also has a relatively high income tax, so another viable option is to transfer funds through such intracorporate pricing systems to subsidiaries in low tax countries. Government officials everywhere will complain, and even the U.S. government insists that all transfer pricing between an American firm and its foreign subsidiaries be undertaken at arm's length. But much of world trade is indeed intracorporate trade, and for many components there is no market through which one can accurately access an arm's length price. There is a wide gap between the actual cost of transferring technology, and the cost of developing that technology anew overseas, and thus there is considerable latitude which the firm has, subject to bargaining power, in regard to transfer pricing. Indeed, even the developer of the technology often has no more than a ball-park estimate of a proper price.

The reason that top management gets involved in this intracorporate transfer pricing problem very quickly is because, very quickly, millions, or even hundreds of millions, of dollars may be at stake. Moreover, given government interest everywhere in this problem, it may take top level public and government relations people to convince suspicious revenue agents that the prices being charged are warranted. What one country loses, another might gain, so joint consultations with representatives of the two governments might be necessary even if the MNC has no design whatsoever to fiddle with taxes or to otherwise artificially tamper with returns.

There are also other reasons, many associated with the daily changes in the value of currencies (which will be discussed in the next chapter), why headquarters, in its supervision over international operations, exercises its tightest control in the financial area. By contrast, decisions in the marketing area are relatively decentralized. It is not fully accurate, however, to suggest that financial decisions are thus centralized in the MNC, while marketing decisions are decentralized. Instead, variations are possible within each function. In the financial area for example, capital expenditures and intercurrency exchanges might be centralized, while profit responsibility is decentralized. Similarly, research is relatively centralized and production relatively decentralized, but there are variations within each of these functions. Moreover, under certain conditions, typically decentralized decisions can be quickly overturned by headquarters. Top management must step in, for example, to stifle intracorporate warfare when an aggressive marketing manager of one foreign affiliate decides to invade a territory historically belonging to another affiliate of the same firm.

This last example may suggest just how critical it is for top management to act as judicial referees in the inevitable conflicts that occasionally occur between branches. If the multinational is profitable and growing, it will have a large number of good junior people, all of whom are trying to look better by whatever criteria the corporation ranks its younger and junior personnel. As the branch managers deal with each other, they will try to gain advantages, and it takes a sophisticated central management to make sure that the rules are both fair and followed, and that evaluations are just. One major penalty for being unjust is that the firm loses good people to other companies.

SUMMARY

We have briefly considered the major core strategies critical to the success of the multinational firm. We looked at locational strategies in Chapter 5, along with questions pertaining to the type of international involvement the firm could or should select in regard to entry and ownership patterns. We viewed, in Chapter 6, the highly critical issue of technology transfer, and then considered the basic structural options available to the firm. All of these decisions depend on the firm's interests and capabilities as well as on the inevitable competitive and local environmental constraints.

These core strategic issues determine the future of the multinational. Sometimes they evolve through intensive analysis and careful, reasoned decision making. One suspects that often, in the past, they have just evolved as the company grew. Frequently, some are forced on the company, such as when a country closes off a lucrative export market, thus forcing the firm to withdraw or to make a commitment to become more actively involved in the foreign operations. Whatever the choice that is made, it is crucial; which is why these are *core* strategies. No firm can ignore them, nor their implications, for long.

It is critical for the firm that its top managers have a global view of its activities; its input and output markets, and its competition. Once such a global view is taken, it is necessary to fit the firm into as many local environments as the countries in which the firm chooses to operate. This fit needs to be efficient, in the sense that the firm takes full advantage of its competitive strengths in whatever countries it can enter. Once it enters a country, the firm must adapt to the local environment as best it can. Thus a dual focus is needed to keep in proper perspective the requirements of global integration, on the one hand, and the requirements of the local environment, on the other.

Because local environments differ so substantially, it is necessary to have good insight into which problems and successes are caused by the environment, and which by management. This is easy to say, but extremely difficult to do. Moreover, top management must also be fully aware of the international system, particularly the financial system, and know how to utilize it efficiently. Again, this is easy to say, but probably no one can profess to fully grasp all of the implications of one's actions in this context. The globally oriented firm has no choice but to make the effort. Once it is involved in the international economy, and all its parts, it has to live with it and has to learn to operate efficiently in all relevant environments.

Given all of these problems, once might wonder why any rationally managed firm would bother. Often there are no viable alternatives except the international option. The payoff can be continued growth, continued prosperity, growing reputations and experience for key managers, and recognition in the world of business and elsewhere that this company is one of the world's best. For such payoffs, many will take the risks, even if one of them is losing one's own nationalistic orientation and becoming a world citizen. Such people now exist, but they are rare. They are not likely to be so rare in the future.

DISCUSSION QUESTIONS

1. How does one distinguish between process and product technology, and what implications does that distinction have for the structuring of intrafirm linkages and the firm's propensity towards transferring its technology abroad?

2. What are the advantages and disadvantages of licensing one's technology abroad?

3. Under what conditions will the multinational corporation typically centralize (or decentralize) its international operations?

4. In what industries is one likely to find functional versus product group versus geographical area structures? Why?

5. Why is the intrafirm bifurcation of interests an especially acute problem for multinational corporations?

NOTES

1. Philip Hanson, "International Technology Transfer from the West to the USSR," *Soviet Economy In a New Perspective* (Washington, D.C.: U.S. Government Printing Office, 1976), 786–812.

2. Josef C. Brada, "Technology Transfer by Means of Industrial Cooperation," in *Polish-US Industrial Cooperation in the 1980s*, eds., Paul Marer and Eugeniusz Tabaczynski (Bloomington: Indiana University Press, 1981), 207–223.

3. Lawrence S. Welch and Robert T. Carstairs, "Outward Foreign Licensing," *Les Nouvelles* (September, 1983), 188–192.

4. Jacques Gaudin, "Outlook for Technology Transfer," *Les Nouvelles* (June, 1981), 122–125.

5. Richard D. Robinson, "The Transfer of Technology to the Relatively Wealthy, Resource-Rich, Technology-Poor Countries," in *Private Enterprise and the New Global Economic Challenge*, ed., Stephen Guisinger (Indianapolis: Bobbs-Merrill, 1979), 23–38.

FURTHER READING

1. Casson, Mark. *Multinationals and World Trade*. London: Allen and Unwin, 1986.

2. Daniels, John D., and Lee H. Rodebough. *International Business: Environments and Operations*, Fifth Edition. Reading, MA: Addison–Wesley, 1989.

3. Davis, Stanley M. *Managing and Organizing Multinational Corporations*. New York: Pergamon Press, 1979.

4. Pitts, Robert A., and John D. Daniels. "Aftermath of the Matrix Mania." *Columbia Journal of World Business*, Summer, 1984, 48–54.

5. Ramo, Simon. *The Management of Innovative Technological Corporations*. New York: John Wiley and Sons, 1980.

6. Rugman, Alan M., Donald J. Lecraw, and Laurence D. Booth. *International Business: Firm and Environment*. New York: McGraw-Hill, 1985.

CHAPTER 7

▼

Strategy Implementation: Production and Marketing

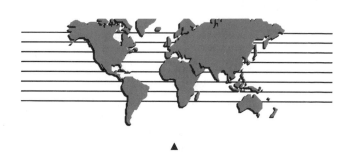

▲

As corporate and business level strategies become more global, functional strategies must also be adjusted. This adjustment is necessary because functional strategies, both in design and implementation, must be subordinate to, and congruent with, the overall corporate and business strategies. Earlier, we noted various examples of how a company can reduce costs and expand sales by taking a total world view of production, marketing, finance, and other functional areas. In this chapter, we explore in greater detail the problems and prospects involved with further internationalization of global productive systems.

It would particularly benefit the small- and medium-sized domestically oriented firms, often family-owned, to have, as part of their strategic concerns, the possibility of global sourcing. Licensing-in from foreign firms can be an excellent substitute for one's own research and development, and a viable method of rejuvenating an over-mature product line. Offshore sourcing of production, through subcontracting at arm's length, taking on a joint venture or cooperation partner, or operating fully owned facilities abroad, can improve price competitiveness, especially in the more mature industries. Capital can be sought from abroad, either through the capital markets or through inviting the participation of a foreign partner in equity, a strategy which Hesston Corporation and American Motors have successfully implemented. Often, there is little choice for the firm that wishes to maintain or restore competitiveness. Whether one wishes it or not, the product, sourcing, financial, and technological markets are international in nature. This, in turn, has far-reaching implications for the selection of functional strategies, even for those firms which prefer, often for very good reasons, to not become actively engaged abroad.

PRODUCTION, PROCUREMENT, AND LOGISTICS

The management of production has assumed greater significance in recent years for both domestically and globally oriented firms, especially in the relatively mature industries. Domestically oriented firms can find new growth opportunities by viewing their production operations from a global viewpoint. Foreign markets may be served by either domestic or foreign production; conversely, even firms that prefer to market only domestically may find viable offshore production opportunities to serve the domestic market. For the firm that chooses to produce abroad, critical decisions include those relating to the location, size, number, and manufacturing processes of foreign facilities.

Production and Procurement

In considering the option of offshore sourcing, the initial question is whether to make or buy. The choice between contracting production by others or operating abroad oneself depends on such factors as comparative capital and operating costs, control of quality, and continuity of supply. Several basic offshore plant configurations should be considered. One is to produce everything at one location and supply all markets from there. Another is to use an integrated network of plants, strategically located throughout the world. Within this second configuration, there are further alternatives. Each plant may specialize in particular products that it exports to all markets. Or, primary manufacturing plants may each specialize in one or more components that are then shipped to a larger network of assembly plants. This second

145

option has been widely adopted by the pharmaceutical and automobile industries. A third alternative is basing production on regional rather than global networks, a strategy pursued by Volkswagen.

In mature industries, such as automobile manufacturing, European firms are increasingly opting for externally sourced components (which may well comprise 60 percent of total product value). Here the strategic choice tends to favor subcontracting (producing to the precise specifications of the main contractor) rather than suppliers (who produce and sell their own standard products). The subcontracting strategy gives the main contractor greater flexibility at less capital investment. The tendency is to outsource more and more complex operations, so the subcontractors gain from the general qualitative upgrading of their own operations. The relationship between main contractors and subcontractors is undergoing a qualitative improvement also. This is because the main contractor has greater interest in establishing more stable and balanced relations with dependent firms once the main contractor begins to acquire products or know-how that he no longer produces or possesses.

British automotive production provides a good example of such subcontracting. The Vauxhall Cavalier and Astra, respectively, import 36 and 38 percent of their components, and the (British) Ford Sierra over 32 percent. This is quite different strategy from the "captive imports" of Detroit, through which Ford, General Motors, and Chrysler import from abroad final products to be sold through their own distribution channels and under their own trade names. Detroit is also opting for "transplant vehicles," i.e., vehicles made in the United States in partnership with a foreign auto maker.

Some companies have plants in many countries, but have made no serious attempt to integrate the production operations. Such firms, referred to as "multidomestics," establish production facilities dedicated to serving individual markets or countries. This approach is not necessarily inferior to the more global outlook, because under certain conditions there are good reasons for maintaining independent production facilities. Nevertheless, in general, there are clear benefits to the global orientation.

The question of production process has been settled in the simplest possible manner by most multinationals: they make only the most necessary concessions required by different plant capacities, materials and machinery availability, and different levels of labor skill. That is, they have attempted to use similar processes worldwide. This means that some plants may be more capital intensive and less labor intensive than local factor costs would suggest as the optimum. Advantages to such an approach are found in the facilitation of cost and productivity comparisons, and of product quality and uniformity.[1]

In effect, the globally oriented firm tries to obtain the best inputs from around the world while producing components and products wherever it is most efficient to do so. This flexibility is a basic determinant of the modern international production system. The manufacture of a product may require some unskilled labor, a bit of highly skilled technical and managerial work, plus energy and various components from outside the firm. If unskilled labor is needed in quantity, then the firm can go to a country where such labor is relatively abundant and cheap, and import the handful of key technicians and managers needed to make the system run. It can easily obtain money and real capital from wherever it is available, buy locally or import key components, and export the finished product to anywhere.

In highly industrialized countries, unskilled and semi-skilled labor is relatively expensive. Hence, in industries that are highly labor-intensive, production moves toward less industrialized countries such as Mexico and Brazil, if these countries are willing to allow the total production system to operate. Countries have learned that it makes sense to allow for key importations, if the resulting production is largely exported. They will gain capital, employment, tax revenues, hard currencies, and new skills in this way. Rarely, however, does the firm take such production to extremely poor countries, since the infrastructure to support production is typically lacking. The firm does need electric power, adequate transportation and communications facilities, and other infrastructural supports. The semi-developed countries offer the best possibilities, and can provide high quality performance.

Note, however, two qualifying conditions to the production rationalization process. First, and unfortunately, for many American firms the global rationalization of production has seldom been implemented as part of a new opportunity-seeking strategy. All too often, it has emerged, instead, as a defensive response to serious difficulties.[2] Secondly, the process technology of production in many industries has substantially changed the approach to rationalization in recent years. For example, in the past the rationale for conventional specialized equipment and automation centered on economies of scale and intensive capital investment. Firms sought increased efficiency of production, but gained that at the expense of reduced flexibility. Much of the new technology is based on economies of scope rather than of scale. A broader range of capabilities is possible in computer controlled machines, which makes possible the production of many small runs. Thus, automated production capabilities formerly economical only in very large plants, and for production of many identical units, are now possible in much smaller operations.[3] Such flexible manufacturing systems make differentials in unit labor costs less important, and may serve to maintain at least final assembly operations near the major markets.

Yet production should still be globally oriented. We now hear about world cars, which are designed to be sold everywhere. Such a car may have its body stampings made in Canada, its transmissions in West Germany, its electronics in Japan, its glass in Belgium, and its engines in the United States. Often there are multiple sourcings of individual components as well, to reduce the potential impact of strikes, riots, wars, or arbitrary changes in government policies. Then cars are assembled wherever it makes the most economic sense to do so. In the end there no longer is an American or European car industry, but a global one.

These cars are to be marketed worldwide, but tastes, safety laws, and emission requirements vary. Thus the cars are not fully identical. In countries where a significant part of the market enjoys a high-powered image, horsepower is increased a bit; in other countries, special pollution control equipment is added; in still others, headlights are higher on the fenders to meet local legal requirements. Advertising, marketing channels, and numerous other details can differ dramatically among the various cultures in which the car is sold. Today, marketing is beginning to look a bit the same everywhere, possibly because peoples' tastes are converging, given the increasing similarity of the life styles enjoyed by individuals in modern industrial states as well as in some Third World countries.

If the production or procurement of components is based on an integrated network of plants located in many countries, as in the case of the world cars just mentioned, then the firm simply could not function independently in any one country. If it were cut off from several key countries, it would cease to be competitive. It has become a truly multinational company, at least in critical personnel, marketing, purchasing, and production dimensions. Things rarely move evenly and smoothly, however. A firm may be far advanced in international sourcing from suppliers, and still insist that all the top managers be from the home country. It may have a multinational production system and still market its products with total attention to provincial markets and tastes. Hence Japanese multinationals often have multinational sourcing, but almost never hire top managers from foreign countries. The homogeneous Japanese culture is still difficult to penetrate. As a result, Japanese firms are stuck with Japanese talent. If, perhaps a decade from now, it turns out that this talent is not good enough, presently powerful and fast growing Japanese-based MNCs may well begin to stagnate.

All of this is still quite radical in business thinking, even as many MNCs move steadily toward such total internationalization of all inputs, outputs, and the productive process itself. It is radical because large groups within any society still see the world in basically nationalistic terms, and MNCs that go the whole way are seen as suspect. Trade unions, perceiving their own jobs lost when foreigners are hired, will protest and demand new restrictive laws; local firms, noting their own inability to obtain the very best inputs or their losing out as suppliers, will also protest; governments, seeing loss of political control, will be very nervous as well. Legislation will be proposed, and sometimes enacted, barring various proposed internationlization arrangements.

In effect, the globally oriented firm is operating as a global citizen, not a local one. This orientation puts it out of step with most other institutions we have at present. Generally, such behavior is tolerated by others only because the results are so good. These globally oriented firms tend to grow faster and create more wealth for the local economies than do the purely domestically oriented firms. Countries prefer income and wealth to stagnation and poverty, but they find some of the associated consequences of global orientation rather unattractive.

Logistics

Much of the expansion of world trade has been made possible by a revolution in transportation and related functions. Beginning in the late 1940s, we have seen the rapid development of very low-cost bulk ocean-carriers for raw materials and oil; in the 1960s, roll-on, roll-off ships and containers came on the scene; and everywhere we find newly automated ports and specialized bulk ports to handle the new cargoes. Warehouses everywhere have been modernized and automated. Even the lowly forklift, that engine of the materials-handling revolution, is found everywhere. Air cargo traffic has become very popular, providing fast and reasonably priced services for more valuable shipments; and world-class airports everywhere mean that such cargoes can go to almost any country with ease.

Not too many years ago, those engines made in Mexico would have been laboriously packed by hand into a slow bulk-freighter for shipment to Western Europe. Now they can be automatically loaded into containers, which are then easily loaded by cranes at the mechanized port for shipment abroad. At the European port, the containers are put on trucks or railway cars for shipment to the assembly plant. There is a savings in labor costs, and loss and damage are minimized. If the trucks are on the road in a country that has a scarce supply of oil, this is not a serious problem. The oil arrives from Africa or the Middle East in huge bulk-carriers, which discharge their cargoes at special ports to be refined. The refined products will be shipped inland by rail or truck at low costs. The whole system depends on reliable, cheap transportation, and virtually all industrialized countries now have that.

The availability and cost of transportation facilities are considered in the calculations made by mid-level technicians when they first begin exploring the possibility of locating the engine plant in Mexico. In short, rapid declines in the real costs of transportation, handling, and storage have occurred, making a world production system at least potentially feasible. Transportation and logistics experts analyze in detail just what is happening in these areas, and MNC traffic managers can buy services in this new efficient system, so most of this work is really not crucial to top management thinking. The system is crucial, and it makes many new options available. Top management's job is to figure out the new options, given the potential.

As in other areas, rapid developments that affect logistics create new problems. In many industrialized countries, some of the toughest unions of all are in the stevedoring trades, and new systems that can wipe out thousands of jobs are not always welcome. Ports are often government-owned and subject to more political pressures than most businesses. Commercial airports are always government-owned, and the same point applies here. Governments are especially vulnerable to pressure-group activities, productivity improvements may be very slow, and strikes are common. Engines from Mexico will do the manufacturer or assembler no good if they are sitting offshore near Britain waiting for a settlement of a nasty dock strike. The bottleneck in engines, incidentally, might well lead to downtime in the production of axles in West Germany or transmissions in France, since the blockage effectively delays production of the total product and thus of its constituent components. Such occurrences quickly lead to multiple sourcings, where engines may be built in several widely scattered locations. Moreover, the net result of the strike is to maintain highly inefficient procedures, which add much to transfer costs.

Countries also have various lags due to specific institutional priorities, and this can complicate matters. The country may be eager to get new investments, but the port authority, a relatively autonomous unit, has for some reason delayed making necessary investments in modernization. Even after the delay, political factors make the new system much less efficient than it might have been. Or the country really does not see the need for modernization of ports or roads; such issues are rarely the most significant political priorities in less developed countries, and badly needed funds tend to get channeled to areas considered more vital, like defense. Not every technician in every port is totally aware of the latest world developments in materials handling, and no one really forces them to learn very fast, particularly in situations where the authorities are government employees and one's job is secure no matter what happens.

As a result, logistical problems can be especially perplexing. Beautifully designed internal systems somehow get bogged down in bottlenecks created at a key port. We must also consider the blizzard of paperwork that invariably accompanies every foreign shipment, and the need for customs inspectors to painstakingly clear every shipment. It has been estimated that perhaps 10 percent of the costs related to a typical foreign shipment are paperwork costs. Highly organized and productive systems may beat the average, but when you want a port to work 24 hours a day, seven days a week, and the port authority is willing but customs officials say that 8 hours a day, five days a week is all they will provide, frustrations abound. Such situations are more common than one might suspect, and often the MNC has to approach the prime minister or other high officials to get some remedial action. Note that a country can wreak havoc in a firm's transportation schedule by working according to the letter, or by taking it easy during customs inspection. Such delays and problems are common in all transport situations. Sometimes the delays are by design, such as when French authorities, for competitive reasons, drastically slowed down the customs approval of Japanese shipments of video equipment; typically, however, the delays are mainly the unintentional consequence of bureaucratic behavior.

Wars and threats of war are also very real influences on an industry's ability to transport materials efficiently. Ships often traverse narrow channels, and if a country has a revolution or is engaged in war, shipping lanes can be cut off. The debate now going on about offshore property rights is also highly important. Countries now claim two hundred miles from their coasts, whereas twenty years ago they claimed 3 or 12 miles. As a result, some key passages that have been international waterways may now belong to individual nations. This could lead to cutoffs or tolls. Once again, risk assessment is critical, particularly if some unstable countries decide to block sea passages. This is precisely what happened in 1984 in the Persian Gulf, as Iran and Iraq, trying to inflict economic damage on each other as part of their military strategy, began indiscriminately bombing oil tankers doing business with the enemy. Lives were lost, insurance costs for the tankers soared, and superpower involvement intensified.

Governments everywhere have been heavily involved in transportation development and control for centuries, and there now exists an incredibly complex system of price and entry controls for all transport modes, a system that often seems to defy logical analysis. A seemingly perfect MNC logistics system may founder in France, as the MNC's goods are moved inland, because, for some reason, French trucking cannot expand. Prices arbitrarily set by government agencies may be raised unexpectedly to levels so high that the costs wipe out all gains in other parts of the system. An MNC may discover that its containers are four millimeters too wide to pass over the French highway system. Firms involved in international business have highly skilled local experts to straighten things out, but these services do add to costs, and such difficulties can affect productivity more than most managers realize. It is easy to assume that a container can easily pass from point A to point B, moving along two different highway systems and through two ports, but any transportation expert can point to a thousand reasons why smooth passage might be difficult or impossible. Far too often MNCs run into major problems because they fail to anticipate the need for local and international transportation experts who can alert them to potential dangers and suggest solutions.

What typically happens in logistics is that every country tries to maximize for itself. For example, if an international pipeline runs across my country, I naturally want to get the highest transit tolls I can obtain; if a shipment runs over my highways, I want to maximize my share of the total pie; if my port is used, I see political gains in maximizing employment at the port. The usual result is a suboptimal system that leads to high costs. New innovations that might reduce one country's share can be resisted for decades; and they are. The bright side is that countries that try too hard to maximize in this disproportionate manner are left behind as their rivals build better facilities. Even cities in the same country will try to outdo each other, in order to gain the additional business. If the U.S. unions are so tough as to ban building modern ports, the Canadians might ultimately surpass the United States in modern port facilities and services, leaving the American union in a worse position than if it had been willing to meet the modernization requirements.

MNCs have done their bit by planning projects that will go forward only if critical logistical improvements are carried out. Thus an MNC will agree to build an auto engine plant in Mexico only if Mexico agrees to build access roads and to modernize key ports. Mexico, seeing big gains in a high-pay industry, may well agree, and those who resist may not have the political clout to prevent change. But quite often, what seems to be a relatively minor technical problem at an obscure port, or a small difficulty with a few trucks, can foul up carefully laid plans. In this sense, logistics does become a major problem for top-management consideration in the designing of corporate strategies.

MARKETING

Marketing experts note that if you can't sell the firm's product or services, all is lost, and questions of where markets are and how they can be properly tapped occupy a major portion of time in strategic management. One might assume that there can be no such thing as an international marketing strategy. Markets are local in nature, the argument goes, so marketing strategy must be localized. The best strategy for one market (and there are typically many markets in each country) might be disastrous for another, so marketing is not an issue for top MNC management. Still, many MNCs have successfully pursued global marketing strategies, and there is clearly a need for top management to coordinate the marketing function with all other functional strategies, and to integrate marketing into the grand strategic plan of the company. The secret is in knowing which marketing decisions to centralize, and which to decentralize. Product-line decisions, for example, are typically a concern of top management, while pricing, distribution, and promotion decisions may be more easily (but not always) left to subsidiary managers. In all cases, however, it should be noted that there are significant and often substantial differences between industries or even among product groups within the same industry. Nestle produces more than 200 blends of Nescafé to cater to the preferences of different markets, but such a strategy would be inappropriate for most product lines.

The product life cycle model discussed in Chapter 1 establishes a general framework for designing marketing strategy in the international context. It suggests in general which markets are the most attractive, and when to make the shift from export marketing to marketing in conjunction with foreign manufacturing activities. It is less helpful in designing specific strategies, such as whether to adopt a standardized marketing approach versus an approach individually tailored to each separate market, or whether to adopt a strategy of market diversification versus one of market concentration. Such decisions are heavily contingent on the nature of the technology involved; the degree of competition worldwide, as well as in the specific market; and the existing organizational structure of, and constraints on, the firm.

In addition to the inherent problems of satisfying the various requirements for success in individual national markets, the international marketer faces serious problems associated with worldwide trade relations.[4] There has been, for example, an acute imbalance of trade between the developing and developed countries, with the consequence that many less developed countries have had to severely curtail imports as part of more general austerity programs. The recent worldwide recession has also encouraged greater protectionism among the developed countries, which makes foreign marketing much more problematic. Today, many governments are offering financial and other significant incentives, to encourage their own firms to export, which in turn leads to intensified competition in third markets as well as at home. The successful marketing strategy must take such worldwide developments into consideration as well as developments in the individual national markets.

Moreover, several highly effective planning tools used in domestic marketing have to be modified when applied to international settings. These tools, such as the familiar market share/growth matrix developed by the Boston Consulting Group (i.e., the cash cows vs. dogs vs. question marks vs. stars), tend to focus on *products* or product groups as the principal unit of strategic endeavor. Harrell and Kiefer suggest, however, that a *market* rather than product portfolio approach is much more appropriate in the international arena.[5] Thus, West Germany might be a "star," France a "question mark," the United Kingdom a "cash cow," and Portugal a "dog," and marketing strategies in those countries would be adjusted accordingly.

Robock and Simmonds, based on earlier work of Keegan, identify five generic marketing strategies from the perspective of product features and communications.[6]

1. The first of these is "one product, one message—worldwide." There are obviously great cost savings associated with this approach, and it is a strategy which might be appropriate for the marketing of advanced technology goods. For many high-technology goods, product specifications are essentially the same worldwide, and therefore there would be little need for product adaptation to individual markets. Furthermore, the buyers of high-technology goods are, in general, a fairly homogeneous group which would respond similarly to identical messages.

2. Another strategy is that of "product extension, communications adaptation." Such a strategy is appropriate, for example, when the same product or service fills a different need or serves a different function in foreign markets than in the home market. Bicycles are mainly for recreation in the United States, but elsewhere often serve as basic transportation. Such a strategy reaps savings through not having to adapt the product for marketing abroad.

3. Conversely, the strategy might be one of "product adaptation, communications extension." This is a strategy that is highly appropriate for the marketing of many foods, since tastes vary substantially across countries. It is also appropriate for many soap products, which must be adapted to the local water conditions and to the types of washing machines used.

4. One may have "dual adaptation" by altering both the product and the message. This strategy, which is suited for many consumer products, can reap some savings if the required adaptations are not major.

5. The strategy of "product invention" essentially results from the necessity of very basic alteration of the product, and perhaps message, for success abroad. Often the cost of the product is a major factor here, as when the original product is simply too expensive to find a significant market in many areas of the world.

The approaches noted above are tactical in nature. Ayal and Zif take a more strategic approach by designing marketing strategies based on either market diversification or market concentration.[7] Market diversification implies a fast penetration into a large number of markets and diffusion of efforts among them, whereas market concentration implies the directing of one's marketing efforts at only a few markets and then gradually expanding into new ones. Because the first route will probably lead to markets which do not develop and therefore are eventually abandoned, it is possible that the two strategies eventually lead to serving the same number of markets. However, the alternative routes typically generate totally different consequences in terms of sales, market shares, and profits over time.

Actually, four strategies can be derived from this model.

1. Concentrate on specific market segments in a few countries. The "dual concentration" model is appropriate generally for products which appeal to a definite group of similar customers in different countries, but the costs of penetration into each national market are substantial relative to the firm's resources.

2. Concentrate on a few countries but use market segment diversification within them. Diversifying among segments within a concentrated group of countries, requires a product line that appeals to different segments; it is appropriate especially when there are significant economies of scale in advertising.

3. Market diversification and segment concentration is appropriate for firms with a specialized product line and potential customers in many countries. It is especially effective when the cost of entry into different markets is low relative to available resources.

4. Dual diversification (of both segments and markets), is appropriate for firms having product lines that appeal to many segments, and sufficient resources to accomplish fast entry into many national markets.

The successful application of such models is contingent on many complex factors, and varies to some extent according to whether the firm chooses to export to the country in question or to serve the country by establishing manufacturing or other productive operations there. As usual in multinational business, both local and general factors apply. Typically one uses the same tools, techniques, and managerial methods anywhere in the world, but differing environments result in differing outcomes. This is because the critical constraints differ among countries. Thus the British market is about one eighth the size of the American, because British per capita GNP is half that of the United States, and there are about one quarter as many people. If minor products require mass markets of a certain size, just this point alone will preclude entry into the British market in isolation. But note that the method of market analysis for both countries is essentially the same.

Tastes vary, often widely, and it has long been noted that products marketed in a country should mesh well with local tastes. Whatever common sense that seems to make, there are many examples of projects that failed because firms did not consider local tastes in designing, producing, and marketing their products. Nevertheless, there also does appear to be a convergence of tastes in many affluent countries. Marketing experts can spend much time, money, and effort figuring out if a TV set or radio designed for the American market will sell well in Germany. To be sure, the electronic requirements differ, and an unadapted American set will not work at all in Germany. But how about a similar set built to German technical standards? That is a marketing problem, and the technical standards an issue for production people.

Marketing organization is important, and influences the relationship between marketing managers and the managers of other functions. Normally, production and other functions are very intimately involved with marketing problems, as when technical standards vary. Producing 110-volt appliances for the English 220-volt market won't do much for sales. Firms must work out logical and effective organizational relationships, and often the multinational structure is much more complex than local ones.

Methods of Distribution

The choice of marketing channels and distributors in any foreign country is critical. Distribution may be expensive, and constrained by local laws unfamiliar to the MNC's management. Poor initial choices can be binding and literally wipe out growth possibilities. Thus most Japanese auto companies, when they began exporting to the United States, tried to set up their own dealer networks. It took years of work and billions of dollars of investment, but in the end it was a successful strategy.

One major manufacturer, however, chose to use the Chrysler Corporation's distribution system and produce in Japan using a Chrysler brand name. While this strategy worked, in that cars were sold, it did not work nearly as well in this case as having one's own brand name. But now it will be extremely costly and difficult for the company to change its strategy, and worse, ten years have been gained by Japanese competitors in attacking the American market. Even if the Japanese company could break away from its contractual obligations, it could face costly close-out penalties, and it will have to start from scratch to build up its brand name and distribution network in the United States.

This is one example of a multibillion dollar error, made long ago by men now retired.

There are no set rules for determining which strategy will work best. What works for the Japanese auto companies may fail for other industries and/or countries. The few Hong Kong firms that have tried to build good brand images for their toys and textile products and sell down the marketing channel have done badly, while those that linked up closely with Sears or Penneys have done quite well. There is no easy answer to this problem, yet every firm, large and small, has to make the decision quite early in the game.

In quite a few countries, it is virtually impossible to change distributors once a commitment is made. If you pick a loser, you can pay for decades. Here too, firms must commit themselves before they have much experience. In smaller countries, the problem of finding some good distributor not already handling competitive products can be tough. Another complicating factor is that channels and distributor agreements perfectly acceptable at home may be illegal abroad. A firm may not be allowed to suggest retail prices, or it may have to. It may not be able to sell direct, but rather work only through locally owned distributors. Whatever the situation, the MNC has to adjust, and difficulties abound.

It is common to find in some small country that the relative competitive position of MNCs is reversed from that at home. Ford is much larger abroad than GM, for example. One reason for this is that Ford has the better distributors abroad, which is perhaps associated with historical relationships. One of Massey-Ferguson's great marketing mistakes was to ignore the United States market, the biggest in the world for agricultural equipment, until well after Deere and International Harvester were firmly established. Thus, for the Canadian firm to be dominant in, for example, the Swedish market is of small consolation. But firms are tied to their history, and it is difficult to strengthen or otherwise change the nature of distributor relationships already established.

The selection of franchises has implications in many ways similar to those connected with distributorships. It is easy to state in a written contract that a poorly performing franchise can be dropped, but laws in some countries prohibit such a move. Huge markets can be lost through the poor selection of the first few franchisees, and it is important to know of their capabilities in advance.

Licensing agreements can cause similar problems, as noted earlier.

Moreover, many licensing agreements contain restrictive marketing clauses, as when the licensee is prohibited from selling the product in selected countries. The reason for this restrictive clause might be that the MNC has already given exclusive marketing rights in that territory to another licensee. This raises the question of enforcement, which can be very easy or very difficult, depending on the parties involved. As always in multinational dealings, what is simple in a purely domestic context can become extremely complex in an international one, and sometimes top-management attention is necessary to resolve interaffiliate conflicts of interest. In cases of breach of contract, there is no single, all-encompassing international law. The MNC ends up in court in its own country, in the licensee's country, or in a third country mutually agreed upon by the partners in the initial contract, and decisions are made on the basis of local rather than international law. It may be psychologically rewarding to get a favorable ruling in Britain, only to discover that all the action is in Egypt, where British rules don't apply. One result of this type of problem is that there is much more effort to establish mutual trust among partners in international business than at home. Trust and respect may be the only enforcement tools an MNC really has; in contrast, the local firms can fully rely on legal recourse should disagreements arise. Much more than in a purely domestic context, relations with foreign affiliates must be based on a cooperative spirit, for the letter of the contract will not always suffice.

Legal and cultural complications abound in this area, because each country has sacred cows, and each country's laws are different. Some products are banned or discouraged; some prices are fixed or heavily regulated; intricate contractual relationships between buyers and sellers vary; consumers sometimes have much power, and at other times or places virtually none; customs and tradition also play a role. The local marketer is typically able to navigate local minefields better than foreigners, which is why so many good distributors are locally owned. But choices and changes typically merit top-management attention, because the future of foreign operations is at stake.

Product Mix

The question of the firm's world product mix also requires much long-term planning. As it enters foreign markets, the MNC might selectively introduce known products well established at home. But other factors are also important. A lot depends on the foreign environment and the quality of distributors. The logistics and production personnel must be consulted. Thus the minimum optimum scale of production for some product or key component may determine when it is feasible to produce the item in the country under consideration. New transportation improvements can also open a market. No one shipped orchids from Latin America to the United States until air carriers could quote good rates and provide reliable services. New ports which can handle containers efficiently open up new marketing potential. Indeed, the marketing decision cannot be made in isolation from these factors, and the need for very free and flexible information flows among corporate divisions is critical.

A company with four or five major product lines, each with hundreds of products within it, selling in seventy countries and producing in perhaps forty, has real problems of coordination and control. The MNCs are usually up to this task, and they do have long-run marketing plans that also involve all other functional parts of the company. Since hundreds of millions, or even billions of dollars may be involved, top-management involvement is certain in such seemingly simple decisions as when to open up Brazil to the third major product line.

Trademarks

Trademarks are often the life-blood of an MNC, and such names as Coca Cola, Ford, or IBM have enormous value. A very real problem is to protect these trade names all over the world. Most countries belong to an international copyright convention, and most agree to protect trade names and other copyrights, but enforcing the rules can be difficult. Bootlegging and counterfeiting are common, and companies such as Levi Strauss have serious problems in policing their markets. Movie and television producers, along with publishers, have problems in avoiding the easy copying of their products. Retaliation is easy back home, but the counterfeiter may not ever plan to sell in the home market. Moreover, copyright laws vary widely between countries, and coverage is not the same as at home. Consequently, the owners of valuable copyrights, such as that for the film *Star Wars*, are likely to spend a great amount of time and money protecting their copyrights. Bootlegging of products also raises quality image problems, as customers complain about inferior products which they mistakenly believe were produced by the MNC. Protecting one's reputation for quality can be an important strategic consideration.

Market Research

Marketing requires much data, and data are hard to get in most countries. Demographic data readily available at home are often unavailable for foreign markets. Moreover, those data which are available are often highly unreliable, sometimes missing the mark by several orders of magnitude. This is becoming a problem even in highly developed economies, as the underground economy surges. Incomes may be much higher than the tax data indicate in such diverse countries as India, Sweden, and the United States. Data collection is expensive, and there is always a cost/benefit question here. Does the value of getting good information justify the expense? To do good market research would infer that the answer is yes, but in smaller markets one may have to settle for less. The MNC, as usual, has an advantage, in that it can experiment with imported products to test the market, while the local smaller firm may go broke finding out. Initially, for the MNC, this market is at least marginally important, while for the local firm it is all there is.

Sales and Service

Sales promotion policies can vary widely, because of both cultural differences and law. Many countries do not allow radio or television advertising. Countries with high illiteracy rates have few magazines and newspapers, and these are read by only a small proportion of the population. This is where a good local distributor can shine, incidentally, since such a firm will have a good grasp of local realities, and may be able to figure out good sales promotions that the home office never heard of. Again the possibilities of exchanging information between branches gives the MNC an advantage. What works well in one Latin American country, as shown by a clever local distributor, may have possibilities, if suitably modified, in other Latin countries, or in Africa. Knowledge really is power in such marketing and sales promotion situations.

Warranties are a problem, again because law and custom may differ widely. Rarely can the firm merely translate its warranties and transfer its guarantees between countries. Local lawyers and marketing people, along with local distributors, can contribute to workable solutions. Since a warranty is a type of contract, whatever the contract law of the country is will be decisive, and more than one firm has realized, too late, that it made very expensive guarantees it had no intention of granting.

Many major multinationals have grown because of their superb after-sales service capabilities. If you buy a Caterpilar Tractor product, you can rest assured that virtually wherever you are in the world, it can be fixed, and spare parts will be available within 24 hours. The local distributor is intimately involved in this process, and some firms spend millions of dollars on establishing inventory systems; training distributor technicians; and securing warehouse facilities for spare parts. Their reputations are built on their ability to maintain their equipment. Languages also become highly relevant here, as noted earlier, when instruction manuals and parts catalogs are prepared. For firms with strong after-sales service needs, this area can be one of the most important for top management. A simply stated policy, such as "Any spare part for any machine we have built should be available within 24 hours anywhere in world," can set five thousand good people to work for decades building the necessary system to support this statement. Costs can run into billions of dollars, but the payoff is that buyers choose your equipment over cheaper stuff that is not as well supported and hence less reliable.

SUMMARY

Marketing, like all other business functions, is a complex and critical topic. Moreover, as the other functions, it must be integrated into the total system as effectively as possible. Saying this is easy; doing it, given all the things that can happen to a global corporation, is something else again. Very few firms feel that they have it right at present, and probably none has been able to figure out exactly what the optimum structure is. And about the time that the company does feel it is approaching the proper solution, new developments, either by countries, by competitors, or by internal changes, force the system out of equilibrium once more. Getting the marketing pieces put together properly is a never-ending task. But that is what management is all about.

Similarly, international sourcing and production, especially if based on a network of interdependent plants located in many countries, require sophisticated coordination and continuous fine-tuning. Information flows assume increased importance, whether regarding the sourcing of key components, competitive developments, or sudden changes in local environments. It is difficult to coordinate the individual functions in the globally oriented firm, and more difficult still to integrate the functional strategies into a worldwide corporate strategy. The gains in efficiency and competitiveness by adopting the global perspective, however, make the efforts well worthwhile.

DISCUSSION QUESTIONS

1. International investment in a political context is more controversial than business in a purely domestic context. What issues related to technology transfer, production, or logistics demonstrate this point?

2. What are some international marketing strategies, and how do they differ from domestic marketing strategies?

3. The globally oriented firm has a great advantage in having the world as a source of inputs. Discuss.

4. There can be no such thing as a "world car," because consumer tastes and government regulations vary substantially in what are, and will remain, "local" markets. Discuss.

NOTES

1. Heidi Vernon Wortzel and Lawrence H. Wortzel, *Strategic Management of Multinational Corporations: The Essentials* (New York: John Wiley and Sons, 1985), 313–314.

2. Yves L. Doz, "Managing Manufacturing Rationalization Within Multinational Companies," in *Strategic Management of Multinational Corporations: The Essentials*, eds., Heidi Vernon Wortzel and Lawrence H. Wortzel (New York: John Wiley and Sons, 1985), 350–362.

3. Mariann Jelinek and Joel D. Golhar, "The Interface Between Strategy and Manufacturing Technology," *Columbia Journal of World Business* (Spring, 1983), 26–36.

4. T. Cannon, "Managing International and Export Marketing," in *Strategic Management of Multinational Corporations: The Essentials*, eds., Heidi Vernon Wortzel and Lawrence H. Wortzel (New York: John Wiley and Sons, 1985), 253–265.

5. Gilbert D. Harrell and Richard O. Kiefer, "Multinational Strategic Market Portfolios," in *Strategic Management of Multinational Corporations: The Essentials*, eds., Heidi Vernon Wortzel and Lawrence H. Wortzel (New York: John Wiley and Sons, 1985), 286–294.

6. Stefan H. Robock and Kenneth Simmonds, *International Business and Multinational Enterprises*, 3rd Ed. (Homewood, Ill.: Irwin, 1983), 433–439.

7. Igal Ayal and Jehiel Zif, "Market Expansion Strategies in Multinational Marketing," in *Strategic Management of Multinational Corporations: The Essentials*, eds., Heidi Vernon Wortzel and Lawrence H. Wortzel (New York: John Wiley and Sons, 1985), 265–277.

FURTHER READING

1. Ball, Donald A., and Wendell H. McCulloch, Jr. *International Business: Introduction and Essentials*, 4th Ed. Homewood: Irwin, 1990.

2. Buzzell, Robert D. and John A. Quelch. *Multinational Marketing Management: Cases and Readings*. Reading: Addison–Wesley Publishing Company, 1988.

3. Cateora, Philip R. *International Marketing*, 5th Ed. Homewood: Irwin, 1983.

4. Cundiff, Edward and Marye Tharp Hilger. *Marketing in the International Environment* 2nd ed. Englewood Cliffs: Prentice Hall, 1988.

5. Douglas, Susan P. and Yoram Wind. "The Myth of Globalization", *Columbia Journal of World Business* Winter, 1987, pp. 19–29.

6. Frank, Isaiah. *Foreign Enterprise in Developing Countries*. Baltimore: Johns Hopkins University Press, 1980.

7. Jain, Subhash C. *International Marketing Management*. Boston: Kent Publishing Company, 1984.

8. Lane, Henry W. and Joseph J. DiStefano. *International Management Behavior*. Scarborough, Ontario: Nelson, 1988.

9. Kefalas, A.G., *Global Business Strategy*. Cincinnati: South–Western, 1990.

10. Robinson, Richard D. *Internationalization of Business: An Introduction*. New York: The Dryden Press, 1984.

11. Root, Franklin R. *International Trade and Investment*, 5th Ed. Cincinnati: South–Western Publishing Co., 1984.

CHAPTER 8

▼

Strategy Implementation: Finance, Research and Development, and Human Resources Management

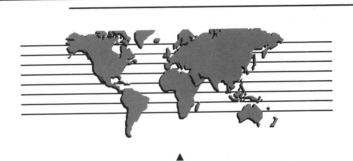

▲

It is clear that the functional strategies of production and marketing must be congruent with, and reinforced by, strategies implemented in the areas of finance, research and development, and human resources management. In turn these functional strategies all together must be subordinate to the core strategies discussed in earlier chapters.

FINANCE

International financial management has become one of the most highly centralized of all MNC functional areas, which is one measure of its strategic significance. The increasingly tight control of financial matters by top management is partly a consequence of the extremely turbulent international monetary environment, and of the growing sophistication of financial managers in devising strategies for currency exposure, transfer pricing, and so on. More basically, however, financial management has assumed strategic rather than merely operational significance because decisions in this area can change the very nature of the company, affecting all other functional strategies.

Volkswagen of West Germany, for example, experienced phenomenal growth during the sixties to become Germany's largest industrial enterprise and the fourth largest auto-maker in the world. The German mark strengthened during the seventies vis-à-vis other currencies, however, and VW's position quickly eroded worldwide. What began as a purely financial problem spilled over quickly to other areas. Product policy was changed, and the Volkswagen Beetle was replaced (in America by the Rabbit, for example) in order to cater to less price-sensitive markets. National markets were diversified in order to be less dependent on the North American market, with its weakening currency. The firm began production abroad, and even encouraged its West German suppliers of components to set up operations abroad. Production standardization was increased, and there was greater integration of subsidiary activities. There were personnel changes at the highest levels of the organization. The focus of promotional strategies shifted from economy and durability to style, convenience, and service. It is evident from this example that dealing with exchange risk is not just a financial issue. It also affects an MNC's production, marketing, sourcing, personnel, research and other strategies, and is clearly of strategic importance.[1]

Money Markets

When a firm goes multinational, the usual pattern in its early years is to rely on its local money market for funds. Its transactions are denominated in the currency of its home country, and foreign currencies are viewed as an inconvenience. Slowly, however, top managers begin to realize that they can now tap global money markets rather than merely local ones, which enormously increases the capital raising potential of the firm, and thus gives it a significant advantage over purely domestic firms, especially in view of the varying availability and costs of capital.

This development also leads to the gradual evolution of global financial planning. Instead of compartmentalizing each currency for use in specific markets, the MNC can plan its sources and uses of funds globally. If the English subsidiary generates a good cash surplus while the Italian branch needs funds, then transfers can be made easily. There is a cost for such exchange moves, but it could be much less than that of borrowing in a variety of local money markets. Modern communications make daily cash statements from all branches possible, and modern budgetary planning makes good estimates of cash requirements feasible as well. Moreover, if the MNC is generating a substantial overall cash surplus in its operations, it can invest these funds in a variety of money markets, including the Eurodollar market.

The ability to utilize money markets everywhere means that managers must know of all the legal constraints in these foreign markets. A bond issued in London may have quite different constraints than one in New York, and French laws may be quite different regarding bank loans than the laws in Switzerland. Hence institutional knowledge is critical. American business schools, long accustomed to teaching students about domestic problems, have barely begun to explore this problem, and many students leave school without any formal knowledge of foreign markets. Europeans, long accustomed to working in smaller markets and thus often forced to use international markets, have an advantage here.

However sound it may be to utilize global financial markets, the amount of detailed planning required to operationalize the concept is enormous. A very real problem in this regard is the provincial attitude of local branch managers, who cannot see the whole picture and who get annoyed at frequent raids on their cash by headquarters. Some home-country managers can be rather provincial as well, and the idea of utilizing foreign currencies can upset them. Education is necessary, but even that is made difficult by the rapidly changing nature of the markets themselves.

Foreign Exchange Rates

In the modern world, the value of one currency in relation to others is determined by supply and demand in the international foreign exchange market. Values fluctuate daily, often dramatically, and a deal made today payable in French francs, rarely yields the same number of dollars thirty days later, when the bill is paid. A firm could win or lose here, since the franc could go up or down relative to the dollar or any other currency. These fluctuations mean tht all MNCs, and all importers and exporters, are subject to foreign exchange risk. There is simply no means of avoiding this when a firm deals with other countries. Many U.S. managers think that they are avoiding exchange risk by dealing only in dollars; but an exporter who demands dollars for a million dollar order to be paid for in 60 days is, in effect, betting that the dollar will not fall relative to the buyer's currency. If it does, the exporter gives the exchange gain to the importer. If the dollar rises, the exporter gets the gain, even though he or she may not be aware of it.

The exchange risk is so pervasive that it occupies much top-management time. It is not uncommon to find that an MNC literally lost its entire operating profit for the year in exchange losses, or conversely, that it doubled its profits because of exchange gains. Because the swings can be so huge, the future of the firm could be in jeopardy without very careful monitoring of exchange rate movements. MNCs and major importers and exporters everywhere are acutely aware of the problem, and financial people who really understand what is going on are in demand everywhere.

Consider a large exporter, such as Boeing, which is offered an order for $300 million worth of jet transports by Lufthansa, the German airline. Delivery is to extend over a three year period, and the question is, which currency should Boeing request? In this case, West German marks or U.S. dollars would be most likely, although Lufthansa is an international airline earning currencies all over the world, so payment in Swiss francs, Swedish kronen, or even Japanese yen might be possible.

The problem that both buyer and seller must consider here, is that the mark/dollar exchange rate has fluctuated widely in the recent past, and it may again. Suppose that Boeing agrees to accept marks, and the mark rises by 10 percent against the dollar before the order is paid for. When Boeing converts these marks into dollars, it will receive $330 million, not $300 million. Lufthansa will pay the same number of marks it originally agreed to, but in effect it will pay 10 percent more for the aircraft than it had anticipated. Lufthansa, having its own currency forecasting unit, might have offered dollars, and if Boeing had accepted, then the exchange gain is in favor of Lufthansa. Thirty million dollars merely from a currency shift is substantial, and top management will be involved in the decision.

The obvious solution is to forecast exchange rates, and much effort has been expended by MNCs to develop models that will do just this. Unfortunately for harrassed top management, forecasting exchange rates is about as easy as forecasting stock prices; and so far, experts have had about the same degree of success as stock-market forecasters, which is to say they do badly. But the thought of explaining to one's board of directors just how it was that $30 million of profits somehow melted away is enough to bother any CEO.

To cope with such problems, many of the largest multinational companies have begun operating big money-servicing operations through separately managed and accountable divisions. Such corporate "mini-banks" tend to have four core activities: banking, investing surplus cash, borrowing and currency management. Of these, dealing with foreign exchange has become the most active component. However, the activities in aggregate have vastly expanded the basic functions of traditional corporate treasury management.

Hedging Strategies

Firms may adopt hedging strategies to protect themselves from changes in currency values. There are various types of hedging tactics, but the three most common are those associated with forward markets, money-markets, and restructuring of the company's balance sheets. Forward markets entail the buying or selling of currencies to be delivered at a future date but at a price agreed upon today. The problem here is that the cost of the hedge, especially if the markets are anticipating a major movement in the value of the currency involved, can be greater than the exchange loss would have been had the risk not been covered. If the desired currency is expected to strengthen, for example, the buyer pays a premium over the spot rate (today's price); if the currency is expected to weaken, the buyer gets a discount (i.e., the currency sells forward for less than the spot rate).

Money-market strategies involve borrowing a currency that is expected to depreciate or placing a currency that is expected to appreciate. That is, the MNC holds its liabilities in currencies which are expected to lose value and thus require fewer dollars in the future to repay. The idea is that repaying the loan in depreciated currency will offset the losses which stem from holding assets denominated in that currency.

A firm may opt for zero exposure on the balance sheet (balancing liquid assets and liquid liabilities in a given currency). Perhaps more common is the use of leads and lags. Suppose that foreign MNCs are confident that the British pound is going to fall in value quite rapidly during the next six months. Major bailouts, as discussed below, might be counterproductive. Instead, the MNCs minimize British pound holdings and maximize the holdings of other currencies. So the firm ships goods out of England to its foreign branches and other customers. For itself, it does not hurry intracorporate payments into Britain. For others, it informally lets them know that delays in payments will be tolerated. In effect, it avoids getting paid in pounds for as long as possible because the longer it waits, the more pounds it will receive for any given transaction denominated in another currency.

The British branch also buys items from abroad, and these invoices are paid immediately, or even in advance. To do this, pounds must be converted into dollars or other currencies. The swings here, even for fairly small firms, can be quite large, and when or if the British pound does fall, the company gains.

In this case, note that the standards for middle- and upper-middle-level managers are unusual. We reward our credit managers when they shorten collection times; here, we give our person a bonus if he or she manages to delay collections. We normally want to pay our bills as slowly as possible; here we pay in advance and are eager to do so. The local credit people, who may be unaware of the overall situation, can be totally baffled by the seemingly irrational behavior of their bosses. In order to prevent suboptimization, and indeed a very expensive one at that, this strategy necessarily becomes a top-management issue.

It is difficult for large MNCs to bail out of foreign currencies in large amounts over a short period. For one thing, throwing multi-million-dollar amounts on the sometimes thin foreign exchange markets may do exactly what the MNC is trying to avoid, namely the weakening of the currency which it is holding. Moreover, governments monitor such actions very closely through their own central banks and local commercial banks, and they can apply all sorts of legal and extralegal sanctions if the MNC do not behave as the monetary authorities believe they should. Thus a major English firm that tried to flee from dollars might find itself embroiled in a nasty U.S. antitrust suit, or its key factories in the United States would be found to be in violation of pollution control laws. Customs inspectors might suddenly demand that every shipment be inspected individually, which might move the time required for customs clearance from two days to six months. MNCs are well aware that they must remain in the good graces of host governments, and any highly visible vote of no confidence in a country's policies could be disastrous. For this reason, financial policies that are otherwise quite logical may not be acted upon because of the strategic consequences involved; and the decisions on which policies to follow must be made at levels that have a proper purview of these interrelationships.

Japanese companies have followed five basic strategies in responding to the yen's strengthening. They have cut costs by squeezing suppliers, by offering early retirement to (or redeploying to affiliated firms) large numbers of managers, and by product redesign and increased automation of manufacturing processes. They have substantially increased foreign investment in Southeast Asia (to reduce labor costs) and North America and Europe (to get closer to the markets and to avoid trade disputes). They have moved up market by cutting the production of low-priced goods and increasing the output of higher value-added, upmarket goods. Technological innovation to stay ahead of international competition has been stimulated through increased expenditures on research and development. Finally, companies in mature markets have diversified their product lines. These too are hedging strategies, in the broader sense of the term.

The MNC can also run into difficulty within its own home government by frustrating the efforts of monetary authorities to implement national policies. Suppose that the U.S. administration wants to restrain economic growth to avoid overheating of the economy, so it restricts money supply and tightens credit. Local firms may be caught in the credit squeeze, but MNCs merely borrow on the Euromarket or in the Far East. They keep right on expanding even when the domestic economy is not. Such activities reduce the effectiveness of governmental macroeconomic policies, and add yet one more reason to the long list of those that make the MNC suspect to all governments.

Exchange Controls

Many strategic financial options available in relatively stable financial environments are not universally available, so global financial strategies must take into consideration regional constraints. The Latin American financial environment for example is currently characterized by forced reschedulings of national debts, excessive inflation, monetary instability, and recurrent devaluations. No forward markets exist to speak of, and dividend repatriation in most countries is limited to a small percentage of capital or is taxed excessively. Price controls restrict the freedom to compensate for devaluation and inflation, and exchange controls make the usual methods of reducing exposure infeasible. Under these conditions, the affiliate's debt in the domestic currencies should be maximized, but funds are generally not available and the cost is prohibitive. Regulations change rapidly, which often makes long-term financial planning highly tenuous. On the bright side, such turbulent conditions present a fine training ground for corporate treasurers.

From time to time, of course, during balance-of-payments crises, industrialized countries also impose exchange controls to prevent capital flight. Britain has long had such policies, and so did the United States during the late sixties and early seventies. More recently, France has introduced such controls, which can totally disrupt an MNC's financial planning system when major currencies are involved. The very reason for the controls is that most firms want to reduce their holdings of French francs (for example). Without the controls, billions of francs would flow out, the demand for francs would fall while the demand for stronger currencies would rise, and the value of the franc would progressively worsen. Those unhappy firms stuck with francs then lose much money, which is what exchange risk is all about.

The ultimate form of exchange control is currency inconvertibility. Many currencies, such as those of India and all communist countries, cannot legally be exchanged for any other currency without special government permission. Therefore, a firm with good profits in India may find that it cannot change the rupees into dollars and repatriate the profits, and it cannot include the rupees in its global cash planning: they must be spent in India.

Countertrade

The inconvertibility of currencies, in addition to the hard currency shortages in most of the Third World, has led to a very rapid increase recently in the use of countertrade, in its various forms, nothing but a sophisticated version of barter. It is a highly inefficient means of trade, and runs directly counter to the multilateral payments system which, since World War II, has led to an unprecedented growth of international trade and investment. We need not discuss here the various forms of countertrade or the motivations of those involved. What is important to note here is that it is a financing strategy which intimately affects the marketing and production strategies of the MNC.

Volkswagen of West Germany, for example, recently agreed in principle to sell technology and related equipment to East Germany for the production of auto engines. Payment is to be made in engines produced by the technology and equipment delivered. Consequently, several of the firm's engine assembly lines in West Germany are to be closed down. This form of countertrade, termed compensation deal or buy-back, is typical of East–West industrial corporation. It has worked beautifully in some cases, disastrously in others, but always affects production planning for the Western firm.

Greater problems typically arise when the goods received from the partner are fully unrelated to the product lines of the Western partner. Consider a Western film company that had a major hit this year. A country wishing to rent the film has no currency available, but it does have a surplus of cattle hides. The filmmaker agrees to the counter-trade, but has absolutely no use for cattle hides. It finds a barter broker who, for a very substantial commission, will eventually find someone in need of cattle hides, and the filmmaker eventually receives cash. Barter deals of this sort can involve huge sums of money, and they are an excellent marketing tool for selling to customers who, ordinarily, are completely out of reach. The imaginative marketing manager of the film company surely would have had to present his case to top management for approval. But note that in this case, the firm's risk is small. It risks the cost of making a few extra film prints and sending them abroad. Whatever it can get for the hides above these minor costs, is an addition to net profit. Hence such deals can be attractive, and many firms get involved in them. Often, however, the goods received in return are of such low quality that they cannot be sold on Western markets except at huge discounts, and real marketing problems arise. Generally, finance addresses the question of how, not whether, to trade. Sometimes, however, the tail wags the dog, and the structure of trade is determined by the nature of finance.

Currency Options and Swaps

The task of international financial management is to minimize the cost of funds and to maximize the return on investment over time, through the best combination of currency of denomination and maturity characteristics of financial assets and liabilities. Implementation is exceedingly difficult, however, and requires substantial variations among individual units of the corporation. New techniques are continually being introduced and experimented with, such as the use of currency options or swaps. An option is very similar to an insurance policy: in return for a specified premium, the buyer obtains the right to buy or sell currency at a specific rate within a given period. Unlike the forward transactions described above, however, there is no obligation to exercise the option.

If currency rates move in favor of the corporation, it simply lets the option lapse.

Currency swaps have become very common among corporations active in Latin America, where the debt crisis has led to the introduction of severe controls on financial transactions. The main result of such controls is that subsidiaries are in effect blocked from repatriating funds to the parent corporation. By preventing the company from deploying the funds where it can earn the highest return, such controls tend to downgrade the quality of the company's investments. These controls affect companies differently; the firms that supply vital inputs into the economy, such as agricultural products or drugs, receive high priority in the country's allocation of scarce foreign exchange. For other types of firms, swapping is a very viable strategy, seeking another multinational whose subsidiary in the given country is short of domestic currency. Thus the local subsidiary of one MNC gives local currency to the local subsidiary of another, and the parent company of the first in turn receives an equivalent sum in dollars from the parent of the second.

Implications of International Accounting Practices

Closely associated with the financial strategies are the numerous accounting problems that arise, typically tactical in the domestic context but strategic in the international context. Accounting practices are culture-bound, in that every country has its own accounting rules. These can range from complex, highly sophisticated rules in industrialized countries to almost no rules at all in some Third World countries. But local accountants have to meet local requirements.

To be sure, there are ongoing efforts by several organizations to draft basic reporting standards that would be agreeable to all. Consensus is not likely, however, for a number of reasons. Efforts along such lines in the United Nations have been motivated by a strongly anti-business sentiment. Many nonfinancial disclosure requirements would be included, such as MNC practices regarding transfer pricing, employment and production data, and investment plans. Similarly, EEC drafts would include many nonfinancial disclosures, due to the insistence of labor organizations. MNCs strongly oppose such requirements, partly due to the competitive disadvantages that would arise from having to unilaterally disclose future plans.

The fact that each country has its own unique accounting practices poses a problem for MNCs, which use accounting records for comparative purposes. Even if one assumes that the standards of different countries were largely harmonious, MNC financial reporting is made difficult by different rates of inflation in various nations. The Netherlands allows the use of inflation accounting, while the United States does not. The usual result of such accounting in periods of rapid price-level increases is to depress earnings drastically. Assume that an MNC's American operations show a net profit of 12 percent after tax on its capital for this past year, while its Dutch branch lost 1 percent of its capital. Shall it fire the Dutch manager and promote the American? Not necessarily, since if there was 11 percent annual inflation in the United States, it is quite possible that under Dutch rules, the American branch would have lost 5 percent on capital. Top management is always looking at critical data, and must know what the data mean before reaching conclusions. Recasting this Dutch and American data with similar rules would give a much different result than using two different sets of local rules.

We shall later consider some difficulties of evaluating the performance of foreign affiliates in light of the widely differing environmental constraints on performance. Another complicating factor is that the overseas units often should not be judged solely on the basis of their own individual performance, for they sometimes have a strong influence on the profits of other units in the system (through the purchase of components, transfer pricing, management fees and royalties, and so on). Here, however, our major concern is with the difficulties of judging performance from accounting records.

The financial statements of any foreign subsidiary of a U.S. firm are recorded in the currency of the country in which that subsidiary is based. In order to consolidate its accounts with those of the U.S. parent, it is necessary to translate the foreign currency into dollars. The problem is, no one has yet been able to draft fully suitable translation rules. That in itself has strategic consequences for the MNC in a number of ways. Rules there must be, but what makes sense in one industry may not in another, and what holds for relatively stable currencies may be precisely the wrong thing for the peso or cruzado. For both legal and control purposes, however, the MNC requires accurate and comparable reporting of performance. These issues are not merely of academic interest or solely the concern of the accounting division.

U.S. firms are subject to American law and regulations, and one very important accounting rule is the one governing how exchange rate gains and losses are translated. Prior to the issuance of FASB 8 (Financial Accounting Standards Board Statement Number 8) in 1975, corporate treasurers had a choice of translation methods. This led to difficulties in comparing the performance of one company with that of another, however, so Statement Number 8 mandated the use of a single method for all. It was the so-called temporal method, under which the current rate of exchange was applied essentially to monetary items, and historic rates of exchange were applied to nonmonetary items (e.g., plant and equipment). All foreign-exchange gains or losses, whether realized or unrealized, had to be reflected in the balance sheet and income statement. This caused profits to be extremely volatile, and it also often reflected purely accounting rather than truly economic performance.

In order to cushion the impact of the rule on the earnings statement, MNCs were often forced to undertake tactics that sometimes did not make economic sense. Debt structures were changed, as were inventory levels. Remittance policies were adjusted, and hedging increased. The collection period of both accounts receivable and payable were affected, and risk management became more highly centralized. It was another example of the tail wagging the dog, and there was little wonder why corporate executives referred to Statement Number 8 as "Section 8," an irreverent reference to the mental discharge provisions of the armed services.

Statement Number 8 was replaced in December of 1982 by Statement Number 52, which (wisely) allows for reserve accounts to be used for foreign exchange gains and losses, thus somewhat alleviating the yo-yo effect on earnings that the previous rule had. Statement Number 52 provides greater flexibility in other respects also, but the rule-makers have yet to resolve one basic problem: It is misleading to judge affiliate performance strictly in terms of dollars or strictly in terms of its domestic currency. One can spend a lifetime exploring international accounting problems, and it is a complex and highly technical field. We mention it here because without some top-management sensitivity to what the data are saying, and to what assumptions they are based on, decision errors will be common.

We have touched elsewhere on the problem of intracorporate transfer pricing, so we shall not discuss it in detail here. Nor need we go into detail to stress that all of the financial problems discussed above are intimately interwoven. The complexity of that alone is great, but consider also that an MNC may be dealing in perhaps 30 or 40 foreign currencies rather than just one, on which our examples have been based. Even that complexity is compounded by the fact, which we have repeatedly stressed, that financial management has a profound impact on other functional strategies, and that it therefore must be strategically coordinated at the highest of corporate levels. Money is the lifeblood of the company even in a purely domestic context. In the international arena, however, completely new and extremely difficult problems emerge which merit continual strategic financial planning, monitoring, and control.

RESEARCH AND DEVELOPMENT

Multinational corporations, especially those whose competitive advantage derives primarily from technological leadership, have long been known for their strength in research and development. They have pools of technically trained personnel; access to both private and public funds, vital to sustaining research and development efforts in spite of the high risks involved; and markets whose size and sophistication encourage continuous innovation. All of these factors, when combined with competitive conditions, have fostered the rapid development of new products, new manufacturing processes, and new applications of existing technologies.

Many firms have fostered innovation through the relatively recent establishment of "new venture" groups, which are internal diversification efforts of the firm to develop and nurture a portfolio of innovative projects. Often, however, such an approach leaves the rest of the organization plodding along unchanged, and even if the new ventures are successful, there are often problems connected with subsequently fitting the new lines into the old structures and corporate culture.

Dow Chemical's European group has therefore taken an opposite approach; that of trying, and so far very successfully, to change the attitudes of managers throughout the entire organization in order to stimulate innovation. This approach has led to the following changes:

1. The company has been restructured into smaller units (to increase the focus of research and to foster closer collaboration between marketing and product development).

2. There has been a relative shift away from the refining of existing processes towards the development of new ones.

3. The lines of communication have been shortened and the speed of the product's flow into the marketplace has been increased.

4. More attention is given to higher-value specialty products, and less attention to commodity chemicals.

The strategic importance of R & D, in this case, is suggested by the impact of these changes on all of the company's operations.

Most multinationals conduct the lion's share of their R & D at home rather than abroad, and there are sound reasons for this. The nature of research depends heavily on the close interaction and proximity of those involved. Research facilities and personnel are exceptionally expensive, and under such conditions the duplication of efforts must be minimized. It makes little sense to reinvent the wheel in some small African country, especially when the size of that country's market alone could not justify the research costs. Moreover, for historical reasons, the MNC's basic technology and research programs are heavily oriented to the domestic market. For that reason, when R & D work is done in foreign affiliates, it typically takes the form of product modification or adaptation to meet the particular needs of local markets.[2] Beyond this, there is a clearly competitive reason for centralizing R & D activities. If the competitive strength and comparative advantage of the firm are associated with its technological leadership, then R & D must be closely controlled, not only because of its strategic importance relative to other functional activities, but also in order to keep the leadership in-house (i.e., out of the hands of potential competitors).

Nevertheless, during the second half of the 1980s American corporations increasingly expanded their research outside the United States. IBM, Eastman Kodak, W. R. Grace, and Merck and Upjohn have all opened research laboratories in Japan, and many other firms are targeting Europe for such activities. The key motivation in establishing foreign research and development activities seems to be the need to monitor (and capture!) breakthroughs in countries where research flourishes in specific technologies.

The major input for R & D is highly trained minds, and this is another reason why most R & D activities occur in the highly developed countries, where training is available. As usual, the MNC has an advantage in this regard, since brilliant and well-trained citizens of poorer countries can be hired and sent to the R & D center to work with equally brilliant men and women from other countries. The MNCs thus get involved in the brain-drain issue, as poor countries allege that the rich part of the world is draining them of their scarce talent.

Like most people, individuals employed in this type of labor tend to prefer pleasant environments, and since output is often on paper in the form of ideas, patents, and licenses, R & D centers can be situated virtually anywhere. They are often found in a country-club atmosphere, far away from grimy plants but near major universities and research institutes. Since the most qualified research personnel are highly mobile, companies tend to make their workplace as pleasant as possible.

MNCs must have a steady flow of new ideas, ranging from fundamentally new processes and products down to minor production or office improvements. Anything can be copied in time, usually a short time, and if an MNC does not have new things to offer, it becomes redundant, and other MNCs or even local firms replace it in the marketplace. In a very fundamental sense, what MNCs are selling is a better way of doing things. Hence there is much top-level concern about the flow of R & D, and what new prospects are becoming economically viable. Such basic strategies as those determining the basic future direction of the firm depend critically on what its researchers and laboratories have in the works.

Another key point, and one which indeed baffles many observers, is that most R & D is very subtle and seemingly unimportant. This can be explained in association with our earlier distinction between product and process technologies. We have all heard stories about people like the industrial genius who finds some wonder drug and wins a Nobel prize, to say nothing about his making his employer rich. But no one knows or much cares about the machinist in Detroit who devises a slightly better way to cut steel; the clerk in Munich who streamlines a troublesome form; the programmer in Tokyo who debugs a nasty routine; or the janitor in Mexico City who figures out a slightly better way of cleaning delicate machinery. The MNC can pick up ideas everywhere and send them around the world, and the steady accretion of minor gains can add up quickly to big wins. For every Nobel prize idea, there are tens of thousands of these little, useful developments. Those not familiar with the industry or with the technology involved can easily overlook such small gains, but then, much later, it becomes clear that they are critical. Moreover, well managed MNCs have clear communications channels everywhere, and they also can buy the best information from outside experts when needed. A troublesome problem with a chemical reaction in Sao Paulo leads to a request from that branch manager for help; perhaps our man in Lyons knows what to do, and if he doesn't, a firm of consulting industrial chemists in Manchester can be hired to figure things out. Local firms often don't have the knowledge or expertise to do as well, particularly in countries where all information is subject to careful scrutiny by the authorities.

R & D activities are closely subordinated to the overall objectives of the firm, and knowledge of what world markets want can be a critical factor in determining what to work on. A Nigerian subsidiary might note that a certain tropical disease is rampant; perhaps as a result, our biochemists in Houston begin work on drugs to cure it. If they succeed, many Africans will lead happier and healthier lives, and the firm will substantially profit from its research on the disease. This ethical problem bothers many people, but without the proper incentives which permit the pharmaceutical companies to recoup research costs, the disease might not have been controlled.

Similarly, research on auto safety in the United States, perhaps mandated by law, may be used in Europe; or new electronic circuitry developed under contract for the U.S. Air Force might prove invaluable in air-traffic control in Asia. With the world as a marketplace to permit sufficient recouping of research costs, useful ideas can pop up in many places in many guises, hence enriching the firm.

The means through which R & D costs are recovered vary. For successful product introductions, the market price reflects, in part, the recouping of funds so that research on new products may continue. But for every successful new product, there may be literally dozens of projects that fail to materialize in marketable innovations. For basic research that has the potential of benefiting the entire company, the firm may recoup the costs through company-wide allocations, royalties, or technical assistance fees. For work specifically requested by overseas affiliates, however, as in the case of the Nigerian drugs cited above, the total cost of the project might be charged to the overseas unit.

Not all firms are innovative, and not all are or choose to be technological leaders. Whether the firm conducts its own R & D or not, all can benefit from the R & D conducted by others, either at home or abroad. U.S. firms would do well, for example, to look at French innovations in nuclear power and aviation, at German innovations in chemicals and pharmaceuticals, at Eastern European innovations in metallurgy, or at Japanese innovations in optics or production engineering. Cooperative research projects with foreign firms have become increasingly popular, especially projects involving "precompetitive research." One may acquire or merge with foreign research firms, or one may enter any number of viable agreements to license-in technology developed abroad.

The concept of precompetitive research collaboration has gained strong government financial backing in Europe in recent years. Its aim, in general, is to restore European competitiveness in certain high-tech fields by encouraging collaboration in basic research among firms that then directly compete against each other in applied research and subsequent product development. Thus Europe has promoted ESPRIT (the European Strategic Programme of Research in Information Technology) to encourage long-term research cooperation among European firms in the electronics sector. Participants in the project so far include GEC, ICL, and Plessey of Great Britain; Siemens, AEG, and Nixdorf of West Germany; Thomson-CSF, Honeywell-Bull and CIT-Alcatel of France; Olivetti and STET of Italy; and Philips of the Netherlands. The collaboration serves to foster innovation among firms handicapped in relation to U.S. and Japanese firms due to smaller national markets, less venture capital, and greater managerial conservatism. Another joint research committee brings together the automobile manufacturing firms of BL, Fiat, Peugot, Renault, Volvo, and VW; all collaborating to pool basic research on such issues as energy conservation, safety, and environmental protection. U.S. firms competing in these sectors should follow the progress of joint research efforts, not only to keep abreast of innovations in the field, but also as a purely defensive strategy of anticipating strategic moves by major competitors.

HUMAN RESOURCES MANAGEMENT

Companies invariably begin in a very restricted geographic environment. Their operations in all dimensions branch out from the center, but usually very slightly in early years. As the firm grows, it necessarily takes in a larger area, and it must hire managers, workers, and technicians who are also working in a broader geographical range. But the firm is still in one country, under a unified legal and economic system, with relatively homogeneous personnel. Even after decades of development, firms may retain a strong regional orientation. Often all key managers come from a very narrow segment of the total population. "Our kind of people" run the show, and anyone who does not accept this attitude can leave. Many do.

But continued expansion for a U.S. firm eventually leads to a national corporation, and in a heterogeneous society, outsiders are necessary to manage affairs. That Southern branch might be unmanageable, except by one familiar with local mores and folkways down there; key technicians no longer come exclusively from M.I.T., but also from Cal Tech and Purdue. The firm begins to understand that if it is to remain an expanding, viable organization, it must tolerate diversity. Yet some firms over fifty years old still have a strong regional flavor, even though they are spread over the entire country. The center manages; the branches respond.

Somewhere along the line, the firm makes its first foreign direct investments, often in a nearby country, such as Canada, and the foreign branch is brought into existence. The initial managerial predilection is to have its branch managers be as much like headquarter's types as possible; and indeed, in the days of gunboat diplomacy, it was not uncommon for a firm to send a full staff, all the way down to the janitors, to an enclave in some foreign country. The government-owned Panama Canal Company, among others, started this way.

In the modern world, however, it soon becomes apparent that foreigners find such enclaves undesirable. Virtually all countries have entry visa and work permit requirements for aliens, and such visas are increasingly difficult to obtain. Countries also often have laws restricting the percentage of foreigners who can work in given activities. Moreover, in the modern world, a totally foreign staff is extremely expensive.

So the company hires locals. In most cases, it would plan to use local workers anyhow, but increasingly it becomes more useful and much cheaper to employ local managers and technicians as well. This is politically astute as well as economically sound. If the firm is in a developed, highly industrialized country, it is quite likely that such personnel will be more efficient than foreigners anyway. They know the local language and culture, and they are as well trained as foreigners.

Many multinationals are presently at this stage. It is common to find as few as one, two, or even no Americans working at a European subsidiary employing 5,000 to 10,000 people. Even the subsidiary's manager is a local, usually because he or she is the best person available for the job. Foreign firms operating in the United States often show the same pattern in reverse. There are plenty of well-trained and highly skilled Americans to handle almost any job.

This emphasis on using locals often disappoints younger Americans who, having perhaps linguistic but no business experience, try to join a large firm in the hopes of travelling to far off places and seeing exotic parts of the world. But few young people go overseas in the private sector, since one must first learn the company, business, and industry before representing the firm abroad; and few corporate personnel of any age or experience really spend much time abroad these days. Only in Third World countries where skill levels are low, or in a few really critical positions requiring long years of managerial or technical experience, does one find many foreigners.

Events to this point are in part forced on the MNC by local law, in part by economic logic, and in part by the feeling that it makes good public relations sense to staff a local branch with local citizens. But nothing stays static for long. Top managers at home notice that some of those foreigners are doing a superb management job, better than anyone else at that corporate level. Sr. Gomez in Mexico, for example, a very able young branch manager for an American firm, is already head of Mexican operations. The MNC, having evolved to an organization having vice presidential control across country lines, is looking for a new vice president for the consumer-goods division. Gomez speaks fluent English and has an MBA from a good Mid-Western university. He has been to headquarters often, and people there like him. They like his managerial ability even better, since his group, by all objective standards, is the best in the company.

At this point, the firm is about to make a very fundamental strategic decision, namely whether this is an American-oriented firm where only Americans dominate top management, or a globally-oriented firm where the very best are chosen. Sr. Gomez is clearly from a different culture, he is Mexican and a Roman Catholic, and some of his views are bound to seem strange and different in the American headquarter's homogeneous environment. But he is unquestionably a superb manager.

To date, most American MNCs will go for the best American, most German MNCs for the best German, most Japanese MNCs for the best Japanese for corporate appointments. But a very few firms have, in effect, decided to join the entire world, to get the very best no matter where. This firm promotes Sr. Gomez to corporate vice president, and in that company from now on, all good people in all remote branches know that they are very much in the running to the top, if they really produce.

The scenario above may suggest one more reason for the very real power of the truly globally oriented firm. It can get the best from the world, not just from any one small corner of it. Its potential talent pool is widened enormously. The decision may be taken consciously, with top managers well aware of what long-term effects such a personnel decision will have, especially on the performance of their personnel overseas; or it may be a relatively casual, ad hoc decision. But in the end, the decision to see the world as a whole and take the very best inputs from it can have profound long-term consequences.

The internationalization of management cadres is a major step toward truly global operations. Major firms typically have rather detailed personnel plans for key positions, and they know far in advance who is likely to get promoted, retire, or otherwise be unavailable. Moreover, they have good people supporting present key managers and technicians, and if they begin a plan to consider foreign-country nationals, then it is only a matter of time before these people will move up to key positions. But if the personnel planning is provincial, then qualified foreigners will not be considered, and the firm will lose in the long run.

There are several reasons, however, why MNCs, at least in their initial expansion abroad, use home-country personnel to staff even the key foreign positions. Because of sometimes significant gaps in technical and managerial education, it is difficult to find highly qualified management talent in many countries. Moreover, cultural barriers often lead to the foreign national's unfamiliarity with Western business concepts. While foreign nationals unquestionably have a better understanding of the local environment, it takes considerable time for them to become sufficiently familiar with the policies and traditions of the headquarter's unit.

Today, most assignments abroad for home-country nationals are almost always of a temporary nature. Job rotation has become an essential element of executive training and development, and for the large multinationals with substantial investments abroad, foreign assignments are becoming more and more necessary in order for top executives to develop a basic appreciation of the multinational dimensions of the company, and to become familiar with the executive talent abroad. Such foreign assignments often lead to culture shock both going and returning, and are always expensive, but they are essential in the evolution of a truly multinational perspective.

Labor Relations

Labor relations are of course as strategic an issue for the MNC as for domestic firms, but the MNC, in addition, faces a multitude of problems in this area not faced by the purely domestic firms. MNCs are politically suspect, and trade unions everywhere are dubious about them. The MNC's flexibility of location cannot be matched by that of labor. Not only does this give the MNC an advantage, but it additionally undermines the bargaining power of unions at home. Strikes, for example, would be less effective if the MNC has alternative sources of supply from abroad for the same components or products manufactured by a local branch. This, at least, has been an argument on behalf of labor in its efforts to internationalize labor union activities, an inevitable consequence of the growth of MNCs.

The argument assumes, however, the existence of excess capacity in the foreign plants and the interchangeability of the output of various plants. Indeed, in some cases worldwide sourcing makes the MNC more, rather than less, vulnerable to strikes. For example, a 1974 coal strike in Britain led to a three-day work week in Ford's plants in that country, which forced Ford to cut production and employment in its West German plant, which was dependent on component supplies from Britain.

Efforts to internationalize trade unions have led to the establishment of international trade secretariats, organized by broad industry types and affiliated with national unions virtually everywhere. The power of the secretariats has been minimal, however, and they have not been able to exert any significant pressure on the MNCs. Their activities appear essentially limited to giving advice to local chapters, gathering varied information, and approaching international organizations (such as the United Nations) to get political support for their efforts.

A number of factors make multinationally coordinated collective bargaining by unions highly unlikely, at least in the foreseeable future. National customs and laws for example make it virtually impossible for a national union to recruit members in a foreign country and to bargain on their behalf. An exception here is the expansion of U.S. unions into Canada, although there exists notable friction between the Canadian and U.S. locals in such cases. In addition to such legal barriers, other factors include strong nationalism, union rivalries, in many countries a tendency toward bargaining at the plant level, and resistance by MNCs to the concept of multinational bargaining.[3] Cultural barriers are also relevant, as are historical antagonisms. Efforts to consolidate West German and British unions would be to little avail, given the wide variations in labor law between the two countries and the irreconcilable differences in both ideology and tradition.

Above all, the major interest of trade unions is to improve the position of labor in their own countries. If they are successful, then their members will do better economically than workers in other countries. Based on historic patterns, these differences can become quite huge. Some of the highest paid union workers (e.g., airline pilots) may well earn over $80,000 per year in some countries, while unskilled workers in other countries might earn $200 a year working ten hours a day and six days a week. Even international comparisons between workers in roughly equivalent jobs show variations of perhaps ten or twenty to one. The diversity of working conditions and pay has clearly undermined efforts to internationalize unions. Suppose that U.S. trade unions succeeded in forcing MNCs to pay U.S. wages in Haiti, where present wages are perhaps one twentieth of the U.S. rates. The net result would be that no MNC would operate in Haiti, given the relatively low efficiency of workers in that country.

Such problems are a key factor in the European Community's delay in approving its proposed social charter of workers rights in preparation for the "finalization" of the Community's economic integration in 1992. Workers in the northern tier countries (especially in West Germany) fear "social dumping", i.e., a competitive devaluation in the labor market due to the potential of losing jobs or having to take pay cuts or a deterioration in work conditions to avoid being replaced by workers from the member countries in which labor wages and standards are much lower. Realistically, it must be recognized that pay levels within the Community vary greatly, but so too the labor competitiveness and productivity. Discussions now underway on the issue suggest that the charter, once adopted, will call for "decent" wages and "adequate" unemployment compensation, leaving it to existing national arrangements to determine precisely what those levels should be.

We have mentioned that MNCs, taking a global view, frequently move to low-wage countries if their production process is labor-intensive. Of equal importance may be the work rules. Five decades of tough bargaining at home or in other developed countries can result in many restrictive work rules that inhibit productivity, but in many countries such work rules might not exist. In Western Europe, for example, MNC managers are faced with strict rules constraining their ability to lay off workers. If the firm expands into a less developed country, it might have the best of both worlds, namely lower wages and greater flexibility in regard to work rules. When the MNC moves to such locales, its runaway action in effect raises incomes in low-wage countries and lowers them (or perhaps more accurately, slows their growth) in high-wage countries. Trade unions at home are understandably upset by such actions. They fight to prevent runaway plants, and they lobby for laws that will keep the work at home. At times, they even succeed in such efforts. The usual result is that the country has high costs, declining exports, and sluggish economic growth, unless it is very lucky. MNCs from other countries take over third country markets, and workers are left with the home market, which is smaller than before because prices are now higher.

In theory, the MNC works for the world, while the union is provincial. However, the head of a union local in New Jersey that is losing jobs to foreigners has little choice but to fight for more controls. It is a difficult fight, since any given union, no matter how large, controls only a small piece of the total industry, and if the union wins, it loses. That is, the better it does, the more likely it will be that some other piece of the industry in some other country will be the winner, expanding and capturing new markets, while the unionized piece stagnates. The sad fact for too many workers is that if someone in the world is willing and able to do the same job for less money, he or she is likely to end up doing it. Astute trade union leaders know this, but it does not make their jobs any easier.

Governments, usually dependent on elections and in any case charged with the welfare of all citizens, not just that of the MNCs, tend to sympathize with labor, and every country has its own restrictive rules regarding labor practices. Often these rules work against the MNCs multinational expansion. Various forms of industrial democracy in Western Europe have given labor powers of a fully different nature than those possessed by labor in the United States. Thus in West Germany, through the institution of codetermination, labor has equal representation with management on the governing boards of the larger companies. In most cases, such boards are reluctant to allow the German firms to go abroad because of the perceived impact on employment

187

at home. Indeed, this way the very factor that delayed Volkswagen's move to the United States for about two years, letting the Japanese producers gain a valuable market share in the meantime. For American MNCs operating in West Germany, similar production decisions have been affected by labor's representation on the government board. For the unions (and governments), suboptimization is the name of the game, and if foreigners lose, well, that is their problem.

Or is it? Ford Motor Company decides to build an engine plant in Mexico instead of Detroit. The American trade unions object, but are insufficiently prepared to make concessions. Such discussions are not particulary harmonious, since unions perceive that they may lose hard-won gains in the process of negotiations. And they are right. But note the difficult bargaining problem. The union may well resist, but the engines will be built in Mexico, and jobs will be lost. If the United States imposes very high tariffs, these engines will go to Europe or Asia to fit into the global company's world cars, and only what is left of the American market will remain for the American auto union. It is a very difficult situation for any union. European experience is quite similar, and Japanese unions face the same problem now.

This whole process has been strongly influenced by two major factors. First, MNC management thinking has become increasingly global, and ideas such as building auto engines in Mexico are no longer rejected as too wild or infeasible. Competitors are producing in Mexico, and the MNC has to follow suit or lose key cost advantages. If the MNC does lose out on costs, it will inevitably begin to lose its world market share immediately, or become insufficiently profitable in the long run to keep pace with the capital expenditures of its competitors.

The second critical factor has been the gradual relaxation of trade barriers all over the world, in spite of much talk in recent years about increased protectionism and in spite of many temporary government measures to give domestic industries time to gain footing after several years of turbulence in world markets. We have by no means reached a state of totally free trade, but it is true that in many industries and sectors, trade can take place with little government interference. This liberalization may be more pronounced on a regional basis, such as that made possible by the formation of the European Economic Communities in 1958. But even on a global basis, mainly under the auspices of the General Agreement on Tariffs and Trade (GATT), trade negotiations have allowed Third World countries to export to rich countries much more easily than in the past. Tariffs have been reduced substantially in the developed countries. Political and economic developments in the late sixties and during most of the seventies significantly reduced barriers to trade with the communist countries, and conditions seem favorable today for a further expansion of East–West trade in general. Indeed, following the political developments in late 1989, during which every East European country, with the exception of Albania, introduced fundamental political and economic reform, we can anticipate a substantial increase of East–West trade in the 1990s. During the 1960s many of the less developed countries demonstrated outright hostility towards MNCs, but throughout the seventies such feelings were tempered by a more realistic appreciation of the role that MNCs play in their development process. As a result of all this, when the MNC examines the nature of the trade barriers that still exist, it may well find that what was infeasible just a decade ago is now quite possible.

The unskilled and semi-skilled workers in affluent countries are losing out the most in this development. Their wages tend to rise along with rising wealth in general. To the extent that it is labor-intensive production that is transferred to less affluent countries, it is the blue-collar workers in the developed countries who are in trouble. The highly skilled technicians and managers are much less vulnerable. Indeed, they may well find more employment options, as they spend some short periods of duty abroad helping to set up production systems. They will also stay home, along with management, and do the research and design work necessary for efficient operations.

There appears to be no easy way out of this problem as long as there are literally billions of unskilled workers ready to take jobs in poorer countries. The one viable option that Japan and others are working on is to automate and robotize home country plants, but this solution also eliminates blue-collar jobs. Every affluent country now has a welfare problem created by this global shift, and efforts to resolve the issue range from semi-permanent doles to very tight protection via tariffs and quotas in a few selected sectors.

If the end result is to restrict world trade, and to return to a more autarkic world, then the evolution of the global production system may well come to an early end. We will go back to production at home at higher costs, and income growth will slow. Productivity will decline, as countries begin once more doing things they are ill-structured to do, and MNC growth also will slow dramatically. Those many poor workers in Mexico will remain poor, and a few fortunate Europeans and Americans will temporarily do a bit better.

Whatever happens in this respect depends more on government and intergovernment activities than anything the MNCs do. The managers of MNCs can work within the system, but the system itself is beyond their control. This situation suggests why the MNCs, like it or not, are forever embroiled in political controversy. Their system is the most productive, and it is easy to demonstrate that this is so. But the system also involves potentially large losses for specific groups of people, so political pressures are certain. We discuss this further in the following chapter, but we mention it here due to its fundamental importance in the management of human resources.

Sustaining Morale

If labor relations seem intractable for many of the largest unionized firms, many others face great difficulty in keeping top technical and managerial personnel. Firms that thrive on technological innovation have quickly found that the care and nurturing of genius is a difficult task at best. Multinationals can pay well, provide good working conditions, and try to make sure that their R & D personnel are happy, but it is difficult to keep them happy. And if they are exceptionally good at what they do, and have an entrepreneurial spirit, as many of them do, they may well leave and set up a competing company. Very frequently one reads in the business press about a stock issue for a new high-tech firm that has some innovative concept or product with potential to change the world. At times, the new firm really does do great things, and a new high-flyer and potential MNC is born. Too many independent creative thinkers just don't like to work for big bureaucracies, and competition thrives. Meanwhile, those firms that manage to hang on to their share of the very scarce great talent continue to perform successfully.

Performance Evaluation

For top managerial personnel, it is the evaluation of performance that is critical. As with all other dimensions of the firm, the process of evaluation becomes increasingly complex as the firm becomes internationally involved. For example, a basic question, such as "What is this company worth?", is virtually impossible to answer when its assets are held in forty countries with forty different currencies. Since values fluctuate from day to day, and often represent accounting more than economic reality, the reported value of an MNC may fluctuate even by the hour. Thus a firm may have a plant in West Germany valued at $100 million. Today the German mark might be worth 1.74 to the dollar; tomorrow it is 1.72; last year, it was 2.21. What is this plant worth?

Such value questions are complicated by accounting practices as well. Under West German law, such a plant might be written off completely in five years; under American law, in ten years. The firm is American based. After five years, what does the MNC have in Germany? The German answer is nothing; the American answer is about $50 million (depending on what depreciation technique is used). Who is right?

All financial figures will be subject to the problem of currency conversion, including sales and cash positions. In an MNC, it is not known how much is sold in any given time period. Further complications arise because some currencies are inconvertible to foreign currencies. Knowing that you had a profit of 300 million Indian rupees from that branch operation this past year is all very well, but if you cannot bring the money out of India, what have you got?

Note that the questions above are very directly connected to accounting and financial operations. An extremely important aspect of both these disciplines is to give management feedback on results in an accurate, concise way, so that managers know what they are doing, and so that they can plan properly for the future. In both fields, the international dimension is a fast growing area, simply because MNC managers would like to know what is going on. So would tax collectors, consumer groups, trade unions, United Nations officials, and many other interested parties. But the very nature of the international monetary system and local accounting differences precludes any accurate measurement of results.

MNCs, in spite of not knowing completely what is happening, keep right on growing. How can they measure results? What many appear to do is to work out cash flows very precisely. If various branches, after suitable development periods, are generating healthy cash surplusses, then the MNC is probably doing well, no matter what the usual money measures show. If cash deficits are being incurred, as when a major expansion is underway, but if credit is available and prospects for surplusses in the future are bright, this is also a good sign. In short, MNC managers work, by necessity, with somewhat cruder evaluative techniques than their local counterparts.

The above does not preclude the use of refined and highly sophisticated money controls at the various local levels. Local managers are knowledgeable about cost accounting, budgets, and similar performance measures. Because they are, the firm does well locally in most cases. And back at headquarters, many highly skilled accountants and financial experts constantly struggle to refine and modify various evaluation techniques. But the very nature of the multinational problem makes such work extremely complex.

Managers usually assume, in discussing policy issues, that their staffs are first rate and competent, and that the information received from them is accurate. In the multinational world, such assumptions are not necessarily as valid as when the firm is local. Companies depend upon their information systems, and in the complex international world, no one can be sure that his or her system is completely accurate. The tools and techniques used abroad to assess performance are the same as at home. The difference lies in the difficulty of interpreting what is reported. Sales are rising and the company is doing very well in a particular country, but the revolutionaries there have recently won some important positions that may threaten the firm's stability. Sales in Brazil are skyrocketing, but there are reports that the Brazilian government will impose tough new exchange controls within a year, making it impossible for the company to repatriate those profits. Is the company as well off as it thinks? Here the financial experts and exchange rate forecasters may give sound advice, but it is a bit like forecasting the stock market. Even the best are not right every time.

Sales may also be skyrocketing in El Palo, but no one told the home office managers that under El Paloian accounting rules, sales on consignment are counted as firm sales. Here we need very good international accountants who are keenly aware of such local differences, and who can point to potential problems.

Physical measures of performance can be easier, but still difficult. Notions of what are adequate quality control checks can vary widely from one country to another, but in the end one can check the product and see if standards are being met. If the firm needs 50,000 four-cylinder auto engines a month from its Brazilian plant to go to Canada to be put in cars to be sold in the United States, management can count and see if performance was adequate. But even here problems arise. The Canadians may raise the import tariffs on engines, nullifying the careful calculations. A dock strike in Brazil can also foul things up, idling the Canadian operation. Labor laws in Italy can mean that we keep our personnel there fully employed, even though the plant must operate, under present conditions, at only 50 percent of capacity. And so on.

In the end, the MNC can make broad assessments of how well its chosen strategies are working. It may anticipate certain money and real growth in markets in given countries, and in a general way its managers can evaluate given data and come to conclusions about results. Overall financial results can be evaluated, subject to all the difficulties noted above. And any of the micro details about local personnel, quality control, production norms, pay rates, supplier relations, and much more can be analyzed with exactly the same tools that are used in the United States or any other advanced industrial country. The difference is always that the local environment may make some adaption necessary. One does not fire a Mexican manager because worker productivity is half the American average. In Mexico, that would mean that this manager is working at a level three or four times as high as the average Mexican industrial plant. Here one needs relevant comparative data, not absolute numbers; the harassed Mexican manager has to live with Mexican constraints, not European or American ones, and these can be very different. The way we measure worker productivity is exactly the same, but the numbers come out differently because of that environmental difference.

These evaluation issues are particulary difficult for provincial managers to understand, and much, much confusion has resulted when reported results seem wildly at variance with accepted home office norms. The problem of assessment is made more difficult by the very human attitude most branch managers have of trying to bail out from disasters. Perhaps sales are up 10 percent in Peru for this year, as compared to last year, in the local currency. The local manager will proudly call this to the home office boss's attention. But the value of Peru's currency might have fallen by 20 percent, so dollar sales are actually down. Moreover, assume inflation in Peru the past year was 80 percent, so a 10 percent sales gain is actually a serious loss. However, the whole economy had a nasty recession, and your main competitor's sales were actually off by 15 percent in local currency. Besides, your local manager averted a strike which paralyzed your industry there, and dealt brilliantly with the Minister of Commerce, averting a 20 percent increase in import tariffs. These positive facts should certainly be considered.

How good is your local manager? Should you fire him or promote him? Perhaps two of the MNC's four major goals for Peru last year were met, while two others were not. Was the manager responsible, or was it that dreadful, uncontrollable environment in which he was stuck that was the culprit? At this point, top management had better have some experts who can give unbiased reports on what is really going on in Peru. The top managers cannot know what is happening everywhere in the world, yet in the end they must know if they are to judge their branch managers properly; otherwise their company will stagnate. When a firm goes international, its communication needs expand because it needs enough information to properly evaluate its foreign branch in the multinational context.

Things get even more complicated when one compares branch managers to decide who deserves a promotion. The firm wants the best, yet it is very difficult to judge just how well the Peruvian performed compared to the El Paloian manager, who worked under quite different environmental conditions. Such evaluations can be made, but they require much more information and many more insights than we need judgments about our man in New Jersey compared to our woman in California.

In the end, good assessments can be made by MNCs, but they are based on factors more subtle and complex than any local assessments. The managers who have a truly global view of their company and the world, and who are keenly aware of how local environments can affect operations, will be better able to assess effectively. A provincial manager is likely to make some major errors, which is why that global view of the world, and the firm, is so critically important.

Given these evaluation problems, how is overseas performance measured? The way in which the profitability of foreign operations is measured varies considerably among and within firms. This variability depends, for example, on the function of the foreign unit (e.g., manufacturing versus marketing versus assembly operations); on the ownership pattern (e.g., fully owned subsidiaries versus joint ventures); on the organizational relationship to the parent company (e.g., licensee versus cooperation partner); and on corporate policy objectives set for the foreign operations (e.g., market-share and long-term growth versus more immediate pay-back criteria).

Whatever the case, as we have stressed above, it is critically important to clearly distinguish between evaluation of subsidiary or affiliate performance and the evaluation of managerial performance. It is entirely possible, (and frequently occurs), that a manager can do a superb job while his unit is doing very poorly, and vice versa. There are some things that neither the individual manager nor the parent company can control, such as rampant inflation and price controls or other arbitrary government decisions. Some factors are beyond the control of the individual manager, and are determined by the parent company, such as transfer pricing in order to optimize globally rather than locally. Unless the manager of the foreign unit is aware of corporate policy to evaluate him on things only within his control, he will be motivated at times to take steps in conflict with the intentions of the parent organization.

The management of human resources by the globally oriented firm is indeed a complex matter, and it requires shedding much cultural baggage which one inevitably acquires in one's earlier years. Very few firms have reached that stage. Coca-Cola has, which is one reason for its recent splendid performance. Its top officer comes from Cuba, and its next two ranking officers come from the Arab Middle East and the American Midwest. In that company, it is performance that counts.

SUMMARY

We have covered the various functional fields in international business in this chapter. Those interested in more details can explore the large literature now available on each function in an international context. Here, our interest was to note just how these functional areas impinge on top management of the globally oriented firm, how decisions made by functional managers must be coordinated across national boundaries, and how frequently a decision in one functional area has spillover effects on others that would not occur in a completely domestic situation. Because of these factors, top management becomes quickly involved, and critical problems of integration or differentiation cannot be shoved down the pyramid of command very easily. Local managers tend to think in provincial terms and to suboptimize in regard to operations. One of the critical jobs of top management is to help these people relate better to the global problems and opportunities of the company, and to indicate just how local activities do affect the total firm. Often this involves doing things which seem dysfunctional from the perspective of the foreign unit, but we have tried to indicate why this is necessary. Eventually, if the MNC cannot do this, it is unlikely to survive and prosper for long.

DISCUSSION QUESTIONS

1. What major factors make the financing of operations abroad much more problematic than the financing of domestic operations?

2. What are some of the practices commonly used to reduce the risk associated with exchange rate movements?

3. Countertrade seems to thrive during adverse economic conditions, and it may be used to gain competitive advantage as well as defensively. Discuss.

4. Why is the evaluation of managerial performance particularly difficult for the multinational firm?

5. Why does the multinational tend to conduct most of its research and development activities at home?

NOTES

1. S. L. Srinivasulu, "Strategic Response to Foreign Exchange Risks," *Columbia Journal of World Business* (Spring, 1981), 13–23.

2. Michael G. Duerr, *R & D in the Multinational Company* (New York: The Conference Board, 1970), 2–9.

3. David C. Hershfield, *The National Union Challenges the Multinational Company* (New York: The Conference Board, 1975), i–ii.

FURTHER READINGS

1. Henning, Charles N., William Pigoty, and Robert Haney Scott. *International Financial Management.* New York: McGraw-Hill, 1978.

2. Lessem, Ronnie. *Global Management Principles.* New York: Prentice Hall, 1989.

3. Levi, Maurice. *International Finance.* New York: McGraw-Hill, 1983.

4. Ramo, Simon. *The Management of Innovative Technological Corporations.* New York: John Wiley and Sons, 1980.

5. Roman, Daniel D., and Joseph F. Puett, Jr. *International Business and Technological Innovation.* New York: North-Holland, 1983.

CHAPTER 9

▼

Government Relations, Social Responsibility, and Conflict Resolution Strategies

▲

Until recently, most business firms could achieve respectable growth and profitability rates while focusing solely on domestic input and output markets. When the competition becomes global, however, or when competitors in the domestic market adopt a global orientation by scanning the world for critical inputs or for product markets, then the domestically oriented firm is placed at a distinct competitive disadvantage. The globally oriented domestic competitor may license-in a superior technology, enhance its price competitiveness through the use of imported components or intermediate products, and gain greater economies of scale through serving foreign markets. Consequently, competitive forces encourage all firms, not merely the giants, to become more globally oriented.

It is easy to demonstrate the efficiency gains associated with the global orientation, both at the level of the individual firm and at the level of aggregate allocative patterns. Nevertheless, such internationalization is not always viewed positively by others. In aggregate, global economic integration at the micro (firm) and macro (national) levels can mean rapidly growing world income, but any given country can also lose out, as resources and investments shift away from it. Even countries gaining a great deal may perceive, correctly, that some local groups (such as blue-collar workers in the developed countries) become adversely affected, at least in the short run, and are losing power in relative terms. Thus, even countries that gain significantly from the internationalization of business might resist the efforts of domestic companies to assume the global orientation. Politicians, trade unions, domestic supplier firms, and the general public in a country may see more losses than gains, and they may try to slow down the process of internationalization, which to them means a potential loss of jobs, income, and power. Many individuals outside the firm are affected by the firm's decisions along these lines, and top management must take this into consideration when planning its strategies.

Strategies can be devised, evaluated, and approved, but they must also be implemented to make the firm move. Although strategy implementation has typically been viewed as a final step in the strategic management process, it is such a critical step that strategy cannot be evaluated adequately without explicitly considering the firm's capacity to implement its strategy. This capacity to implement strategy, in turn, must be evaluated from the viewpoint that strategy implementation is an administrative task, and inherently behavioral in nature.

In this chapter we address the behavioral aspects of global strategies from the perspective of the firm's role in society. First, we consider the issue of corporate legitimacy. Next, we consider the issue of corporate social responsibility from the viewpoint of foreign governments that are hosts to the multinational corporation. Not all globally oriented firms are multinationals, of course, but the rich experience of the multinationals abroad contributes much to our understanding of the general climate in which foreign firms often operate. That climate is frequently a hostile one, and while this fact is by no means the full picture, we emphasize it here in order to stress the basic behavioral implications of foreign investment. Third, we consider the issue of corporate social responsibility of the globally oriented firm from the perspective of the home government. This perspective is sometimes in direct conflict with the perspective of the foreign government, and the multinational corporation is consequently often faced with the dilemma of meeting conflicting demands. As a result, strategies of conflict resolution, covered in the fourth section of this chapter, become a highly salient issue for the globally oriented firm.

CORPORATE LEGITIMACY

The privately owned corporation is fundamentally a creature of the law, and it must behave in a legitimate and socially responsible manner if it is to be allowed by society to function in the long run. All companies have a bewildering variety of legal and social constraints upon their activities, as societies try to manipulate these institutions to meet real or imagined social issues. Thus, in the United States, firms must observe antitrust laws, child labor laws, pollution-control laws, and other legislation. But the law may be obscure at times, and firms are constantly in court working out what the rules really are. Such legal tests establish precedents for future action for other companies, and reflect the fact that laws are not written in stone.

There are continuing debates in the United States, as elsewhere, about what precisely is meant by corporate social responsibility. Some still argue that the single social responsibility of privately owned firms is to make profits, while at the other extreme there are many in this world who believe that profit-making in itself is the epitome of irresponsibility. It does seem clear, however, that the issue of legitimacy involves considerably more than obeying the letter of the law, paying enough taxes to avoid invetsigation, and marginally adjusting to local economic conditions. For some companies it can mean giving to acceptable charities and performing routinely humanistic acts. When a flood occurs, the firm lends the community its trucks for aid, and does not send a bill. When a serious blizzard hits, the firm's canteen may serve as a relief center, even if it interrupts some of the firm's other functions. The firm may beautify its factories and offices, although no law says that it has to. Smaller companies can survive by doing a good business job, in the sense of making a good product, paying its workers reasonable wages, and simply trying to be economically efficient. But the larger firms are typically expected to do more, and truly outstanding corporate citizens accept duties far beyond those stated in the law.

For the multinational company, the expectations are even greater. Local firms, even large ones, escape some of the demands that are placed on foreign firms, simply because the public senses that the former belong to the community at large, while foreign enterprises are somewhat detached and thus suspect. Often the owners and managers of the local firms live nearby, and such firms can be counted on to give moral and financial support to important civic causes, such as rebuilding a decaying downtown. Both managers and owners may well be members of important civic committees, key members of the Chamber of Commerce, or important laypersons in local churches. If something happens within the firm that bothers local people, they know where to go to get redress.

Such factors are important to the multinational because, by definition, it is the outsider. The local manager may be a well-known person from nearby, but citizens sense that he does not really have much power to control the behavior of the firm that he nominally heads. To be sure, this problem can be somewhat alleviated if the multinational's affiliate adapts to local conditions. An American firm in Canada, or a West German firm in the United States, is likely to be quite similar to local firms. Its managers and technicians do things that Canadians and Americans understand and appreciate, and work processes are generally indistinguishable from those of locally owned firms.

A Western firm in Iran can be very alien, however. Foreign managers live lifestyles that locals find repugnant, and few Iranians are familiar with the types of work done in Western factories. Under such conditions, managers, both local and foreign, make demands that local workers find incomprehensible, and not occasionally distasteful. Perhaps the local Iranians who adopted Western ways were more repugnant to traditional Iranians than were foreigners. At least foreigners would eventually go home, but the Iranians would stay, and their lifestyles and thinking would change the traditional culture in basic ways. They became Westernized, scientifically and managerially oriented; their new values came into direct conflict with Iranian heritage. The conflict reached the point at which, overnight, many foreign based firms in Iran lost their legitimacy when the Shah's regime was overthrown.

Foreign observers noted, correctly, that the end result for Iran would likely be much lower incomes, deteriorating quality of life, and possibly political chaos. Such factors may not be important, however, when one's basic culture is threatened or when one's religious beliefs are brought into question.

There is at base, however, an even deeper, inherent conflict of interest between the multinational and the host country. The objectives of the multinational, which optimizes globally, are always to some extent incompatible with the policy priorities of national governments, which optimize locally. This poses no inordinate problem for developed countries, whose macroeconomic guidance mechanisms and regulatory policies are sufficiently sophisticated to assure compatibility of multinational corporate operations with national interests. Nor is it often a problem in communist countries, where the conditions of entry for multinationals generally assure performance in strict conformity to state guidelines and priorities. In many less developed countries, however, the frequent perception is that the affiliates of multinational firms are beyond control of the local administrations and that they often behave contrary to the interests of the state. In particular, there is concern that foreign firms control key sectors of the economy and behave in ways that make the implementation of key government policies ineffective. Indigenization laws (requiring majority ownership by nationals), exclusion of foreign firms from certain industries, pressures for local participation, restrictions against foreign personnel, and even expropriation are some of the direct means of addressing the problem. The introduction of much stricter operating rules is indirectly aimed at the nation's gaining control of foreign owned operations.

These actions stem from fundamental concerns over the very legitimacy of the globally oriented firm. Often the host countries have fully valid complaints about the consequences of foreign-controlled operations on their soil; but overreaction to the real or perceived conflicts between multinational corporate behavior and the interests of the host states has often placed the multinational in a "no-win" situation. For example, if the multinational brings in the latest, modern technology, that technology is often inappropriate because it is typically labor-saving technology; the less developed country suffers from high unemployment and underemployment, and thus needs labor-creating technology. If the multinational brings in more appropriate (e.g., labor-creating) technology, it is then accused of selling outmoded machinery and equipment at inflated prices and keeping the host country technologically behind and thus continuously dependent on foreign sources for new technologies. This is not simply a problem of securing machinery and equipment more suitable for capital-rich and labor-scarce countries, however. Multinationals tend to build large plants abroad compared to the existing domestic plants, which are geared predominantly only to the domestic market. But for a given product, the efficient large plant tends to be more capital intensive than the efficient small plant. Moreover, less developed countries often encourage the use of modern equipment through investment incentives. For example, they sometimes provide for accelerated depreciation of plant and equipment as well as the right to import capital equipment without payment of duty. Others clearly insist on the latest of technologies and equipment for reasons of prestige, or in order to somewhat alleviate the widely perceived technology gap that confronts these less developed countries.[1] Inevitably, the multinational's behavior is subject to valid criticism from one faction or another no matter what the firm does.

Other examples of these conflicting pressures and responsibilities abound. If the multinational repatriates the bulk of its profits, it is perceived to be depriving the country of the newly created wealth; if it reinvests the profits in the host country, it is perceived to be further increasing its control of the economy. If the multinational pays the going rate of wages, it is perceived to be exploiting cheap labor and gaining excessive profits; if it pays more than the prevailing wages, it is perceived to be siphoning off the best of the labor supply and rendering local firms noncompetitive. The multinational exports from the host country and brings in foreign exchange, but according to some, does not use enough local components and therefore stifles the supplier industry; however, when the multinational is forced by local regulations to use more domestic suppliers for components, the inefficiency of the local industries leads to high prices, making it impossible for the multinational to compete further on international markets and to bring in the foreign exchange. If the multinational does not promote local managerial talent, some feel it is discriminating against them; if it does promote that talent, some feel it is guilty of the "brain drain." Whatever it does, it creates some negative repercussions.

For this reason, multinationals serve as convenient targets when governments, especially in the developing world, are unable to satisfy the needs and aspirations of their people. This creates one mammoth public relations task for the firm, and places its very legitimacy in question. The multinational is big, and draws the hostility of those who see it as smothering the small local entrepreneur and threatening to dominate the domestic economy. The multinational is foreign, and is seen as an alien influence subverting the indigenous culture and acting as a tool of its home state. The multinational is typically private, and is viewed as a rapacious pursuer of its own gain at the expense of the public welfare.[2] Above all, it is the most visible symbol of a world-order that allegedly systemically discriminates against the less developed countries, and in that sense the legitimacy of the multinational corporation is inherently subject to dispute.

This problem of defining socially acceptable behavior is greatly exacerbated by the fact that what is considered quite legitimate in one country is often fully unacceptable in another. We shall discuss some of these issues later in this chapter, but note that it is all part of the larger dilemma that the globally oriented firm faces. Firms have to live within the local environment as well as the global environment. The large multinational faces the problem of conforming to anywhere from 2 to 150 societies, each with its own laws, customs, traditions, and culture. What is an abomination in one culture is the norm in another, and realization of this fact must be built into the decision-making process of the multinational. Thus the issue of legitimacy is a very complex one for the multinational, which is forced to cope with conflicting requirements far beyond its control. The globally oriented firms are not the uncontrollable rogue elephants that many people consider them to be. But often, whatever they do is considered by someone, somewhere, somehow, to be completely unacceptable. Thus the question of legitimacy is a much more salient issue for the multinational than for the domestic firm, which operates basically under a single, relatively clearcut set of rules, values, and expectations.

THE FIRM'S RELATIONS WITH HOST GOVERNMENTS

Underlying the legitimacy dilemma of the globally oriented firm are fundamentally different philosophical perspectives. The economic policy orientation of the Western industrialized countries, and also that of the major international institutions (the International Monetary Fund, the General Agreement on Tariffs and Trade, and the International Bank for Reconstruction and Development, or World Bank), tends to focus on the maximization of economic growth, efficiency, and the optimal allocation of resources for national growth in the context of a global economy. It is in connection with these policy priorities that the major Western states and institutions encourage specialization, free trade, and the production of goods and services based on comparative advantage. It is a positive-sum view of international economic relations based on mutual advantages and minimal conflicts of interest between the participating states.

In contrast, the economic policy orientation of the less developed countries is based on quite different priorities. While growth and efficiency are clearly desirable objectives, equally important objectives are to create a more equitable income distribution among countries and to sharply increase economic self-determination of the less developed countries. These two latter goals are frequently interpreted by leaders in the less economically developed countries as being incompatible with the increased integration into the global economy, and are thus frequently in conflict with the tenets of Western economic policies. That is, the economic orientation and priorities of the industrialized nations are viewed as inherently exploitative, in the sense that the relationship between the rich and poor countries appears to favor the rich and to sustain the dependency position of the poor. This essentially zero-sum view of international economic relations leads to policy prescriptions quite different from those that are associated with the market orientation of the industrialized nations. Consequently, there is also a fundamental difference of opinion between developed and less developed countries in regard to the legitimacy of multinational corporate behavior.

It is easy to find specific examples of corporate behavior that is legitimate in one country but not in another, but it is important to note here that the question of legitimacy is not solely one of specific government policies or corporate practices, but also one of philosophical orientation. This conflict is most obvious in the case of market-oriented Western firms operating in the plan-oriented communist countries. It is also evident in the case of Western multinationals operating in many of the less developed countries. In brief, national economic policies and corporate strategies that are appropriate for Western industrialized countries are not necessarily appropriate for, or compatible with the interests of, the less developed countries.[3]

During the 1970s, as many governments in the less developed world gained experience and confidence in dealing with multinationals, the environment for multinational firms investing in the Third World became much harsher. The rules of the game were changed unilaterally to assure closer compatibility of multinational operations with national interests. There were outright expropriations, as in the oil industry, and creeping expropriation, as in the manufacturing sectors, through which foreign subsidiaries were forced to take on local partners. Severe limits were placed on profit repatriation, interest and royalty payments, and other financial flows to foreign parent firms. Subsidiaries faced demands to reduce prices, limit imports, increase exports, use more local labor and components, and borrow less local capital.

One result of all this is that multinationals frequently appear to be shifting their operating strategies in response to every new or potential threat that appears. On the other hand, there do appear to be predictable patterns on which the multinational might base its long-term strategy. One set of such regularities relates to the nature of competition in less developed countries, and another to the way in which national attitudes towards multinationals change over time.

The competitive strength of the multinational lies in its ability to provide what is needed most in the less developed country: essentially a combination of capital, access to markets, and human skills and technology. The strengths of the multinational are typically greatest when it first establishes a subsidiary in the host country. Thereafter, the relative strengths decline and the bargaining power of the multinational obsolesces. Once the plant is built, the mineral discovered, or the skills transferred to nationals, the multinational is increasingly vulnerable. Less vulnerable, of course, are those multinationals that maintain control over critical components or markets, or that are on the leading edge of rapidly changing technologies. This vulnerability has been greatly exacerbated in recent years by intensified competition among multinationals for the major Third World markets. No longer is Latin America an area ceded by others to American multinationals, or French-speaking Africa an area mainly for French multinationals. Multinationals from the developed, industrialized countries now clearly see the world as their beat, and industrial firms based in the more rapidly developing countries of the Third World are also spreading multinationally. One consequence of this is that the total investment package typical of perhaps a decade ago is becoming increasingly unbundled, as less developed countries play off one multinational against the other for specific components of investment (i.e., marketing channels, capital equipment, or technology) rather than for the package in its entirety. Especially in the more mature product lines, licensing agreements or other cooperative arrangements tend to replace direct investment.

But the phenomenon of the obsolescing bargain is not universal. Changes in products, technologies, and markets periodically serve to restore the bargaining power of the multinational, and new alliances with domestic firms may well serve to buttress the foreigner's position in any given market. It is out of this congeries of trends and possibilities, according to Vernon, that each multinational corporation must build its strategies in the less developed countries.[4]

It is also important to note that changing economic conditions can lead to a reversal of host country policies in this regard. In May 1989, for example, Mexico announced a sweeping liberalization of its foreign investment rules. The move was designed to attract foreign capital to stimulate economic growth, which for years has been depressed by the consequences of low oil prices and a massive foreign debt burden. The liberalization is part of Mexico's process of opening the economy to global economic forces, reflected above all in the decision to join the General Agreement on Tariffs and Trade (GATT) in 1986. The relaxation and in some cases reversal of the stringent foreign investment rules that had been applied in Mexico can lead to new opportunities for foreign-based enterprises, and reduce the difficulties they have had in the past of reconciling global strategies with specific operating requirements.

Public Relations Strategies

The public relations function in purely domestic firms has typically been of relatively little importance. In the multinational corporation, however, as we shall see, the public relations function often holds a critical and highly prestigious position. One reason for this is that the demands of the office clearly surpass those of its counterpart in domestic firms. Multinationals face critical government relations problems wherever they go, not, of course, just in the Third World. In Europe, in many key sectors, they must compete directly against state-owned firms, which changes the rules of the game considerably. They must also adapt to very stringent labor standards and performance disclosure requirements. Because they pursue global rather than national strategies, the multinationals are suspect wherever they go. And in the industrialized nations, this problem is made worse by the apparent tendency of many governments to give less and less importance to purely market mechanisms in that they are pursuing protectionist national strategies that restrict international competition.

Thus, public relations is crucial to the globally oriented firm, given the highly volatile political environment in which it operates. At one extreme, the multinational has been subjected to expropriation or nationalization virtually throughout the world. At the other extreme, it has been able to secure extremely favorable conditions under which investment is made or operations continued. But nowhere are the multinational's actions consistently perceived to be fully legitimate. Here the public relations strategy of the firm takes on added dimensions.

The function of public relations aims not only at projecting an image of legitimacy and social responsibility, but also at representing the firm's viewpoint on relevant policy decisions made by the government and at exerting influence to obtain favorable operating conditions (such as permits, subsidies, etc.).[5] These tasks should be performed in a very low-key manner, due to the sensitivity of many countries to what they perceive as foreign interference. Nevertheless, public relations are critically important in addressing acute problems.

How acute the problems are depends on a number of factors. No amount of public relations will help in cases such as Cuba, where, for ideological reasons, the government indiscriminately nationalizes all foreign assets in the country. Thus the nature of the government and the direction in which it appears to be heading are factors that are of vital concern to the public relations personnel. The French government nationalized several sectors during the early eighties, and it required intensive public relations work to help negotiate the terms of the eventual agreements reached between the government and the MNCs.

Some economic sectors require a greater public relations effort than do others. The extractive, agricultural, and infrastructural industries, for example, have been found to be much more vulnerable to expropriation than others. These are industries that are clearly of national importance. The recent scarcity of many raw materials, and the heavy dependence of some countries on the exploitation of these materials, strengthened the desire of many countries to regain full control over their natural resources. By its nature, agriculture is a highly emotional issue, for sovereignty itself implies that the land belongs to the people. MNCs active in agriculture or mining (including oil operations) easily become the target for local radicals or other aggrieved people, particularly given the image of wealthy foreigners living in the midst of general poverty. The infrastructural industries (including utilities, communications, and transportation) are sectors naturally sensitive to foreign involvement since control of them is deemed necessary, even in the developed countries, for the proper implementation of public policy. The sensitivity of these industries to foreign operations varies from country to country, but generally, the more important it is economically, the more vulnerable a given sector will be to government intervention (such as a country's depending on one or two basic commodities for 70 percent of export earnings).

Some sectors are not politically sensitive, or are not a source of national pride or income, and in these sectors the public relations effort need not be stressed. A producer of toys, for example, especially if its operations are not sizable, will escape the public notice. So too will those firms following the adage: when in Rome, do as the Romans do. Some highly visible major multinationals, such as Woolworth's or Marks and Spencer, have done this so well that many people do not even know that their affiliates are foreign owned. For such firms, it is common to find no foreigners at all in the local branch, and the local CEO is typically a person of influence and prestige.

Keeping a low profile is generally an excellent public relations strategy. Many billions of dollars of Indian capital have been invested in other countries, but few have ever heard of the companies. If the Ajax Tool Company in Boston is owned (via an Andoran holding company) by a person from Hong Kong, then few people are likely to know or care. And if the same individual owns the Starlight Motel in Wyoming, or the Plains Peanut Packing House in Georgia, then no pattern emerges. The foreign owner may do interesting things with intracorporate transfer pricing and the like, but as long as he more or less follows local laws and customs, his public relations bill can be very small indeed.

The problem is, most MNCs are extremely visible because they are extremely successful. The public relations task then becomes one of proving to suspicious locals that the firm's net contribution in the country is highly positive. In effect, the MNC argues that it plays a positive-sum game: when it wins, locals also win. Few will deny this. Still, the MNC must cultivate local journalists, politicians, lawyers, trade union leaders, religious people, and other persons of influence and power. In the end, MNCs are only tolerated when it is perceived locally that their net contribution to the economy is far greater than their cost. Indeed, perhaps the best public relations the MNCs have is what happens to countries that keep them out. The usual results, namely stagnation and backwardness, do not appeal to many political leaders for long. A classic situation is the revolution, followed by confiscation, followed by economic decline, followed by some sort of reentry by the multinational. Countries that have fully severed ties to the multinationals, such as Albania and Burma, are not seen in many circles as highly desirable models.

Public relations lies at the very core of the multinational's survival. If it is evicted, the whole game ends, and there are always strong local groups aiming at precisely that. It is common to find that the vice president for public relations occupies a critical role in the multinational firm, and that his task clearly exceeds in importance the task of his counterpart in a purely domestic firm. He or she has to justify constantly the firm's reasons for existence, and if this effort fails, then all is lost. Public relations work in the international arena is rarely delegated very far down the corporate pyramid, and major public relations efforts typically require top management approval and monitoring, if not participation.

THE FIRM'S RELATIONS WITH THE HOME GOVERNMENT

The recession in the West during the early 1980s fostered increasingly intensive economic competition among Western industrialized nations. Industrial policies introduced by governments to revitalize domestic industries have led, in effect, to what Barton refers to as technology-based mercantilism.[6] This new form of protectionism complicates considerably the firm-level choices in regard to product design, facility location, and competitive strategy. The protectionist measures apply not just to the troubled smoke-stack industries, but more and more to the industries of the future, as governments attempt to ensure their nation's competitiveness in the high-technology sectors.

The industrial policies of subsidizing and otherwise aiding the development of domestic industries are often linked to trade policies restricting international competition. The U.S. Congress has on its agenda the consideration of literally scores of protectionist bills. The French government is pushing for the "Europeanization" of certain high-technology industries, aimed in part at assuring that a high percentage of components for the resultant products are manufactured in Europe. Canada's "world product mandate" gives subsidization priority to Canadian firms producing for global markets. Around the world, governments of the major trading nations are taking steps to enhance the global competitiveness of their industries. Sensitivity to national priorities requires highly sophisticated analytical skills on the part of corporate management, especially since government policies and priority objectives necessarily shift over time. And for the American multinational, it is especially important to remain highly sensitive to the U.S. government's priorities along these lines.

Note first the general problem. Political power is lost when the production system assumes a global orientation. No longer can the U.S. Congress enact laws telling auto companies what to do when half the industry is beyond the jurisdiction of U.S. law. Foreign countries also have limited power in this situation. Politicians may well prefer less wealth and more power. But in most countries the outcome of the political process is still uncertain, and in spite of many, many complaints, the world trading system has tended to become increasingly and remarkably liberal.

This straightforward approach to thinking about production on a global basis gets even more complicated when one considers military and diplomatic power. The United States can pass new laws and raise tariffs to prohibitive levels to keep out any production the country chooses. But this may well mean that the Japanese or Europeans will come to dominate the industry, as it shrinks back to a high cost base in America. Now, what diplomatic influence does the United States have in such a case? The probable answer, very little, does not thrill U.S. diplomats. For example, if we ban Mexican engines or Japanese cars while negotiating mutual defense treaties, how will the Mexican and Japanese governments respond? The probable answer also does not please military thinkers.

We begin with the problem of where to build an auto engine, and we end up discussing grand, strategic diplomatic and military issues. But this is inevitable, because these engines, and other products, represent both wealth creation and income for a number of countries. They also represent the potential economic linkages of dozens of countries into an inseparable configuration quite new in this world. From 1955 to the present, the increasing globalization of the world production system has worked very well in the West, as per capita incomes have perhaps quadrupled or at least doubled in most industrial countries, as well as in quite a few newly industrializing countries. This new wealth and economic power is important to everyone. But no one has yet figured out how to avoid the inevitable social and political costs, and as the system accelerates toward total internationalization, problems grow. The multinationals can point proudly to their role in the creation of this wealth, but they also have to bear the heat from those who do not do as well. In the end, the future will depend really on how countries decide to join the world, or conversely on how they decide to leave the world and become isolationist again.

There is a political risk-assessment problem here that is absolutely critical for any multinational. If an engine plant is built in Mexico, and if the United States and Western Europe ban these engines, then the multinational loses a lot of money. But if the international trading system becomes more liberal, than failing to build in Mexico would give the advantage to competitors who took the risk. Top managers may literally be betting the entire company against a set of environmental constraints that they can only indirectly influence. It can be a very high-risk game.

Since the early 1970s, U.S. labor unions in particular have argued that the international involvement of American firms has been detrimental to American interests. One of the contentions is that U.S. firms export jobs through a variety of activities such as serving foreign markets from subsidiaries located abroad instead of through exports; moving labor-intensive operations to low-wage areas throughout the world and then importing into the United States goods once produced at home; and destroying export markets abroad by creating future competitors through the licensing of technologies abroad. High unemployment in many sectors of the economy during the 1970s gave political clout to such arguments.

Labor's concern about the multinationals is, of course, not merely a question of exporting jobs. One perceives also that the bargaining power of labor in relation to the multinationals is weakened through the relative immobility of labor. That is, the individual worker is largely stuck to one geographical area, whereas the multinational can relocate worldwide wherever it wishes to, depending on, among other things, favorable labor contracts. Thus, the firm can play-off workers in one country against those in another in search for better terms.

These issues are the center of intense debates, but can probably not be resolved except on a case-by-case basis. In many instances, foreign investment has led to a substantial increase in the export of components and machinery to support the foreign operations. In other cases, even if exports are sharply reduced as a consequence of foreign investment, the firm has no choice except to invest abroad or lose the market completely to other firms that are willing to invest in the foreign country. In particular, the direct effect of foreign investment on exports cannot be determined except through a detailed analysis of the countries, conditions, companies, and products involved.

Some highly labor-intensive products must be produced abroad or not at all by the firm, given competitive conditions. In this case, jobs are created abroad by relocating production in low-cost labor areas. Some countries, especially given the serious debt crisis of today, have completely banned the import of many products, so that the firm that wishes to serve those markets is forced to locate abroad. In aggregate, however, it might be safe to assume that foreign investment by U.S. firms creates white-collar employment at home and displaces blue-collar employment at home. While the government's policy on such matters tends to be neutral overall, there are strong spokesmen in government, especially in Congress, to support labor on such issues.

Not all industries are labor intensive of course, and multinationals have other motivations for going abroad. Certain firms are dependent on extractive raw materials, and locate abroad where such materials can be found. In such cases, the financial, managerial, and technological contributions of the multinationals have played a very basic role in the development of both production and markets for countries initially lacking sufficient resources to exploit their materials base themselves. But the MNCs must be sensitive to the political consequences of their actions because political controversy rapidly emerges. Indeed, the origins of OPEC and its pricing and embargo practices are closely associated with the perception by national governments that the multinationals were unfairly taking advantage of them. The extractive industries in particular have proven to be especially vulnerable to the expropriation or confiscation of multinational assets by host governments. In such cases, the U.S. government inevitably gets involved, and its involvement is not always in favor of the multinationals in question.

Firms competing on the basis of high-technology advantages also become involved in political controversy, as reflected in the running battle between IBM and Western European governments over the company's share of the EEC market. Firms involved solely in consumer goods, and luxury items at that, also run into problems. Coca-Cola Company pulled entirely out of India due to that government's insistence that the company reveal to nationals the formula of its major soft drink. No matter what the nature of the industry, political controversy is a fact of life for multinationals, both at home and abroad, and the U.S. government is consequently involved.

But how and to what degree the U.S. government enters the picture are highly circumstantial. The United States does not have an overall, coherent policy towards foreign investment or trade, and thus its position is highly ambivalent. Instead, our government's policy towards trade and investment matters has been subordinated to other, overriding concerns. The policies that affect trade and foreign investment are diverse in nature, and indeed often conflicting among themselves. Moreover, decisions bearing on trade and foreign investment issues are often made with little consideration of their implications for trade or the competitiveness of U.S. firms, which creates a great deal of uncertainty for the globally oriented firm.

One reason for the U.S. government's ambivalent approach to trade matters is that U.S. trade policies are highly fragmented and implemented by numerous and diverse administrative units. The Department of Commerce is concerned with the international competitiveness of American industry. The Department of State gives priority to foreign policy matters, and the Department of Defense is concerned primarily with national security. The Department of Agriculture, the Treasury, and SEC all have their own priorities. Yet each of these units has a very substantial voice in the determination of trade policies, and internal disagreements are frequent. Add to this the fact that it is Congress, rather than the executive branch, that is granted constitutional powers to regulate trade, and the politicization of trade policies is certain. If the steel industry is protected against foreign competition, the auto industry pays through higher input prices and reduced competitiveness. If the textile industry is provided protection against Chinese imports, that country retaliates by reneging on anticipated purchases of American grain. These are inevitably political issues, and they affect the distribution as well as generation of income.

U.S. Government Policies Supporting Business

To be sure, the U.S. government has some tools to help American business in general, in addition to the macroeconomic policies that are so important in establishing the fundamental environment of business. Tariffs protect some industries, although this form of protection goes against the grain of the country's basic trade orientation. Anti-dumping duties are sometimes applied on foreign goods sold at less than fair value in this country. Countervailing duties are sometimes applied when imports into the United States have benefited from foreign government subsidies. The escape clause and market disruption procedures provide potential redress in case injury has been caused to domestic producers through rapid import surges. Orderly marketing arrangements have been negotiated, for example with Japanese auto producers, concerning the levels of imports into the country. The procedures in applying the remedies noted above are often not fully satisfactory, and the implementation is far from consistent because the administration may typically waive the protection if it is determined to be in the interest of the country to do so. In any event, invoking such measures requires ongoing contact between the firm and government.

The U.S. Export-Import Bank helps finance the export of big-ticket items, such as aircraft. However, it has typically suffered from budget constraints and has seldom been able to offer terms on a sufficiently flexible level to compete with the official export credit arms of European governments. The Commodity Credit Corporation provides export financing for agricultural goods, but has often been undercut by European credits which mix aid with trade financing. Foreign economic aid is typically tied to the purchase of American goods, and the Commerce Department has a variety of export promotion programs. Probably more important than any of these, however, have been the general efforts of the U.S. government, both under the auspices of GATT and through bilateral negotiations, to establish the basic ground rules of international trade and investment. Recent efforts along these lines have gained substantially from intensified input from the business community, although progress has been understandably slow. Meanwhile, initiatives at the state level throughout most of the fifty states have been largely successful in stimulating exports and in inducing foreign direct investment in the states.

The Conflict Between Economic Policy and Foreign Political Policy

Apart from the measures just mentioned, the government has pursued a number of policies that have been largely detrimental to American business interests in many respects, at least according to large numbers of firms. The general complaint is, that the United States pursues domestic economic policy (such as antitrust regulations) and foreign political policy (such as the embargo on the Soviet-West European pipeline) with no regard to the effects on the overall competitiveness of American firms on international markets. Some of the more salient issues are discussed below.

Apartheid

South African apartheid policies have become a highly controversial foreign policy issue of the American Government. On the one hand, a "divestment campaign" that has gained considerable support calls for legislation, already enacted by a number of states and cities, prohibiting the investment of public or pension funds in U.S. companies that operate in South Africa. In 1984 the U.S. House of Representatives amended its version of the Export Administration Act to require that American firms with investments in South Africa adhere to the Sullivan Principles, which since 1977 have been a strictly voluntary code of standards for equal treatment of people of all races and for explicit aid to South African blacks through training, education, and housing programs. Those who favor the withdrawal of foreign investments from South Africa contend that such investments support and perpetuate the white minority government at the expense of the well-being and human rights of the black majority.

The administration has opposed the proposed sanctions, mainly on the grounds that U.S. companies in South Africa act within the system as a force for racial integration in that country. The proposed sanctions, it is argued, would prompt American companies to pull out of South Africa and thereby worsen rather than improve the plight of South African workers. Beyond that, the current administration is concerned with continuing its "constructive engagement" with South Africa in order to maintain some influence in a continent that is deeply troubled politically. Businesspeople in general point out that if U.S. business does withdraw, there would be virtually no effect on South Africa's apartheid policies since many of the plants and facilities which would be left behind would be quickly purchased, at rock-bottom prices, by less constrained competitors from Europe and Japan. In the long run, it is contended, increased standards of living brought about by the foreign investment will induce economic pressures that eventually will lead to the demise of apartheid.

Foreign Corrupt Practices Act

The Foreign Corrupt Practices Act of 1977 was aimed essentially at preventing the bribery of foreign officials by American businessmen in order to gain or maintain business abroad. Framed during the aftermath of the Watergate scandal, the legislation applies to corrupt practices at home as well as abroad, and imposes relatively severe sanctions (up to five years in prison and $1 million fines). The legislation was enacted on ethical grounds, but also out of concern about the image of the

United States abroad, and about the possible misallocation of resources through unfair competition. Whatever the merits of the letter and intent of the law, it is essentially flawed according to many observers. The legislation, and so far the courts, have not yet clearly distinguished between what is and is not illegal. The law is ambiguous and so far lacks sufficient interpretative case law to provide concrete standards of behavior. Some forms of payment to foreign officials are permitted, and others are not, but no clear distinction is made between the two. The language of the act indicates that the duties performed by the individual receiving payment, not the intent of the payor, is the important factor in determining the legality of the payment. Moreover, liability arises from proof of making payments "corruptly," which is also not defined in the act. Throughout the act, such vagaries as "having reason to know" are left unexplained.

Probably the strongest complaint brought by businessmen against the act derives from its unilateral nature. Foreign competitors are not only untouched by the law, but indeed are sometimes encouraged by their own tax laws to extend bribes which increase the competitiveness of the firms. Were every major country to introduce antibribery legislation, few businesspeople would object, since bribery is an expensive way of conducting business. But it places U.S. businesses at a competitive disadvantage to have to follow laws that others do not have to follow, especially when bribery is rampant in some of the world's most lucrative markets. Thus, while the purpose of the law is fully defendable, its implementation has been far from satisfactory.

Human Rights Legislation

This legislation authorizes the withholding of financial credits from, and the placing of export controls on, foreign countries that violate our concept of human rights. Like the anti-apartheid and antibribery efforts, this legislation is associated with highly ethical issues over which few would argue. Implementation, however, has been flawed in several regards. The legislation has been unevenly and inconsistently implemented, in that priority concerns have prompted exemptions in significant cases, for example, earlier in the Shah's Iran and in the Philippines, two flagrant violators of the established standards. The legislation has been counterproductive in some cases, in that it initially contributed to a tightening up, not a loosening, of Soviet policy towards the emigration of Jews in that country. The legislation has been viewed by others as interference in their domestic affairs, a charge induced by other pieces of U.S. legislation as well. And businesspeople complain, as so often is the case, that it places a unilateral constraint on them which gives their foreign competitors distinct advantages.

U.S. Strategic Controls and Embargoes

These have been aimed primarily at the Soviet Union, and they subordinate U.S. business interests to those of national security and foreign policy. When the Soviet Union invaded Afghanistan, a U.S. grain embargo on the Soviet Union gave Argentina the opportunity to replace American sales in that market. Caterpillar was no longer permitted to sell construction equipment to the Soviet Union, so Komatsu of Japan took over its 85 percent share of that huge market, becoming internationally competitive by doing so. The U.S. administration attempted (unsuccessfully) to block the equipment supplies for the Siberian–Western Europe pipeline, thus drawing complaints from Europe about the extraterritoriality of U.S. laws. American companies, although often having the world's leading technologies, have become suppliers of last resort in markets that they once dominated. Few American businesspeople would question the necessity of placing national security interests above those of business concerns. They do find it frustrating, however, when their contracts are simply replaced by those of West European or Japanese competitors, and argue that our government should take into consideration the foreign availability of similar goods when imposing trade embargoes.

There are many similar issues. Our antitrust laws, proposed environmental protection laws, anti-Arab boycott rules, and tax laws all fail in general to sufficiently take into consideration the changing configuration of international competition. Clearly there are some issues that are of such overriding importance that the competitiveness of American firms on international markets is of peripheral concern. But in many cases, business interests have been neglected in part through the failure of business to present its case to the U.S. government in a positive and effective manner. Under today's competitive conditions, it is imperative that U.S. business adopt a firmer and more participatory approach to government relations, especially in its own home country.

CONFLICT RESOLUTION

Should Dresser's French subsidiary have exported gas pipeline compressors to the Soviet Union in 1982? It was ordered not to do so by the American government, and to do so by the French government. Should an American firm's subsidiary in South Africa accept the practice of apartheid, as the South African government insists? If it does, other units of the firm will be subject to boycotts and harsh criticism from many circles. Clearly, the mandate "When in Rome, do as the Romans do" is not always feasible for the firm that has to weigh conflicting claims of legitimacy against each other. Socially responsible behavior varies from country to country, and the multinational is frequently caught in conflicts that are beyond its power to resolve. These and many other issues already discussed suggest that methods of conflict resolution are of considerable importance to the multinational or globally oriented firm.

Even domestic firms face conflicts, of course. However, conflicts involving the MNC vary much more widely in terms of content, frequency, intensity, forms of expression, and duration. This is probably due to the diverse economic, social, political, and institutional contexts in which the MNC operates. Conflicts can arise at home over a domestic matter, as when unemployment results from an MNC's new operations in a low-wage country. Conflicts can arise at home over foreign matters, such as church-group opposition to investment in South Africa. They can arise in a host country over a domestic matter, such as the perceived exploitation of cheap labor. They can arise in a host country over foreign matters, such as the subsidiary's support of U.S. foreign policy. But increasingly, MNC conflicts are international in scope, which perhaps reflects the growing economic and political interdependencies in today's world.[7]

Conflict can be functional as well as dysfunctional, beneficial as well as detrimental, constructive as well as destructive. One key to conflict resolution is to maintain a balanced perspective, or, in other words, to maintain the global as opposed to the provincial view. It is also important to keep in mind what we have contended all along, that much of the conflict faced by the MNC is inevitable. Such problems are rarely solved and the best that one can do is simply to try to manage them. Thus, the task is often not one of conflict resolution per se, but of reaching the most satisfactory of alternative outcomes. If one must give up majority ownership of the Mexican affiliate, for example, that does not preclude maintaining quite profitable operations in that particular country.

The discusion so far has centered on conflict between the MNC and several of its external stakeholders. The general public, consumers, governments, stockholders, creditors, competitors, and suppliers all exert pressures on the MNC. Quite frequently, these demands are in direct conflict with each other. Thus the American government exerts pressure on Ford of Detroit to prevent its Canadian subsidiary from exporting autos to Cuba, but the Canadian government insists that the cars be shipped. A firm might have affiliates in both Pakistan and India, but intracorporate flows between those two units are interrupted by war between the two nations. Creditors in the United States may be no longer willing to finance the MNC's operations in Argentina, due to that country's resistance to austerity measures proposed by the IMF.

There can also be serious conflicts within the firm, among its various units. Managers fight each other for resources. A subsidiary in Canada argues convincingly that it should manufacture certain components instead of having to import them from the United States. The French subsidiary objects strongly to the transfer prices it must pay for parts made in West Germany. The Italian subsidiary insists on exporting to the North African region, which has traditionally been served by the affiliate in Spain. Workers in Mexico note with disfavor the wage differentials between their plant and plants north of the border. The affiliate in Chile is upset about delays in the supply of components from the plant in Peru. These intracorporate conflicts are very real, but our focus in this section is on conflicts between the MNC and external bodies.

Conflicts between the MNC and outside groups are inevitable. They do not stem simply from misunderstanding, and therefore cannot be resolved simply through discussion and enlightenment. As long as the objectives of the MNC differ from those of the host country, and they necessarily do, the conflicts are not amenable to easy resolution. Misunderstandings do occur, but they do not constitute the crux of the problem. The outcome of many conflicts is decided by the relative bargaining power of the parties involved. Both sides have strong power in that they may unilaterally end the relationship. The MNC can fully divest and withdraw, and the state may expropriate or nationalize. But both sides suffer great losses by such extreme solutions, which is one reason why conflict resolution is so important.

It appears as if bargaining power is shifting in favor of the host countries. This has political causes, for foreign governments are vigorously seeking a degree of economic independence commensurate with the political independence that many of them won during the post-World War II process of decolonialization. It has institutional causes, for many countries have just recently developed international linkages, either on a regional basis or through the United Nations, allowing them to jointly confront the MNC. It has resource transfer causes, for by its very success, the MNC has strengthened the economic position and the managerial capabilities of the Third World. It has historical causes, for once the foreign investment is sunk in plants and marketing networks and sourcing arrangements, the MNC loses much of its flexibility. And above all, it has economic causes, for the highly competitive international business environment today encourages MNCs to yield to certain host country policies when major competitors are willing to do so.

The bargaining power of the MNC is associated with the very reasons it came into existence in the first place. These reasons are essentially economic in nature, and of overriding importance to the welfare of every nation. Note, however, that economic weakness might be a negotiating strength. When firms such as International Harvester, Chrysler, or Massey-Ferguson come to the verge of bankruptcy, there is little the negotiating rival can demand.

Gladwin,[8] and Gladwin and Walter,[9] have identified numerous conflict strategies available to the MNC.

1. The MNC may adopt a competitive, uncooperative stance and directly oppose the other party, as in the battle between IBM and the U.S. federal government regarding antitrust concerns. This strategy seems appropriate when the MNC's stakes and power are relatively high, and when interest interdependence and relations are relatively negative.

2. The MNC may avoid conflict by withdrawing, as when both Coca-Cola and IBM left India. This strategy is feasible when the firm's stakes and power are relatively low, and when interest interdependence and relations are relatively negative.

3. The MNC may accommodate by yielding to the negotiating rival's demands, as when U.S. MNCs in Mexico agree to give up majority ownership of their affiliates. This strategy is appropriate when stakes and power are relatively low, but when interest interdependence and relations are relatively positive. The objective is appeasement, which makes sense when the issues involved are of more importance to others than to the firm itself.

4. The firm may collaborate in seeking a positive-sum solution, as when

the MNC agrees to experiments involving worker participation in decision making. This strategy is effective when both sides agree on objectives, but differ over means. It is appropriate when the MNC's stakes and power are relatively high, and when interest interdependence and relations with the opposition are relatively positive.

5. Finally, the MNC may compromise by having both sides drop some demands, as when the American Jewish Congress negotiated a middle-of-the-road course for MNCs in connection with the Arab boycott of Israel. This approach seems to be useful when the firm's stakes are moderate and power advantage slight, and when interest interdependence and relations are mixes of positive and negative elements.

These are, of course, ways of coping with, and not fully resolving, conflict. Moreover, they are not mutually exclusive choices. But given the choices, the MNC must weigh various factors in selecting its approach to conflict. The most critical factor is the extent to which the foreign operations in the given country are a vital component of the firm's global strategy. If they are of only marginal importance, the MNC can readily yield to external pressures. If, on the other hand for example, a foreign government demands the surrender of proprietary control over a key technology, as India demanded of IBM and Coca-Cola, then no accommodation of any sort is possible. It is for this reason that the issues involved affect companies in different industries differently. Some MNCs readily agree to accept a passive managerial role in foreign affiliates, while others, dependent perhaps on tight quality control of production or marketing, cannot relinquish managerial control. Firms in the capital-intensive extractive industries depend on long-term, reliable sources of supply, and cannot accept short-run contracts favored by some firms in the light-manufacturing sectors.

Knowing when to be nice, when to apply pressure, and when to stay quiet or speak out is an art not fully amenable to textbook analysis. This is true of many of the behavioral and administrative aspects of MNC management. We can only suggest the magnitude of the task here, and not explain in detail the many variables that must be taken into consideration.

In the end, conflict-resolution strategies must be linked to the basic corporate goals of long-term profitability, growth, and survival. These goals themselves may come into conflict, as when short-term measures to assure survival are detrimental to the long-run profitability of the firm. But then, without short-run survival, there is no long run to consider. Ultimately, the best defense against conflict is a policy of good corporate citizenship, but as we have suggested already, there are very basic conflicts even in the perception of what good corporate citizenship is.

SUMMARY

Corporate legitimacy and social responsibility are especially perplexing issues for the globally oriented firm. Even within any given country, the same corporate behavior may be viewed positively by one constituency and negatively by another. The problem is compounded when the corporation is active in more than one country, for national priorities vary widely, and corporate behavior actively encouraged in one country is frequently unacceptable in another. Consequently, two types of conflict emerge. First, the firm that attempts to optimize globally by integrating its strategy on a worldwide basis runs counter to the understandable tendency of governments to optimize on a national basis. Thus, the firm, for example, that seeks to rationalize production and procurement by sourcing its components from various low-cost areas worldwide is often pressured by host countries to increase the local content of production in order to generate employment and to improve the country's balance of payments. While this makes sense from the national perspective, for the multinational corporation it often means suboptimizing behavior and makes it more difficult to integrate strategy on a global basis.

Second, there are conflicts among the constraints placed on corporate behavior by the different countries in which the firm operates. In this regard we referred to the case of some European subsidiaries of U.S. firms, which have been ordered by the U.S. government not to trade with the Soviet Union and by the European governments to do the opposite. Similarly, subsidiaries based in South Africa are expected by that government to abide by the apartheid laws, but governments elsewhere put pressure on the firms to behave contrary to those laws. Such dilemmas are an ongoing fact of life for the multinational corporation, and the resolution of such conflicts is difficult, if not impossible. Consequently, the globally oriented firm faces critical public relations problems wherever it goes, and high-level corporate attention must be given to methods of conflict resolution.

QUESTIONS

1. What dilemmas are associated with the firm's pursuit of social responsibility in an international context that would not be found in the purely domestic context?

2. What are some of the basic approaches that the globally oriented firm might take in regard to conflict resolution?

3. What is perceived as fully legitimate behavior in one country is often totally unacceptable in another. How does this affect the strategies of the globally oriented firm?

4. The globally oriented firm optimizes globally, while the nation-state, by definition, suboptimizes. How does this affect the ability of the firm to implement its desired strategy?

NOTES

1. Raymond Vernon, "The Future of Multinational Enterprise in Developing Countries," in *Private Enterprise and The New Global Economic Challenge*, ed., Stephen Guisinger (Indianapolis: Bobbs-Merrill Educational Publishing, 1979), 1–21.

2. Isaiah Frank, *Foreign Enterprise in Developing Countries* (Baltimore: The Johns Hopkins University Press, 1980), 28–29.

3. David H. Blake and Robert S. Walters, *The Politics of Global Economic Relations*, 2nd ed. (Englewood Cliffs: Prentice-Hall, 1983), 5–10.

4. Raymond Vernon, "The Future of Multinational Enterprise," op. cit.

5. Ashok Kapoor and J. J. Boddewyn, *International Business-Government Relations: U.S. Corporate Experience in Asia and Western Europe* (New York: American Management Associations, 1973), 2–3.

6. John H. Barton, "Coping With Technological Protectionism," *Harvard Business Review* (November–December, 1984), 91–97.

7. Thomas N. Gladwin, "Conflict Management in International Business," in *Handbook of International Business*, ed., Ingo Walter (New York: John Wiley and Sons, 1982), 41.

8. Gladwin, ibid.

9. Thomas N. Gladwin and Ingo Walter, "How Multinationals Can Manage Social and Political Forces," *Journal of Business Strategy* I (1980), 54–68.

FURTHER READING

1. Banker, Pravin. "You're the Best Judge of Foreign Risks." *Harvard Business Review*, March–April, 1983, 157–165.

2. Bergsten, C. Fred, Thomas Horst and Theodore H. Moran. *American Multinationals and American Interests.* Washington, D.C.: The Brookings Institution, 1978.

3. Guisinger, Stephen. *Private Enterprise and The New Global Economic Challenge.* Indianapolis: Bobbs-Merrill Educational Publishing, 1979.

4. Jones, Ronald W. and Anne O. Krueger, eds. *The Political Economy of International Trade.* Washington, D.C.: Sidney Kramer, 1989.

5. Moyer, Reed. *International Business: Issues and Concepts.* New York: John Wiley and Sons, 1984.

6. Stern, Robert M., ed. *U.S. Trade Policies in a Changing World Economy.* Cambridge: The MIT Press, 1987.

CHAPTER 10

▼

Epilogue

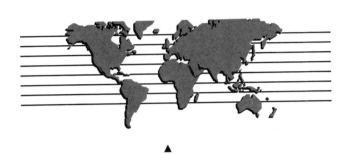

▲

The economic performance of U.S. business firms is affected by international economic and competitive conditions. This holds true regardless of whether the firm is large or small, and regardless of whether the firm is oriented to domestic or global markets. American economic performance in general, which is a key environmental determinant of success at the firm level, is more than ever before dependent on international linkages. The recession of the early 1980s, which dampened demand in virtually every industrial sector, was a global phenomenon, not an American one. The cost of energy, a key input for most businesses, is essentially determined by global, not domestic, forces. American firms are increasingly dependent on foreign sources of raw materials, capital, and technology. The recent strength of the dollar vis-à-vis other currencies has adversely affected not just U.S. exporters, but every U.S. firm that competes against imports. Conversely, the strength of the dollar has favorably affected those American firms that import from abroad. Reverse effects are seen when the dollar falls.

Some industries have become globalized, in that the strategic position of competitors in major geographic or national markets is fundamentally affected by their global position. But even in industries that are not globalized, the firm that fails to scan worldwide sources of technology, or other critical inputs, faces the risk of seeing its competitive position rapidly erode. Long-run strategic planning must take into consideration the global economic and competitive developments that directly affect the economic environment in which the firm operates and to which the firm must respond. No firm, whatever its size or market orientation, can fully escape the consequences of increased international economic and business linkages. Business is a game more akin to chess than to Trivial Pursuit; what happens anywhere on the board directly affects the strategy and competitiveness of the player.

Clearly not all industries provide significant synergies through internationalization. Instead, the configuration of input and output markets or the regulatory constraints on such industries may preclude substantial benefits from strategic or operational linkages beyond national borders. Even here, however, a portfolio approach of having relatively independent operations at home and abroad may make sense. And in any event, a global orientation is necessary in long-run planning to assist in the forecasting of macroeconomic trends in the home environment, and the inwards or outwards licensing of technologies by domestic competitors must be monitored. The global perspective may lead to high pay-offs at very marginal costs.

If the firm adopts a global orientation, what difference does it make? There are major differences to be found within both the firm and the environment. If one approaches the problem from the perspective of business-policy literature, the focus might well be on management as a proactive or opportunistic agent, with emphasis on the strategy variable. If one approaches the problem from the perspective of the literature on organizational theory, one might take a more reactive stance by viewing the environment as a deterministic force to which organizations respond. In this book, we have viewed these issues as two sides of the same coin, in keeping with the strategic-management literature.

For the firm that expands abroad and enters international markets, perhaps the most obvious difference is that the firm now operates in many national environments instead of one. To the extent that any managerial problem is affected by the local environment, the firm will have to take into account complex and diverse environmental constraints not faced by the purely domestic firm. Indeed, the internationalization of the firm today takes place under highly turbulent environmental conditions, including very volatile exchange rate movements; dramatic shifts in cost structures; economic stagnation or even negative economic growth in many areas of the world; intense nationalism and political unrest; and increasingly restrictive measures adopted by many countries. The firm that internationalizes operates in an environment in which the rules of the game are extremely ambiguous, frequently contradictory, subject to unilateral and recurrent change, and sometimes, in fact, quite different for the individual competitors. These highly unpredictable conditions, however, create opportunities as well as threats, and new avenues of growth as well as new sources of frustration. In general, firms have shown remarkable flexibility in successfully coping with such problems.

Much of our recent experience in internationalization comes from the recent activities of multinational corporations, and they have been very instructive in this regard. We learn that a global view is necessary if the firm is to compete successfully in this increasingly interdependent world. In some industries, such as aircraft, computers, and telecommunications, economies of scale and/or scope are made possible by technological developments and the gradual relaxing of barriers to trade and foreign investment. In industries such as construction equipment and motor vehicles, the segmentability of the production process permits multiple-site sourcing of components from where they are most efficiently produced. In certain high technology industries, the costs of research and development must be spread over many markets to make the projects economically feasible. Firms in the extractive industries must seek their raw materials wherever they happen to be found. A global perspective is necessary even for those many firms that are not engaged in international operations. For example, a firm may benefit from this perspective if the competition is international; if the cost of energy rises around ten-fold, as it has in the 1970s; or if an important industrial client that receives components from the purely domestic firm changes the nature of its operations because of foreign competitive pressures. Thus, even those firms not directly engaged in international business must be fully aware of what is happening in the global context.

The global view is necessary also for cultural and political reasons, since the more successful firm is the one that breaks away from the constraints imposed by traditional provincialism. If the host government suddenly insists on nonequity arrangements or joint ventures in which locals hold majority control, it is the firm capable of adapting that succeeds in the long run. If foreign environmental conditions necessitate a change in certain operating procedures, the successful manager is the one who modifies corporate policies accordingly.

Thus, the MNC faces two basic and frequently conflicting tasks. One is to integrate the global activities of the firm by coordinating at the top the development of product and markets, sourcing and finance. The other is to respond adequately to the environmental conditions of individual countries or regions. The simultaneous achievement of both integration and differentiation is problematic even in the purely domestic context. In the much more complex international arena, it assumes dimensions that present a far greater and continuous challenge.

To be sure, the increasingly restrictive measures of host governments have considerably reduced the options available to the MNC, and the foreign investment climate has substantially deteriorated in some respects. In some regions, direct foreign investment is not at all possible. In others the traditional form of fully owned subsidiaries is being replaced, under pressure, by interfirm linkages of a qualitatively different nature. There are two immediate consequences of these developments as far as the MNC is concerned.

1. They have forced the MNC to basically reappraise its overall strategy in a search for approaches more amenable to the changed environmental conditions.

2. They have made it much more difficult for the MNC to globally integrate its functions and activities, since worldwide coordination of those activities is somewhat hampered by local imperatives that inevitably dictate suboptimizing behavior.

Import substitution policies, restrictions on the repatriation of profits, price and wage controls, locally mandated sourcing, indigenization laws, and local content laws are all changing the nature of MNC activities in many parts of the world. These are the more serious risk to MNC operations, not those posed by the bearded fanatics who confiscate MNC assets abroad. The continuous erosion of operating profits, and the undermining of the very assumptions on which direct investment is based, are forcing the MNC to reevaluate its strategy.

Thus, administrative strategies also acquire new significance for the MNC. The basic search for legitimacy and the pursuit of social responsibility are perplexing for the MNC, which is frequently caught in conflicts far beyond its control. Country risk analysis becomes more and more important, as the rules of the game are more and more in flux. Technology transfer, though increasingly critical to economic recovery in the developed world, basic development in the Third World, and modernization in the socialist world, faces increasingly stringent conditions. Conflict resolution strategies assume higher priority, given the diverse and often conflicting economic, social, political, and institutional contexts in which the MNC operates. Planning and control similarly take on added dimensions.

Clearly, the environment one operates in is significant. For example, the requirements for successful technology transfer differ substantially according to whether the recipient is in a developed, less developed, or centrally-planned country. In developed countries, related products and processes already exist, adaptable production facilities are available, a core of indigenous technical expertise can be employed, and a discernible market is present or can be quickly developed. Little of this exists at all in the less developed countries, and systemic constraints impede its efficient utilization in the centrally-planned countries. Note that the environmental distinctions suggested here illustrate basic problems of an extremely high aggregation. The distinctions hold, but only begin to suggest the tremendous problems involved when the focus is narrowed to one of perhaps 170 countries instead of just three basic regions.

In this environment, the MNC behaves amorally compared to locally constrained firms. This behavior is in fact a major source of criticism by many who oppose the MNC. We are all culture-bound, but the MNC is relatively immune to this, going its own way to achieve its goals of growth, survival, and long-term profit maximization. Amorality is both the supreme strength and the ultimate weakness of the MNC. It is a strength because the MNC can, in effect, obtain the best inputs from the entire world; manage them with the best managers from the whole world; and sell its outputs at the best prices in the entire world. In contrast, the local firm is handicapped by being chained to whatever local inefficiencies happen to exist. This does not necessarily mean that the MNCs will own the world, since many local firms have certain major advantages that a distant MNC cannot have; but it does mean that the MNCs tend to be the fastest growing and most dynamic firms around in most cases. The weakness that stems from this amorality is that in some cases the local cultural issues are so strong that they cause the MNC to lose its legitimacy completely.

In spite of much concern and criticism, the globally oriented firm is here to stay. Indeed, in the past decade MNC ranks have swelled with fast growth firms from Canada, Japan, Western Europe, and, surprisingly, India, South Korea, and Hong Kong. Historically, this was basically an American game, with a few old and astute European firms involved as well. Now any good player can try his hand. And in spite of all the controls, taxes, and absolute bans, the MNCs still find plenty of places to thrive and prosper.

These developments have been duly noted by managers of the MNCs, but the evolution has been so rapid that many of our institutions and modes of thinking have become somewhat obsolete overnight. This is particularly noticeable in the United States, with its huge domestic market, relatively low dependence on foreign trade, and, however justified in many cases, its subordination of international trade and economic relations to higher priority issues of foreign policy and national security. These latter issues are of clearly great significance, but what is disturbing in some cases is the apparent conviction of some that all beyond the country's borders is irrelevant.

There are ethical questions here that rarely get explored sufficiently. Nationalistic suboptimization might temporarily leave the individual country better off, but not in the long run, and always at the cost of global welfare. One is baffled by 1980 surveys which indicate that over half the Americans in the country do not even believe that the United States imports any petroleum. Apparently, this half of the public believes that our energy problem is an oil-company plot, or something similar. With attitudes like this still prevalent, it is easy to see why governments have such difficulty adjusting to the real world of MNCs we are already in, let alone the still more internationalized world we are likely to face in the 1990s.

Controversy is certain, and in a turbulent and unstable world environment, no one seriously expects the MNCs to have clear sailing. Indeed, one possible future is that the provincials win, and the MNCs are forced to retreat. If this occurs, we can expect the level of international tensions to rise perceptibly. But this is one type of forecasting that MNCs undertake, and among the possible future scenarios there are three major possibilities, as follows:

1. The nationalistic scenario: Here the provincials win, and MNCs are pushed back to their home bases or abolished completely. Local firms do the best they can, and imports and exports are minimized. Trade controls proliferate, countries seek self-sufficiency and plan their local economies, and international relationships are minimized. We have already seen this one, in the 1930s. The most likely outcome here is many local wars, endless sparring for local advantage, the possible re-colonization of significant parts of the world by superpowers, and much lower incomes and economic growth.

2. The way we are scenario: Here we bumble along the way we have been going. A few countries, like Iran, will avoid multinational interaction and drop out and become provincial and consequently suffer. Other countries, including some very important ones in Eastern Europe and perhaps in Asia, join the world and enter into internationalization. In this scenario, the MNCs do reasonably well because their real and potential contributions are largely recognized. Gradually the institutions and rules of the game will adapt to the requirements of internationalization, and steady progress will be made.

3. The more international scenario: The world becomes increasingly international. New customs unions are formed, along the lines of the successful European Community. More countries open their borders to the world, noting that the most dynamic growth in the Third World has been by those who opened their doors far earlier. MNCs thrive because they are welcomed virtually everywhere. World income grows rapidly, and regional conflicts dissipate. By the year 2000 we are well on our way to a world government and uniform rules.

Take your pick. In any case, the MNCs will have something to do with what happens. Perhaps the most likely scenario at present is a mix of one and two, where some countries retreat and others become more international. India and the Soviet Union are the countries to watch, given their huge populations and economic potentials. If they go multinational, the odds on scenario three tend to increase, even if a dozen or more small countries go back into their shells.

These long-term trends are significant to all top MNC managers, simply because they will determine the limits of growth and profitability. Ultimately, the MNC is a servant; a cantankerous and obnoxious servant at times, to be sure, but still a servant. The countries are the masters who decide whether or not the MNC is to be tolerated.

So there is the multinational game. It has changed the world in unexpected dimensions, and we can predict with confidence that all the surprises are not over yet. In the end, the MNCs, along with their managements, will increasingly influence the way the world evolves; and understanding how such firms are managed is crucial knowledge to any manager or scholar.

Index